GENDER IN HISTORY

Series editors:
Lynn Abrams, Cordelia Beattie, Pam Sharpe and Penny Summerfield

The expansion of research into the history of women and gender since the 1970s has changed the face of history. Using the insights of feminist theory and of historians of women, gender historians have explored the configuration in the past of gender identities and relations between the sexes. They have also investigated the history of sexuality and family relations, and analysed ideas and ideals of masculinity and femininity. Yet gender history has not abandoned the original, inspirational project of women's history: to recover and reveal the lived experience of women in the past and the present.

The series Gender in History provides a forum for these developments. Its historical coverage extends from the medieval to the modern period, and its geographical scope encompasses not only Europe and North America but all corners of the globe. The series aims to investigate the social and cultural constructions of gender in historical sources, as well as the gendering of historical discourse itself. It embraces both detailed case studies of specific regions or periods, and broader treatments of major themes. Gender in History titles are designed to meet the needs of both scholars and students working in this dynamic area of historical research.

The feminine public sphere

Manchester University Press

THE FEMININE PUBLIC SPHERE

MIDDLE-CLASS WOMEN IN CIVIC LIFE IN SCOTLAND, c.1870–1914

⇥ Megan Smitley ⇤

Manchester University Press
Manchester and New York

distributed exclusively in the USA by Palgrave

Published by Manchester University Press
Oxford Road, Manchester M13 9NR, UK
and Room 400, 175 Fifth Avenue, New York, NY 10010, USA
www.manchesteruniversitypress.co.uk

Distributed exclusively in the USA by Palgrave
175 Fifth Avenue, New York,
NY 10010, USA

Distributed exclusively in Canada by UBC Press
University of British Columbia, 2029 West Mall,
Vancouver, BC, Canada V6T 1Z2

British Library Cataloguing-in-Publication Data
A catalogue record for this book is available from the British Library

Library of Congress Cataloging-in-Publication Data applied for

ISBN 978 0 7190 7966 5 *hardback*

First published 2009

18 17 16 15 14 13 12 11 10 09   10 9 8 7 6 5 4 3 2 1

Typeset in Minion with Scala Sans display
by Koinonia, Manchester
Printed in Great Britain
by MPG Books Group

For my grandmother,
Phyllis Eileen Smitley (1925–2003)

Contents

Acknowledgements

As this project has evolved from Bachelor's dissertation to PhD thesis to published monograph I have become indebted to a great many individuals and institutions whose support was vital to successfully overcoming the many challenges and obstacles this research has faced. PhD-funding was a particularly difficult challenge, and I can thank my grandmother, Janet Ziegler, and my father, Jeffrey Smitley, for underwriting my first two years of post-graduate study, while my successful application for a PEO loan for the final year's fees owes much to the help of Mary Ellen Rickert and Laurie Beall. Thanks are also due to my mother, Linda Ziegler, for her financial and moral support and to Daniel Soule, who sustained my student lifestyle by hiring me as his tutor. I must also thank the University of Glasgow's Economic and Social History Department for providing me with much needed office-space and interesting company during my PhD candidacy. I am further grateful to the Economic and Social Research Council for awarding me a post-doctoral fellowship, an appointment which allowed me to re-write substantially and re-imagine my doctoral research as a monograph study.

This study would not have been possible without the care and diligence of the archivists and librarians who cared for the materials I relied on, and I am especially grateful for the efforts of: the Ayrshire Archives, the British Library, the Glasgow City Archives, the Glasgow University Archives and Special Collections, the Library of the Society of Friends, the Mitchell Library, the National Library of Scotland and the Women's Library. A special thanks to Denise Brace and the Edinburgh City Museum for granting access to their outstanding collection of BWTASCU material.

This book has been a long time in the making, and over the years I have benefited from the kindness and patience of friends and colleagues. Thanks are due to Luc Russell whose proof reading and forbearance through ups and downs has been vital to bringing this project to a happy conclusion. I am particularly grateful for the insight and encouragement of teachers and mentors: Marc Baer for first inspiring my interest in middle-classness and industrialisation; Lynn Abrams and Eleanor Gordon whose invaluable guidance and critique nurtured my initial analysis of middle-class women's public lives; and Clare Midgley whose friendship and mentoring helped me to re-evaluate and strengthen my discussion. A final thanks to the staff at Manchester University Press for bringing this book to fruition.

Abbreviations

BWTA	British Women's Temperance Association
BWTASCU	British Women's Temperance Association Scottish Christian Union
GNSWS	Glasgow National Society for Women's Suffrage
GWSAWS	Glasgow and West of Scotland Association for Women's Suffrage
ENSWS	Edinburgh National Society for Women's Suffrage
NUWSS	National Union of Women's Suffrage Societies
SFWSS	Scottish Federation of Women's Suffrage Societies
SLWM	*Scottish Liberal Women's Magazine*
SNSWS	Shetland National Society for Women's Suffrage
STL	Scottish Temperance League
SWLF	Scottish Women's Liberal Federation
SWTN	*Scottish Women's Temperance News*
WCTU	Women's Christian Temperance Union
WH	*Women's Herald*
WLA	Women's Liberal Association
WLF	Women's Liberal Federation
WSJ	*Women's Suffrage Journal*
WWCTU	World Women's Christian Temperance Union

Introduction

In 1882, Miss Eliza Kirkland addressed the Edinburgh National Society for Women's Suffrage with the assertion that:

> the sphere of both men and women was to do the duty in the position of life in which God had placed them, to exercise to the full the talents and abilities He has endowed them with not contented to wrap them up in a napkin, but to fulfil earnestly, heartily, and conscientiously all the duties and responsibilities laid upon them for the good of their fellow men and for the glory of God. Therefore, as politics permeated all the duties of life, as there was scarcely a patriotic, philanthropic, social, or religious movement which has not its political side, she said women had a right – nay, it was a duty incumbent upon them – to interest themselves in all that concerned their homes, their friends, their country, and their nation.[1]

Miss Mary White, in an 1898 remembrance of her career in the temperance movement, wrote:

> In closing this fragmentary sketch I cannot help expressing my thankfulness to God for calling me to gospel temperance work. Not only has it brought me into intimate sisterly association with many noble Christian women, some of whom are now 'in the presence of the King' but, amid many disappointments, I have seen wonderful miracles of grace – lives rescued and transformed through the power of Christ. It has, above all, given me innumerable precious opportunities to exalt the power of my Lord and Saviour to break the chains of strong drink and to 'save to the very uttermost all who come unto God by Him'.[2]

For Kirkland and White the informal power structures of female associational life provided opportunities to participate as citizens through public agitation for social and political reform, to express Christian service at a time when women were barred from clerical roles and to organise within influential and highly systematised middle-class women's networks. This investigation of women's participation in associationalism and civic life seeks to provide a fresh approach to the 'public sphere' in order to illuminate women as agents of a middle-class identity and to develop the notion of a 'feminine public sphere', or the web of associations, institutions and discourses used by disenfranchised middle-class women to express their citizenship. The extent of middle-class women's contribution to civic life is examined through their involvement in reforming and philanthropic associations as well as local government.

The analytical usefulness of 'separate spheres' has remained a hotly contested issue since the 1980s. Debates among feminist historians have increasingly developed a more nuanced view of the influence of separate spheres on women's public lives. Simultaneously, they have re-evaluated Habermas' concept of a 'bourgeois public sphere' to include the centrality of gender in its construction. Yet, many analyses of the development of a middle-class civic identity in the nineteenth century have conformed to over-rigid interpretations of separate spheres to largely exclude an exploration of women's role. By examining under-used Scottish material, it may be possible to shed new light on these issues by highlighting the active contribution of women to a middle-class civic identity derived from their participation in public life.

This case study of members of the British Women's Temperance Association Scottish Christian Union (BWTASCU), the Scottish Women's Liberal Federation (SWLF), the Glasgow National Society for Women's Suffrage (GNSWS), the Glasgow and West of Scotland Association for Women's Suffrage (GWSAWS) and the Edinburgh National Society for Women's Suffrage (ENSWS) aims to investigate key ideas in gender and social history. Themes of particular interest include: exploring the relationship between separate spheres ideology and women's public lives; developing a broader understanding of suffragism to recognise the contribution of organisations not normally associated with the Victorian and Edwardian women's movement; and demonstrating the importance of regional and international perspectives for British history.

Firstly, I will argue that middle-class women actively contributed to the development of a middle-class civic identity through participation in philanthropic, reforming and local government bodies. Evidence from the organisations examined here suggests that women in public life were integrated into local elites through kinship, neighbourhood and religious networks. Their involvement in female associationalism was central to middle-class women's ability to join their male peers in defining a middle-class identity through public service. Religion and religious networks, in particular, played a significant role in the development of a feminine public sphere: on the one hand, evangelical Protestantism was fundamental to middle-class women's discursive defence of women's public roles; on the other hand, a commitment to Christian service appears as a key motivation for women's entry into public life.

Secondly, female associational life further highlights the hitherto hidden role of Liberal and temperance women in Scottish suffragism and demonstrates that the BWTASCU and the SWLF were important partners in the campaign for women's enfranchisement. Inter-organisational co-operation among temperance, Liberal and suffrage associations was encouraged by patterns of cross-membership coupled with organisations' shared interest in temperance reform and women's political rights. The affinities between demands for women's political emancipation and temperance reform in Scotland were unique in the British context, and it emerges from this research that the nexus of late nineteenth-century demands for prohibition and the 1881 municipal enfranchisement of women in Scotland cultivated female temperance reformers' support for women's suffrage more effectively than in other areas of the United Kingdom.

Thirdly, the distinct relationship between suffragism and temperance in Scotland further reveals the importance of 'Britannic' and Anglophone perspectives for modern British history. The role of female temperance reformers and Liberal women in Scottish constitutional suffragism shows previously unrecognised diversity in the British women's movement and Scotland's divergence from English organised feminism. Likewise, the evidence suggests that Anglophone networks levied a strong international influence on the development of women's organisations in Scotland. The source material from these organisations – minute books, annual reports, periodicals and personal papers – reveals a community of upper-middle-class women who engaged in civic life at the level of charitable associations, social reform groups and local government.

The feminine public sphere

The notion of the feminine public sphere is based on the active participation of women in the formation of a middle-class identity which was derived from a commitment to civic life and public service. Associationalism was a key feature of civil society in the 1870 to 1914 period, and while women's contribution to philanthropic societies has received some attention this book represents a more concerted effort to link women's public careers with the rise of a middle-class identity. By taking a fresh perspective on the 'bourgeois public sphere' through the lens of local, urban civic life – as opposed to high politics and the upper echelons of industrial capitalism – this research shows that the wives, sisters and daughters of men in the local elite mirrored their male kins' investment in a public profile in order to assert their own social position.

Separate spheres was a potent philosophy of the nineteenth and early twentieth centuries, with meaningful implications for women's public lives. Much of this meaning derived from the relationship of separate spheres with other ideological factors, especially evangelical Protestantism, middle-class ideas of respectability and the notion of 'woman's mission'. The many ideological threads that informed 'woman's mission' in relation to separate spheres presented women with the opportunity to subvert orthodox views on gender by emphasising elements of these ideologies that related to a woman's Christian duty to serve her community. While middle-class women's religiously-inspired revision of women's place in public life was ultimately limited by essentialist notions of femininity which centred on the 'career of motherhood', re-interpretations of separate spheres allowed women to assert a feminine niche in the public sphere. Debates over the usefulness of separate spheres in women's history can be traced to Leonore Davidoff and Catherine Hall's *Family Fortunes*.[3] While Davidoff and Hall's work recognises the inter-penetration of 'public' and 'private' spheres, *Family Fortunes'* greater emphasis on the importance of women's domesticity for middle-class identity tends to overshadow the ways in which bourgeois women might use heterodox interpretations of gender ideology to contribute to middle-class public life. Re-evaluations of separate spheres have challenged the notion of rigidly defined 'public' and 'private' realms, the comparative importance of separate spheres for the opportunities of working-class versus middle-class women and the relationship of separate spheres with civil society and gendered notions of citizenship.

In *Public Lives*, Eleanor Gordon and Gwyneth Nair seek to challenge understandings of the consequences of separate spheres for the lives of middle-class women through a detailed study of the Claremont Estate in Glasgow.[4] Underlying Gordon and Nair's attack on the ability of separate spheres to sequester femininity in the 'domestic sphere' is a more literal interpretation of 'public' and 'private' spheres. Their fine-grained discussion of life in the Claremont Estate of Glasgow challenges popular understandings of a public–private dichotomy and demonstrates women's physical presence in the 'public', for instance in shops, at balls, on the streets and in parks, while further arguing for the 'public' nature of the home, for example, as the preferred site of middle-class entertainment. Yet a demonstration of women's presence in public spaces does not, in itself, provide evidence of women's role in the 'public' world of opinion-making and citizenship. In contrast, the feminine public sphere of this study is the sphere of influence more affluent women carved out of a hostile, male-oriented 'public' through heterodox interpretations of separate spheres; it is the discursive and organisational sites from which women contributed to the socio-political issues of their day while further reinforcing middle-class notions of civic duty. While Gordon and Nair rightly suggest the importance of middle-class liberalism and its relationship with evangelical Protestantism to motivating middle-class women's participation in public life, much of their discussion of this point rests on demonstrating women's physical interaction with the world outside the home, rather than on revealing the ways in which women might seek to practice liberal ideals of citizenship.[5] For example, 'Victorian middle-class ideology *required* a public role for women. In order to acquire the goods and attributes essential to her domestic role, the middle-class woman *had* to enter the public realm of shops, churches, concert halls and so on.'[6] While Gordon and Nair's description of middle-class women's rich and varied lives inside and outside the home is significant for undermining popular notions of Victorian women's sequestered lives, this interpretation of women's 'public' lives is less helpful for understanding the ways in which middle-class women were conscious of themselves as citizens. This is not to suggest that women were absent from civic life at the level of socio-political discourse and agitation, rather my treatment of the feminine public sphere intends to mobilise evidence of women's pursuit of active citizenship outside formalised power structures.

In order to complement existing studies of the Victorian middle classes, I will take a closer look at the dynamics between separate spheres and civil society. Work by historians such as Simon Gunn, Alan Kidd and David Nicholls have shed light on the development of a nineteenth-century middle-class identity through individuals' involvement in civic life.[7] While an increasing effort is being made by scholars such as Simon Morgan, Moira Martin, Sue Innes and Jane Rendall to gender discussions of middle-class civic identity, a robust narrative that tends to portray women as confined to inferior roles in ladies' auxiliaries to male-dominated associations continues to obfuscate the agency of women in civic life.[8] This book challenges those studies of the middle classes, which tend to interpret separate spheres ideology as evidence of middle-class women's absence from positions of public influence or debate.[9] Instead, this approach seeks to demonstrate how principles of liberal democracy and ideas around the duty of citizens to serve the wider community, principles fundamental to middle-class identity, were embraced by women who sought to act as agents of social and political reform in their local communities.

Late nineteenth and early twentieth-century middle-class women's expressions of citizenship tended to emphasise women's particularity and often focused on the perceived needs of poorer women and children. Feminists have noted the relationship between liberal conceptions of the universal, aligned with the masculine, and of the particular, aligned with the feminine, and the development of a public sphere that tended to marginalise the interests of women.[10] In turn, feminist evaluations of citizenship and liberal democracy have highlighted the inherent tension between liberal understandings of the free individual, implicitly male, and the 'natural' qualities of the sexes which assert women's essential role as subordinate wife and mother.[11] Within this fundamentally patriarchal paradigm, which denies the detrimental influence of social inequalities on political equality, it is argued that women cannot be accepted as full and equal citizens.[12] The veil of universality and individualism, which obscures the consequences of power relations between men and women for the development of liberal democracy, has in turn undermined gendered conceptualisations of citizenship. Feminist scholars have sought to gender discussions of citizenship, and for nineteenth-century Scotland, Sue Innes and Jane Rendall have discussed the ways in which 'women made a claim to influence in public life and to a role as citizens that did not depend on formal voting rights.'[13] Innes and Rendall's investigation emphasises women's civic activity, and suggests that women's political participation might reinforce essentialist gender stereotypes by the tendency to seek to extend, 'familial responsibilities within civil society towards the broader terrain of social and national welfare.'[14] Similarly, my own work on a feminine public sphere demonstrates that middle-class women's efforts to participate in liberal democracy relied heavily on essentialist under-standings of gender and justifications for women's public participation were often rooted in claims regarding the equal importance of 'natural' feminine qualities for the common good. Clearly such a strategy was problematic in terms of providing a direct challenge to female subordina-tion, yet my research provides evidence that while middle-class public women might be motivated by essentialist and maternalist ideologies, they were equally self-conscious in seeking to express their citizenship through the informal power structures of their associations.

The feminine public sphere described here shows women drawing strength from the various ideological strands which contributed to separate spheres and subverting prescriptions against women's involve-ment in public life and so contributing to middle-class socio-political discourse and reforming activism. Motherhood was central to separate spheres ideology, and while Davidoff and Hall and Gordon and Nair highlight the importance of mothering and family-life, Julia Bush has more recently demonstrated the centrality of social-maternalism for the public lives of anti-suffragist women. In arguing for the importance of separate spheres ideology for women's identities, Bush notes that: 'The message that strongly differentiated gender roles were beneficial to civic society, as well as a source of satisfaction and empowerment for women themselves, was taken up in the late nineteenth century by suffragists and women anti-suffragists alike."[15] Indeed, the ideological gulf between suffragist and anti-suffragist women was negligible as both sets of women were distinguished by an active commitment to public service through philanthropy, reforming activism and local government work. It is this ability to work within the ideological confines of separate spheres in order to develop a culture of social mothering which then allowed middle-class women to assert their agency in the consolidation of a middle-class identity based on active citizenship in the public sphere.

The notion of a feminine public sphere is borne out by an analysis of the public lives of female temperance reformers, Liberal women and suffrage activists, who operated within an overlapping network of reform, charitable and political organisations. Sources relating to women's temperance, suffrage and Liberal associations, as well as local boards and charitable groups, in particular minute books and organisations' periodicals, reveal in new ways the extent to which middle-class women in the 1870 to 1914 period negotiated a place in the public sphere while simultaneously aiding in the construction of a middle-class civic identity. In this way this analysis of women's associations is aligned with the notion, recently posited by Simon Morgan, that female associationalism empowered women and stimulated their demands for sexual equality.[16] In contrast, Carmen Neilson Varty's discussion of the Ladies Benevolent Society in Hamilton, Canada mobilises a strict interpretation of Habermas' public sphere to argue that a reliance on women's particularity, as mothers and moral guardians, excluded women's charitable associations and activities from public life and as agents of public opinion.[17] While Varty's tightly argued article makes the important point that historians' efforts to 'find' women in public life should nevertheless recognise women's oppression and victimisation under patriarchy, I assert the pressing need for recognition of women's 'important contribution to the emerging ideal of a progressive middle-class based around voluntary associations, local government institutions and a burgeoning civic pride'.[18]

Late nineteenth-century female associationalism was in many ways the inheritor of early nineteenth-century women's participation in the anti-slavery, Unitarian and anti-Corn Law associations examined by Clare Midgley, Kathryn Gleadle and Simon Morgan.[19] Midgley's most recent work on women involved in overseas missionary work and the campaigns against slavery and sati shows that middle-class public women in the later nineteenth century worked within a public sphere rooted in women's activities from earlier in the century.[20] Not only were the middle-class public women investigated by Midgley forerunners of organised feminism, the methodologies and ideologies of their campaigns were echoed by later female associations, in particular the temperance movement. Indeed, the similarities between the slave-sugar boycott and temperance reformers' efforts to impose household abstinence through women's control of domestic consumption are striking. Midgley's investigation of female missionaries highlights the importance of women's Christianity to the development of a heterodox evangelical discourse that opposed 'angel in the house' ideologies. Christian women's desires to serve their communities, locally and in the imperial context, continued in the later period to motivate a subversion of gender roles aimed at justifying women's participation in public life. While the early nineteenth-century activism of women certainly informed the operation and notional correctness of later nineteenth-century women's associations, the later period is distinguished by increasingly formalised and professionalised organisations. The anti-slavery and foreign missionary movements of the first half of the century resisted formal inclusion of women, thus forcing women to carve out what Kathleen D. McCarthy has described as 'parallel power structures' in order to actively support these causes.[21] By the 1870 to 1914 period women's associations were increasingly independent of male oversight, intent on pushing the agenda of women's rights, insistent on women's valuable contribution to public life and opposed to male-dominated policy making.

This new breed of highly systematised women's associations is epitomised by women's temperance, Liberal and suffrage organisations. In temperance, the rise of the World Women's Christian Temperance Union (WWCTU) heralded the movement of women to the fore of the international temperance movement from the mid-1870s. In Britain, the Corrupt Practices Act (1883) encouraged the growth of women's party-political organisations, including the Women's Liberal Federation. This period further saw an expansion of women's suffrage organisations affiliated with the National Union of Women's Suffrage Societies (NUWSS). In the run-up to the formalisation of qualifications for social work in the early twentieth century, the temperance, Liberal and suffrage associations of the later nineteenth century evidenced an advanced degree of professionalism and a businesslike pursuit of a raft of reforming objectives. From within these self-consciously Christian and increasingly professionalised voluntary organisations, elite women subverted notions of sequestered femininity and acted as agents of a middle-class identity through their robust participation in public life.

New views on constitutional suffragism

The feminine public sphere was, in part, the site of organised feminism. Records of women's networks and the policies of women's organisations uncover the important contributions made to suffrage by the SWLF and BWTASCU. Geographically, this discussion focuses on Glasgow and Edinburgh, the urban heartland of Scotland. Evidence from Scottish organisations points to important divergences from organised feminism in England. For instance, the BWTASCU, the most influential women's temperance group in the 1870 to 1914 period, differed significantly from its sister organisation in England, the British Women's Temperance Association (BWTA). Most notably, the BWTASCU officially supported women's equal parliamentary enfranchisement, and paralleled much more closely the progressive policies of the American Women's Christian Temperance Union (WCTU). My work on the membership of the ENSWS, the GNSWS, the GWSAWS, the SWLF and the BWTASCU, facilitated by the use of a relational database, exposes inter-organisational networks running through the women's movement. These networks helped to cultivate a multi-issue approach, and the BWTASCU and the SWLF where characterised by diverse departmental structures. The evolution of increasingly varied departmental structures over time reveals the issues that concerned public women, and importantly the centrality of both temperance and women's political rights for women's reforming organisations. This emphasis on women's Liberal and temperance associations as sites of suffragism diverges significantly from the bulk of histories of British 'first-wave' feminism.

This analysis of Liberal and temperance women's contributions to the women's suffrage movement supports Myriam Boussahba-Bravard's-identification of 'outside suffrage'.[22] Boussahba-Bravard defines outside suffragism as those, 'party and non-party structures that were not specifically suffragist, although suffragists belonged to them'.[23] Boussahba-Bravard asserts that suffragism's inclusive nature, derived from its emphasis on sex-loyalty, ensured that suffragism became increasingly synonymous with female activism by the early twentieth century. Boussahba-Bravard further argues that the synergies between female activism and suffragism led to a dynamic relationship between inside and outside suffragists, where individuals pressured their various organisations in multiple ways with reference to their sex-loyalty and interest in women's rights. I have found this notion of outside suffragism invaluable in my struggle to recognise a broader base of constitutional suffragism in Scotland which can incorporate the efforts of women's temperance and Liberal associations while preserving the complex nature of these organisations. Through a consideration of women's temperance and Liberal organisations as loci of outside suffragism it is therefore possible to move beyond the militant-constitutional dichotomy and to investigate the centrality of suffrage to the public lives of women and organisations not normally associated with the campaign for women's enfranchisement.

The historiography of the British women's suffrage movement has been strongly influenced by a militancy narrative that concentrates on the twentieth-century campaign of the Women's Social and Political Union (WSPU).[24] This narrative, while increasingly challenged in more recent studies of British suffragism, was consolidated by the emphases and ideologies which informed the new women's history of the 1960s and 1970s. The work of historians such as Maroula Joannou, June Purvis and Kathryn Dodd has helped to uncover the influence of suffragists' writings on the construction of dominant historical narratives in the 1960s and 1970s.[25] The links between 'second-wave' feminism and women's history writing have, in many ways, dictated the terms of women's suffrage histories. Melanie Nolan and Caroline Daley have argued that the white, middle-class make-up of many suffrage organisations made for unappealing subject matter for more radical historians, and thus encouraged those who did write about suffrage to do so from the perspective of militant and socialist suffragists.[26] In this way, suffragettes' own notions of the centrality of the WSPU's methods, coupled with feminist interpretations of the 1960s and 1970s, have worked to obscure the nineteenth-century constitutional suffrage campaign.

The militancy narrative in British suffrage historiography came under increasing pressure in the 1980s. The most important challenge came from Sandra Stanley Holton's *Feminism and Democracy*, which demonstrated the fluidity of membership between constitutional and militant societies.[27] The scope of enquiry was further broadened by new studies of the NUWSS, such as Les Garner's evaluation of the ideology and methodology of constitutional suffragism.[28] This period's radical analyses of suffragism were concerned with women's, 'intellectual, social and political worlds' rather than discussions of militancy.[29] This approach responded to the work of historians such as Carroll Smith-Rosenburg who illustrated the importance of a 'female world' to nineteenth-century middle-class women's experiences.[30] Similarly, work by historians such as Philippa Levine and Kathryn Gleadle has helped to destabilise the militancy narrative by seeking to contextualise suffragist and feminist organisation in earlier nineteenth-century women's movements.[31]

This book diverges from existing studies of the British women's suffrage movement in several meaningful ways. Firstly, I will focus on the nineteenth-century women's organisations that would become known as 'constitutionalist'.[32] Recent work on British suffragism has endeavoured to address the long-standing preoccupation with twentieth-century English militancy, however nineteenth-century agitation remains less visible than fresh analyses of militant organisation.[33] My discussion harmonises with re-evaluations of suffrage such as Holton's *Feminism and Democracy* and Laura E. Nym Mayhall's *The Militant Suffrage Movement*,[34] and my treatment of nineteenth-century constitutionalism highlights the still largely unexplored elements of participation by women's temperance and Liberal organisations in Scotland.[35]

Secondly, women's rights activists in Scotland are central to this investigation. The only monograph study of the suffrage movement in Scotland is Leah Leneman's *A Guid Cause*.[36] Leneman's book was rigorously researched and uncovered many similarities and differences between the movements in Scotland and England. Yet, Leneman's narrative is overwhelmingly concerned with twentieth-century militancy, and is less concerned with the role of outside suffragists working in a wider range of female associations. Elspeth King and Lindy Moore have provided some alternative views of the Scottish campaign,[37] yet Leneman's analysis endures as the primary reference work.[38] While the work of these historians has been invaluable in excavating the Scottish women's movement, existing scholarship has yet to deal with the activity of outside suffragists in Scotland.

In contrast, my account highlights the importance of late nineteenth-century female temperance reform for Scottish suffragism. Female temperance reform is integral to analyses of suffragism in other Anglophone contexts, however little work has been published on this connection in Britain. Indeed, the British temperance movement more generally is a somewhat under-researched topic. The main text is Brian Harrison's *Drink and the Victorians*.[39] While Harrison's study examines drink from a variety of angles, his time frame excludes the period of greatest female involvement in temperance reform from the mid-1870s. Lilian Lewis Shiman's work on temperance focuses on England, and dismisses the BWTA as conservative and unimportant for the women's movement.[40] The Anglocentrism of Harrison and Shiman's work has been balanced somewhat by W. R. Lambert's investigation of the Welsh context, albeit without much reference to the Welsh women's temperance movement.[41] For Scotland, the main publications are Bernard Aspinwall's *Portable Utopia* and King's *Scotland Sober and Free*.[42] While both authors deal with women's contribution to temperance, I will aim to provide a much more thorough investigation of the BWTASCU. The British women's temperance movement is attracting more scholarly attention, and chapters by Margaret Barrow, Kirstin Doern and Ceridwen Lloyd-Morgan have gone a long way towards rescuing temperance women from obscurity.[43] Barrow and Lloyd-Morgan have discussed the English and Welsh women's temperance organisations specifically in the context of suffragism, while Doern has challenged Shiman's negative portrayal of the BWTA to suggest that the writings of temperance women provide evidence of a 'separate spheres feminism'. My investigation goes further than the existing literature on the BWTA, and for the first time the unique character of the BWTASCU is made central to an analysis of 'first-wave' feminism and women's public lives.

Britannic and Anglophone perspectives

Scotland is a distinct nation within the United Kingdom, differentiated by its own legal and educational systems, ethnic and linguistic groups, religious denominations, political attitudes and international networks. Women's suffrage histories have been dominated by a focus on the campaign in (south-east) England, yet more recent work has moved towards more 'Britannic' perspectives.[44] Scotland diverges from England in two major ways. Firstly, the municipal vote was only extended to Scotland's female ratepayers in 1881, whereas women in England gained this franchise in 1868. While this can be considered the greatest single difference in the formal political status of women in England and Scotland, little scholarly attention has been brought to bear on this issue.[45] Secondly, the BWTASCU took a pro-suffrage stance, while its sister organisation in England sought to distance itself from suffrage agitation. These two factors were key influences on the shape of Scotland's women's movement, and illustrate the importance of regional perspectives to developing a more sophisticated discussion of British organised feminism.

Women's access to local boards in Scotland increased incrementally between 1872 and 1914.[46] While municipal enfranchisement on the same terms as women in England was delayed until 1881, the Education (Scotland) Act of 1872 stated that all qualified 'persons' were eligible to vote for and to sit on the newly created school boards, and so included women. The Education (Scotland) Act was the first piece of legislation that explicitly recognised the local political rights of Scotswomen. The Municipal Elections (Scotland) Act, 1881 incorporated women into the town council electorate; women who met the property qualification for the parliamentary vote could vote in town council elections. The Local Government (Scotland) Act, 1889 established county councils and required the maintenance of a 'supplementary register' of voters. The supplementary register included persons other than parliamentary electors entitled to vote in county council elections, which included single women and women married but living separately from their husbands. No woman was eligible to act as a county councillor. The Local Government (Scotland) Act, 1894 removed the marriage disqualification for the county, town and parish council electorates, but married women were required to register to vote using a different property than their husbands. That is, prior to 1894 married women separated from their husbands could vote, but the 1894 Act allowed married women to register to vote as long they had access to sufficient means to meet the property qualification independent of their husbands. Hollis has presented evidence from England to show that married women did register for the poor law electorate using properties distinct from their husbands', and my own preliminary research into Glasgow's female electorate suggests that women could negotiate the use of family property to qualify as municipal voters.[47] Secondly, the 1894 Act, which established parish councils, stated that no person on account of sex or marriage was disqualified from candidacy to a parish council. In sum, while the 1881 Act gave female ratepayers greater access to the local government electorate, only the Education (Scotland) Act, 1872 and the Local Government (Scotland) Act, 1894 admitted Scotswomen's right to act as elected representatives. The Town Councils (Scotland) Act, 1900 included as electors all single women who met the parliamentary property qualification as well as married women not qualified with respect to the same property as their husbands, however no woman could act as town councillor until the Qualification of Women (County and Town Councils) (Scotland) Act, 1907. Finally, the County, Town and Parish Councils (Qualification) (Scotland) Act, 1914 allowed all persons regardless of sex to run for county council.

The timing of women's municipal enfranchisement in Scotland seems to have had important implications for mobilising the BWTASCU's support for women's suffrage. Temperance reform was a major political issue in late nineteenth-century Scotland, and in the 1870 to 1914 period, in contrast with earlier nineteenth-century emphases on temperance reform through moral conversion of the individual, temperance reformers increasingly favoured prohibition as the preferred means of reform.[48] Prohibition advocates supported local veto, or the ability of communities to vote to ban licensed premises, and so the local vote and temperance reform were seen by many as intrinsically linked. The relationship between local voting and prohibition in Scotland had clear implications for the BWTASCU's support for women's equal parliamentary enfranchisement.

While a Britannic perspective is necessary for developing a stronger appreciation of diversity within the British women's movement, an international perspective can reveal the importance of Anglophone networks for the women's movement in Scotland. Interest in the 'Atlantic world' has gained currency in British history, but in the context of Empire I find the notion of an 'Anglophone world', which includes the United States and white settler colonies, more useful.[49] Scotland is distinguished by its position in this Anglophone context. The Scots were a strongly migratory population and developed close ties with Australia, New Zealand and the United States, and the immigration networks that spread out from Scotland connected reforming women to the ideas of a global women's movement.[50] These relationships with the Anglophone world had important consequences for the Scottish women's movement, and for example, when the American temperance reformer Mrs Eliza Stewart visited Britain in 1876 her visit was used as the opportunity for establishing British organisations similar to the American WCTU. While the BWTA in England sought to distance itself from the WCTU, official histories of the BWTASCU as well as Stewart's own history of British female temperance reform celebrate the BWTASCU's close ties with the American women's temperance movement.[51]

It is through the lens of these themes – a feminine public sphere, a re-evaluation of constitutional suffragism and an appreciation for Britannic and international perspectives – that key women's temperance, suffrage and Liberal organisations in Glasgow and Edinburgh are investigated. In so doing, this book seeks to be more than a narrow organisational history, but rather an exploration of the social and cultural world of middle-class public women with resonance for the vigorous community of reforming women throughout Britain's urban landscape.

Notes

1 'Scotland. Leith', *Women's Suffrage Journal* [hereafter *WSJ*] 13, no. 151 (Aug 1882): 124.

2 Mary White, 'Recollections of My Temperance Work', *Scottish Women's Temperance News* (*SWTN*) 2, no. 2 (Feb 1898): 22. BWTASCU Collection, the People's Story, Edinburgh City Museums [hereafter BWTASCU Collection].

3 Leonore Davidoff and Catherine Hall, *Family Fortunes: Men and Women of the English Middle Class, 1780–1850* (London: The University of Chicago Press, 1987).

4 Eleanor Gordon and Gwyneth Nair, *Public Lives: Women, Family and Society in Victorian Britain* (London: Yale University Press, 2003).

5 Gordon and Nair, *Public Lives*, 5 and chapter 6.

6 Gordon and Nair, *Public Lives*, 200.

7 See Simon Gunn, *The Public Culture of the Victorian Middle Class: Ritual and Authority and the English Industrial City 1840–1914* (Manchester: Manchester University Press, 2000); Alan Kidd and David Nicholls (eds), *Gender, Culture and Consumerism: Middle-Class Identity in Britain 1800–1914* (Manchester: Manchester University Press, 1999) and *The Making of the British Middle Class? Studies of Regional and Cultural Diversity since the Eighteenth Century* (Thrupp, Gloucestershire: Sutton Publishing Limited, 1998).

8 See Sue Innes and Jane Rendall, 'Women, Gender and Politics', *Gender in Scottish History Since 1700*, eds Lynn Abrams, Eleanor Gordon, Deborah Simonton and Eileen Janes Yeo (Edinburgh: Edinburgh University Press, 2006), 43–83; Moira Martin, 'Single Women and Philanthropy: A Case Study of Women's Associational Life in Bristol, 1880–1914', *Women's History Review* [hereafter WHR] 17, no. 3 (2008): 419–34; and Simon Morgan, *A Victorian Woman's Place: Public Culture in the Nineteenth Century* (London: Tauris Academic Studies, 2007).

9 The literature tends to make this assumption tacitly, however this notion is made explicit in: Graeme Morton, *Unionist Nationalism: Governing Urban Scotland 1830–60* (East Linton: Tuckwell, c.1999), 71–2; and Richard G. Trainor, 'The Elite', *Glasgow, Volume II: 1830 to 1912*, eds W. Hamish Fraser and Irene Maver (Manchester: Manchester University Press, 1996), 237.

10 Joan B. Landes, 'The Public and the Private Sphere: A Feminist Reconsideration', *Feminists Read Habermas: Gendering the Subject of Discourse*, ed. Johanna Meehan (London: Routledge, 1995), 97–9.

11 Ruth Lister, *Citizenship: Feminist Perspectives* (London: MacMillan, 1997), 67.

12 Carole Pateman, *The Disorder of Women: Democracy, Feminism and Political Theory* (Cambridge: Polity Press, 1989), 210–11.

13 Innes and Rendall, 'Women, Gender and Politics', 44.

14 Innes and Rendall, 'Women, Gender and Politics', 60.

15 Julia Bush, *Women Against the Vote: Female Anti-Suffragism in Britain* (Oxford: Oxford University Press, 2007), 24.

16 See Morgan, *A Victorian Woman's Place*.

17 Carmen Neilson Varty, '"A career in Christian charity": Women's Benevolence and the Public Sphere in a Mid-Nineteenth-Century Canadian City', 'Middle-Class Women and Professional Identity', eds Krista Cowman and Louise A. Jackson, *WHR* 14, no. 2 (2005): 254.

18 Morgan, *A Victorian Woman's Place*, 1.

19 See Kathryn Gleadle, *The Early Feminists: Radical Unitarians and the Emergence of the Women's Rights Movement, 1831–51* (London: MacMillan Press Ltd., 1995); Clare Midgley, *Women Against Slavery: The British Campaigns, 1780–1870* (London: Routledge, 1992); and Morgan, *A Victorian Woman's Place*.

20 Clare Midgley, *Feminism and Empire: Women Activists in Imperial Britain, 1790–1865* (Abingdon, Oxon: Routledge, 2007).

21 See Kathleen D. McCarthy, 'Parallel Power Structures: Women and the Voluntary Sphere', *Lady Bountiful Revisited: Women, Philanthropy and Power*, ed. Kathleen D. McCarthy (London: Rutgers University Press, 1990), 1–34.

22 Myriam Boussahba-Bravard, 'Introduction', *Suffrage Outside Suffragism: Women's Vote in Britain 1880–1914*, ed. Myriam Boussahba-Bravard (Houndsmills, Basingstoke: Palgrave MacMillan, 2007), 1–32.

23 Boussahba-Bravard, 'Introduction', 1.

24 This narrative is rooted in suffrage histories from the early and mid twentieth century, including those written by female campaigners, which tend to reserve the greatest emphasis for the militant campaign in the 1903–14 period. For example, see Roger Fulford, *Votes for Women: The Story of a Struggle* (London: Faber & Faber, 1957); Christabel Pankhurst, *Unshackled: The Story of How We Won the Vote* (London: Hutchinson & Co. Ltd., 1959); Sylvia E. Pankhurst, *The Suffragette Movement: An Intimate Account of Persons and Ideals* (London: Longman Group, 1931); Antonia Raeburn, *The Militant Suffragettes* (Newton Abbot: Victorian & Modern History Book Club, 1974) and *The Suffragette View* (Newton Abbot: David & Charles Limited, 1974); and Andrew Rosen, *Rise Up, Women!: The Militant Campaign of the Women's Social and Political Union 1903–1914* (London: Routledge & Kegan Paul, 1974).

25 These authors have highlighted the particular importance of Ray Strachey's *The Cause* (1928) and Sylvia Pankhurst's *The Suffragette Movement* (1931) for women's history writing. See Maroula Joannou and June Purvis, 'Introduction: The Writing of the Women's Suffrage Movement', *The Women's Suffrage Movement: New Feminist Perspectives*, eds Maroula Joannou and June Purvis (Manchester: Manchester University Press, 1998), 1–14; and Kathryn Dodd, 'Cultural Politics and Women's Historical Writing: The Case of Ray Strachey's *The Cause*', *Women's Studies International Forum* 13, no. 1/2 (1990): 134.

26 Melanie Nolan and Caroline Daley, 'International Feminist Perspectives on Suffrage: An Introduction', *Suffrage and Beyond: International Feminist Perspectives*, eds Melanie Nolan and Caroline Daley (Auckland: Auckland University Press, 1994), 7.

27 See Sandra Stanley Holton, *Feminism and Democracy: Women's Suffrage and Reform Politics in Britain 1900–1918* (Cambridge: Cambridge University Press, 1986).

28 See Les Garner, *Stepping Stones to Women's Liberty: Feminist Ideas in the Women's Suffrage Movement 1900–1918* (London: Heinemann Educational Books, 1984).

29 Sandra Stanley Holton, 'Reflecting on Suffrage History', *A Suffrage Reader: Charting Directions in British Suffrage History*, eds Claire Eustance, Joan Ryan and Laura Ugolini (London: Leicester University Press, 2000), 24.

30 See Carroll Smith-Rosenburg, 'The Female World of Love and Ritual: Relations between Women in Nineteenth-Century America', *Signs* 1 (1975): 1–29.

31 See Philippa Levine, *Victorian Feminists 1850–1900* (London: Hutchison Education, 1987); and Gleadle, *The Early Feminists*.

32 Nineteenth-century feminism has attracted increased investigation by historians such as: Barbara Caine, *Victorian Feminists* (Oxford: Oxford University Press, 1992); Gleadle, *The Early Feminists*; and Levine, *Victorian Feminists*.

33 Edited collections include, Eustance, Ryan and Ugolini (eds), *A Suffrage Reader*; Joannou and Purvis (eds), *The Women's Suffrage Movement*; Laura E. Nym Mayhall, Philippa Levine and Ian Christopher Fletcher (eds), *Women Suffrage in the British Empire: Citizenship, Nation and Race* (London: Routledge, 2000); June Purvis ed., 'The Suffragette and Women's History Special Double Issue', *WHR* 14, no. 3 & 4 (2005): 357–602; and June Purvis and Sandra Stanley Holton (eds), *Votes for Women* (London; New York: Routledge, 2000). See also Ann Heilmann ed., 'Words as Deeds: Literary and Historical Perspectives on Women's Suffrage', *WHR* 11, no. 4 (2002) and 12, no. 1 (2003). These edited collections are based on exciting new evaluations of suffrage that recover under-researched organisations and recognise the value of regional and

international perspectives. Even so, analyses of the militant movement, though novel, dominate in these collections.

34 See Holton, *Feminism and Democracy*, and Laura E. Nym Mayhall, *The Militant Suffrage Movement: Citizenship and Resistance in Britain, 1860–1930* (Oxford: Oxford University Press, 2003).

35 Liberal women in England have received limited attention in chapter and article form, see Claire Hirshfield, 'Fractured Faith: Liberal Party Women and the Suffrage Issue in Britain, 1892–1914', *Gender & History* 2, no. 2 (1990): 174–97; and Linda Walker, 'Party Political Women: A Comparative Study of Liberal Women and the Primrose League, 1890–1914', *Equal or Different: Women's Politics 1900–1914*, ed. Jane Rendall (Oxford: Basil Blackwell, 1987), 165–91 and 'Gender, Suffrage and Party: Liberal Women's Organisations, 1880–1914', *Suffrage Outside Suffragism*, ed. Boussahba-Bravard, 77–102; and Martin Pugh, *The March of the Women: A Revisionist Analysis of the Campaign for Women's Suffrage, 1866–1914* (Oxford: Oxford University Press, 2000).

36 Leah Leneman, *A Guid Cause: The Women's Suffrage Movement in Scotland* (Aberdeen: Aberdeen University Press, 1991).

37 See Elspeth King, 'The Scottish Women's Suffrage Movement', *Out of Bounds: Women in Scottish Society, 1800–1945*, eds Esther Breitenbach and Eleanor Gordon (Edinburgh: Edinburgh University Press, 1992), 121–50; Lindy Moore, 'Feminists and Femininity: A Case Study of WSPU Propaganda and Local Response at a Scottish By-Election', *Women's Studies International Forum* 5, no. 6 (1982): 675–84.

38 Reliance on Leneman can be seen in June Hannam, '"I had not been to London": Women's Suffrage A View from the Regions', *Votes for Women*, eds Purvis and Holton, 226–45; and Sarah Pederson, 'The Appearance of Women's Politics in the Correspondence Pages of Aberdeen Newspapers, 1900–14', *WHR* 11, no. 4 (2002): 657–74.

39 See Brian Harrison, *Drink and the Victorians: The Temperance Question in England 1815–1872* (London: Faber and Faber, 1971).

40 See Lilian Lewis Shiman, '"Changes Are Dangerous": Women and Temperance in Victorian England', *Religion in the Lives of English Women, 1760–1930*, ed. Gail Malmgreen (London; Sydney: Croom Helm, 1986), 193–215 and *Crusade Against Drink in Victorian England* (London: The MacMillan Press Ltd., 1988), especially chapter 7.

41 See W. R. Lambert, *Drink and Sobriety in Victorian Wales c.1820–c.1895* (Cardiff: University of Wales Press, 1983).

42 See Elspeth King, *Scotland Sober and Free: The Temperance Movement 1829–1979* (Glasgow: Glasgow Museums and Art Galleries, 1979); Bernard Aspinwall, *Portable Utopia: Glasgow and the United States 1820–1920* (Aberdeen: Aberdeen University Press, 1984).

43 See Margaret Barrow, 'Teetotal Feminists', *A Suffrage Reader*, eds Eustance, Ryan and Ugolini, 69–89; Kirstin Doern, '"Equal Questions": The "Woman Question" and the "Drink Question" in the Writings of Clara Lucas Balfour', *Women, Religion and Feminism in Britain 1750–1900*, ed. Sue Morgan (Houndsmills, Basingstoke: Palgrave, 2000), 159–75; Ceridwen Lloyd-Morgan, 'From Temperance to Suffrage?', *Our Mother's Lands: Chapters in Welsh Women's History, 1830–1939*, ed. Angela V. John (Cardiff: University of Wales Press, 1991), 135–58.

44 In terms of suffrage history, see, for example, Claire Eustance, Laura Ugolini and Joan Ryan, 'Introduction: Writing Suffrage Histories – The "British" Experience', *A Suffrage Reader*, eds Eustance, Ugolini and Ryan, 1–19; Hannam, '"I had not been to London"; and Ursula Masson, '"Political conditions in Wales are quite different…': Party Politics

and Votes for Women in Wales, 1912–15', *WHR* 9, no. 2 (2000), 369–88.

45 Those who have acknowledged the differing status of women in Scottish local government include W. Hamish Fraser, *Scottish Popular Politics: From Radicalism to Labour* (Edinburgh: Polygon, 2000); Patricia Greenwood Harrison, *Connecting Links: The British and American Woman Suffrage Movements, 1900–1914* (London: Greenwood Press, 2000); Leneman, *A Guid Cause*; and Jane Rendall, 'The Citizenship of Women and the Reform Act of 1867', *Defining the Victorian Nation: Class, Race, Gender and the British Reform Act of 1867*, eds Catherine Hall, Keith McClelland and Jane Rendall (Cambridge: Cambridge University Press, 2000), 119–78 and 'Women and the Public Sphere', *Gender & History* 11, no. 3 (1999), 475–88. In contrast, women's position in local government is not a feature of Michael Dyer's discussion of Scottish local government, see *Men of Property and Intelligence: The Scottish Electoral System prior to 1884 Vol. 1* and *Capable Citizens and Improvident Democrats: The Scottish Electoral System 1884–1929 Vol. 2* (Aberdeen: Scottish Cultural Press, 1996).

46 For more information on the laws governing women's access to local government in the 1870–1914 period, see Appendix 1.

47 Patricia Hollis, *Ladies Elect: Women in English Local Government 1865–1914* (Oxford: Clarendon Press, 1987), 206–7. See also Megan Smitley, 'Women in Victorian and Edwardian Politics: The Case of the Municipal Vote in Scotland, 1881–1914', unpublished paper presented to Institute of Historical Research, Women's History Seminar, 7 May 2004.

48 From the second half of the nineteenth century, the international temperance movement came increasingly to support prohibition, and in Britain this is seen in the formation of dedicated prohibition societies such as the United Kingdom Alliance (1853) and the Scottish Permissive Bill Association (1858). See A. E. Dingle, *The Campaign for Prohibition in Victorian England: The United Kingdom Alliance 1872–1895* (London: Croom Helm Ltd., 1980); James Kneale, 'The Place of Drink: Temperance and the Public, 1856–1914', *Social & Cultural Geography* 2, no. 1 (2001): 43–59; and King, *Scotland Sober and Free*.

49 Several historians have highlighted the importance of international perspectives for studies of 'first-wave' feminism. See, for example, Antoinette Burton, 'Rules of Thumb: British History and "Imperial Culture" in Nineteenth- and Twentieth-Century Britain', *WHR* 3, no. 4 (1994): 483–501 and 'The White Woman's Burden: British Feminists and "the Indian Woman" 1865–1915', *Western Women and Imperialism: Complicity and Resistance*, eds Nupur Chauduri and Margaret Strobel (Indianapolis: Indiana University Press, 1992), 137–57; Harrison, *Connecting Links*; Clare Midgley 'Anti-Slavery and the Roots of "Imperial Feminism"', *Gender and Imperialism*, ed. Clare Midgley (Manchester: Manchester University Press, 1998), 161–79; and Ian R. Tyrrell, *Woman's World Woman's Empire: The Women's Christian Temperance Union in International Perspective, 1880–1930* (London: University of North Carolina Press, 1991).

50 For discussions of nineteenth-century Scots' emigration see, for example, Jeanette M. Brock, *The Mobile Scot: A Study of Emigration and Migration 1861–1911* (Edinburgh: John Donald Publishers Ltd., 1999); and Marjory Harper, *Emigration from North-East Scotland Volume One: Willing Exiles* (Aberdeen: Aberdeen University Press, 1988).

51 Eliza Stewart, *The Crusader in Great Britain, or, The History of the Origins and Organization of the British Women's Temperance Association* (Springfield, OH: The New Era Company, 1893), 315–16. The Women's Library [hereafter WL] 178.10942 STE.

I

The organisations

Women's organisations in the 1870 to 1914 period were characterised by a vigorous community of public-spirited women. This community of middle-class public women generated influential inter-organisational networks, networks which were mapped using a database of organisational membership and which cross-pollinated the policies of women's temperance, suffrage and Liberal organisations. That is, individual women's membership to multiple organisations, either simultaneously or at different periods during their reforming careers, made an important contribution to broadening the reform programmes of each organisation. The women's temperance and Liberal associations were particularly prone to a multi-issue approach, and both organisations were sites of energetic agitation for temperance reform and female political rights. Indeed, individuals' membership across several organisations encouraged an inter-penetration of ideas and reforming interests, a process which undermines strict differentiation between organisations as suffragist or non-suffragist.

The constitutional suffrage societies

The Glasgow and Edinburgh constitutional suffrage societies are the central explicitly-suffrage societies in this study. The ENSWS was established in 1867, and was the first dedicated suffrage organisation in Scotland and one of the first three women's suffrage groups in Britain alongside Manchester and London. The records left by the ENSWS include annual reports for the years 1868–78, 1892 and 1907 as well as reports of its work published in the *Women's Suffrage Journal* (*WSJ*) (1870–90). The GNSWS was established in 1870, and while official records for this organisation do not survive, the *WSJ* carries a selection of reports submitted by the GNSWS.[1] The work of Glasgow suffragists is better documented from 1902 when the GNSWS was reorganised as the GWSAWS, and the records for the GWSAWS include minute books spanning 1902 to 1914. This discussion also refers to suffrage societies in Kilmarnock and Shetland. The Kilmarnock branch of the Scottish Federation of Women's Suffrage Societies (SFWSS) was formed in March 1911; the SFWSS was established in 1910 as an affiliate of the London-based NUWSS, and was designed to supervise the constitutional suffrage campaign in Scotland. The minute books of the Kilmarnock society cover the period 1911 to 1914. The Shetland National Society for Women's Suffrage (SNSWS) was formed in Twageos in October 1909, independent of party affiliation and with the understanding that it 'had no connection with the disturbances which had been caused recently by women Suffragists'.[2] The minutes for this society are also confined to the early twentieth century and cover the years 1909 to 1919.

The constitutional societies examined here shared a similar approach to the suffrage campaign across time and space. The uneven distribution of source material means that this analysis of the nineteenth-century campaign must focus on Edinburgh, while evidence from the early twentieth century is more plentiful for Glasgow. While accepting the deficiencies of the source material, it is possible to identify some important aspects of the methodology of these organisations, namely suffragists' agitation in support of parliamentarians' bills for women's suffrage. The annual reports of the ENSWS (1868–78), suggest that the early work of the society centred on supporting the parliamentary work of men such as John Stuart Mill, Jacob Bright and Duncan McLaren. This support most often took the form of petitions to Government in favour of legislation for women's equal enfranchisement. For instance, the 1868 report claimed that fifty-five petitions had been organised with a total of 14,000 signatures in support of the Representation of the People Bill: 'The signatures to the petition were procured partly by the aid of paid Canvassers, partly by the personal efforts of Members of Committee'.[3] In 1871, the ENSWS claimed to have gathered over 24,000 signatures, including the endorsement of the Edinburgh Town Council – the first local government body to petition for women's suffrage – in support of Jacob Bright and Charles Dilke's bill to enfranchise women.[4] From this year, the ENSWS gathered tens of thousands of signatures in favour of legislation for women's equal enfranchisement, an effort which peaked in 1875 with 50,000 signatures.[5] The minutes from the GWSAWS suggest that Glasgow suffragists also focused on support for male politicians' efforts to pass legislation for women's enfranchisement. For instance, the GWSAWS worked closely with Colonel Denny MP to bring equal enfranchisement measures before parliament. In March 1903, the GWSAWS asked Denny to introduce a pro-suffrage amendment to the Representation of the People Act.[6] In November, the GWSAWS asked the NUWSS to rally behind Denny's amendment.[7] In April 1904, the GWSAWS secretary, Mrs Isaac T. Hunter, sent letters to MPs known to support women's suffrage, 'asking them to support a Resolution in favour of Women's Suffrage to be moved on the 16th March by Sir Chas. McLaren and seconded by Col. Denny'.[8] Ultimately Denny's amendment was unsuccessful, and by October 1904 the GWSAWS's attention had shifted to Kier Hardie's women's suffrage bill. What is significant here is that the GWSAWS's relationship with Denny can be seen as representative of its approach to suffrage agitation, and demonstrates the continued co-operation between constitutional suffragists and their male advocates in parliament. This trend is further reflected in the work of the SNSWS, which consisted in the main of lobbying local MPs to support women's suffrage legislation. So, in the run up to the 1911 Conciliation Bill, the SNSWS lobbied the local MP, Mr Wason, to support the measure.[9] While a basic component of constitutional suffragism was co-operation with and support of parliamentarians, suffragists also took on a role in public speaking for their cause.

A prominent feature of suffragists' campaigning was the organisation of large public meetings in order to promote women's voting rights. An important component of public meetings was suffragists' public speaking. Evidence from the annual reports of the ENSWS and the *WSJ* suggests that women had a somewhat marginal role as speakers in the early years of the campaign. While women were listed as present on the platform in reports of annual public meetings, the speakers tended to be male parliamentarians and local leaders with the exception of Miss Eliza Wigham, the secretary, who read the annual report. In Glasgow, Miss Jessie Craigen was renowned for addressing working-class audiences at open-air meetings in the 1870s. The *WSJ* described such a meeting at Glasgow Green in 1872:

> The persons present numbered about 1,000, chiefly working men of the most intelligent type. The meeting lasted more than two hours, and of the immense mass not more than 50 quitted the place from the beginning to the end. All stood in a compact throng till the end of the proceedings. After an address by Miss Craigen, the Chairman opened the discussion. Mr Long, and a young man whose name did not transpire, spoke in opposition, and Miss Craigen replied. When the debate was closed, a motion for the adoption of a petition in favour of the Bill to Remove the Electoral Disabilities of Women was put. A

perfect forest of hands went up for it; for the contrary a few appeared. The meeting was dispersed with some little difficulty, for the people wanted to hear more.[10]

In the following year, the *WSJ* reported that: 'Miss Craigen addressed a meeting in the United Presbyterian Church Manse, St Girbal's [*sic*], Glasgow, on February 17th. The attendance was almost entirely of the working class. A petition in favour of Mr Bright's Bill was carried by a unanimous vote.'[11] Craigen's efforts to gear her speeches towards working-class audiences in the early stages of the suffrage campaign were extraordinary in terms both of women's public speaking and of efforts to engage with the working classes, and Leneman has noted that Craigen's endeavours to enlist working-class support were the exception rather than the rule.[12]

Suffragists' public speaking seems to have become more common practice as the campaign matured. This is most striking in reports of the Scottish National Demonstration of Women, which was organised in 1882 by the GNSWS. The *WSJ* carried an extensive report of the meeting held in St Andrew's Halls, and described the meeting as, 'specially a woman's one, the only portion of the hall to which men were admitted being the balcony'.[13] The spatial segregation of male attendees is significant as evidence of suffragists' subversion of gendered roles in public spaces. As Simon Morgan has noted, by the 1860s the trend towards spatially separating female attendees at public events was increasingly realised in the architecture of public buildings, specifically the inclusion of balconies and galleries designed to accommodate female spectators.[14] By dominating the speaking platform and removing men to the balcony, suffragists at the Scottish National Demonstration symbolically usurped men's dominance of public forums. All of the speakers at the demonstration were women, including the American suffragist, Elizabeth Cady Stanton, and the English editor of the *WSJ*, Lydia Becker. Mrs Priscilla McLaren, who presided, along with Miss Eliza Wigham, Miss Flora Stevenson, Miss Jessie Craigen and Mrs Wellstood represented the Scottish movement. The *WSJ* reproduced Reuben Roseneath's coverage of the demonstration for the Glasgow paper, the *Christian Leader*. Roseneath summarised the arguments of the speakers while critiquing, with much praise, the public speaking capabilities of the women on the platform. He was especially impressed with Craigen's adept public speaking and claimed: 'For twenty minutes Miss Craigen held the audience spellbound. This lady is one of the greatest orators I have ever heard. She gave the impression of being an independent and original thinker, fearless in speaking out her convictions; and some of the passages of her speech might be justly described as logic on fire.'[15] Roseneath pressed his point regarding suffragists' ability to work a platform by issuing a challenge to the male audience to admit the fine performance of the female speakers: 'if any of the gentlemen in the balcony – and among them were sheriffs, professors, ministers, and lawyers – can say that they ever heard the same uniform good speaking at any meeting they attended in their lives before, or as many effective points crushed into the same space of time, I shall be greatly surprised.'[16] Roseneath's commentary is especially revealing in the context of this investigation as he seems to highlight middle-class women's successful endeavours to participate fully in middle-class public life. As Roseneath implies, public speaking was understood as central to the public lives of the local male elite, and this point was further emphasised in the *WSJ*'s reporting.

Suffragists' endeavours to network with MPs, and their ability to publicly lay claim to their political rights demonstrates the positioning of constitutional suffrage societies in middle-class civic life. Suffragists were keenly aware of their male peers' emphasis on civic participation, and in arguing for women's equal enfranchisement Victorian feminists might organise public spectacle of their capacity for full participation as citizens. In other words, the speakers at the Scottish National Demonstration of Women can be understood as an example of suffragists' endeavours to prove their fitness for the parliamentary franchise by demonstrating their own mastery of the skills so prized by the local male elite. While the GWSAWS and ENSWS were loci of middle-class women's public and political activities, other associations, especially the temperance and Liberal women's groups, provided further outlets for women's civic energies.

The BWTASCU

The BWTASCU and the BWTA in England represent British equivalents of WCTUs. A WCTU was first established in the United States in 1874. WCTUs were quickly formed around the world, and in 1883 the WWCTU was formed to facilitate co-operation and communication among an emerging international network of female temperance reformers. The BWTASCU was the most influential women's temperance organisation in late nineteenth-century Scotland, and represents the largest umbrella organisation for women's single-sex temperance unions in Scotland. The BWTASCU and BWTA were established on 21 April 1876 when female temperance reformers met at an International Order of Good Templars conference in Newcastle. British female temperance reformers had been invited to the meeting by the American WCTU, which was represented in Newcastle by the world-renowned American female temperance reformer Mrs Eliza 'Mother' Stewart. An estimated 150 delegates came together in Newcastle, and resolved to establish women's temperance unions in Scotland and England along the lines of the WCTU. In her history of the British women's temperance movement, *The Crusader in Great Britain*, Eliza Stewart suggests that the choice of the name 'British Women's Temperance Association' rather than 'Women's Christian Temperance Union' was motivated by religious belief:

> Several of the ladies composing that convention were Friends, and consistent with their known objection to the use of unnecessary titles or names beyond the simple name denoting the object of their work, they objected to the prefix 'Christian'. Mrs Lucas, especially, maintained that the word Christian was superfluous; it was, as a matter of course, understood that the association was composed of Christian women, actuated by Christian principles and motives ... Sister Lucas, commanding the highest respect, and having unbounded influence among her co-workers, the name was settled upon as she suggested.[17]

Stewart further reports that Mrs Helen Kirk, wife of a distinguished University of Edinburgh professor, was responsible for appending 'Scottish Christian Union' to the name of the organisation in 1879.[18]

The BWTASCU was an autonomous organisation, which determined its own policies, raised its own funds and organised its own branches, yet during the nineteenth century the BWTASCU was affiliated with the WWCTU via the BWTA in England. The BWTASCU broke all administrative ties with the BWTA in 1904 after the Scottish organisation was denied autonomous representation at the WWCTU conference held in Edinburgh in 1900. The BWTASCU had paid its affiliation fee to the WWCTU through the English BWTA, and so was barred from representing itself as an independent organisation. A history of the BWTASCU written by Miss Christina Robertson, editor of the BWTASCU's official journal, the *Scottish Women's Temperance News* (*SWTN*), cites this insult to the BWTASCU's sovereignty as the determining factor in the organisation's decision to disaffiliate from the BWTA and to affiliate directly with the WWCTU.[19]

The BWTASCU was a large, well-funded and highly structured organisation. Its members were known as 'British Women', and by 1908 the BWTASCU claimed 80,000 members across 332 branches.[20] The BWTASCU's funding came mainly from affiliation fees and contributions to the so-called extension fund. Special fund-raising events were organised to top up the coffers, and in 1898 a Victoria Extension Fund scheme raised

£9,993 for the expansion of the organisation, and a 1905 Bazaar organised by the Glasgow British Women in St Andrew's Halls raised £7,700.[21] The BWTASCU headquarters was in Edinburgh, and in 1902, eleven district unions were established to ease its workload: Aberdeen, Ayrshire, Borders, Dumfries and Galloway, Dundee, Edinburgh and Lothians, Fifeshire, Glasgow, Moray and Ross, Perth and Stirling.[22]

Two branches of the BWTASCU are particularly important for this discussion: the Edinburgh Central Branch and the Glasgow Prayer Union.[23] Women's temperance associations had begun to emerge prior to the formation of the BWTASCU, and while the Edinburgh Central Branch developed from a group established in 1876, the Glasgow Prayer Union was based on the Ladies' Temperance Prayer Union which had been formed in 1874.[24] In 1878, the Edinburgh Central Branch invited all Scottish women's temperance unions to unite under its headship, at which point the Ladies' Temperance Prayer Union joined the BWTASCU and was renamed the 'Glasgow Prayer Union'. By 1879 twenty-one women's temperance unions had united under Edinburgh's administration. In 1902, a headquarters office was set-up in Edinburgh, followed in 1906 by a sub-office in Glasgow.[25] Indeed, while the Edinburgh Central Branch was the official Scottish-national headquarters, the Glasgow Prayer Union functioned as a de facto headquarters for the west of Scotland. Source material is abundant for both branches. The minute books and annual reports from the Glasgow Prayer Union span the period 1881 to 1898. The annual reports (1888–1913) and minute books (1908–11) from the Edinburgh Central Branch are useful for studying developments in BWTASCU policies as the organisation professionalised and departmentalised. In 1896, the BWTASCU began publishing its official organ, the *SWTN*, and by 1908 the *SWTN* was credited with a monthly circulation of 4,800.[26] The *SWTN* is an incredibly rich source, which includes biographical accounts of prominent members, discussions of trends in female temperance reform, debates on women's political rights as well as reports on the international women's temperance movement.

The BWTASCU was an international rather than a provincial organisation, and it is best understood in an Anglophone context. Members of the BWTASCU held positions on the executive of the BWTA in England, and, for example, Miss Eliza Wigham (Edinburgh), Mrs George Stewart (Glasgow) and Mrs Henderson (Dundee) were elected vice-presidents of the BWTA in 1876.[27] Members of the BWTASCU were further active on an international stage, and Mrs Margaret Parker (Dundee) acted as the president of the Woman's International Temperance Union at a temperance congress in Philadelphia in 1876.[28]

Temperance reform in the United States exerted a strong and sustained influence on female temperance reform in Scotland, and Aspinwall has noted that, 'America consistently forced the pace among Scottish temperance reformers'.[29] This is particularly evident from the BWTASCU's willingness to adopt the progressive multi-issue approach of the American WCTU. In the early 1890s, Francis Willard, President of the American WCTU, developed the 'do everything' policy which sought to mobilise women's temperance unions in pursuit of all 'women's issues'. As Ruth Bordin suggests 'do everything' illustrated that the WCTU, 'approached temperance as part of a complex of related issues that should be dealt with simultaneously'.[30] 'Do everything' was justified as a means to, 'open up a wide field and give room for diversity of gift', and its practical consequence was an increased departmentalisation of women's temperance unions.[31] The BWTASCU implemented 'do everything' in 1893, and the Edinburgh Central Branch set the tone by forming thirteen departments, which had increased to twenty by 1908. Local branches operated with a fair degree of autonomy and organised departments that reflected the reforming interests of their members. An important upshot of 'do everything' was the formation of suffrage departments, and the BWTASCU is distinguished from the BWTA in England by its accept- ance of suffrage departments and the multi-issue approach inherent to 'do everything'. Scoto-American connections were important for making the BWTASCU more open to the feminist-inspired 'do everything' than was the case in the BWTA in England. These links were facilitated by the BWTASCU's self-construction as a legacy of the American women's temperance 'Crusade' as well as personal networks among female temper- ance reformers in Scotland and the USA.

Female temperance reformers in Scotland and the United States shared an understanding of the origins of the BWTASCU. Robertson's history identifies the BWTASCU as an outcome of the Crusade, while Stewart describes the establishment of the BWTASCU as, 'really a contin- uation of our crusade work, or a legitimate outgrowth of it, and would be better understood and appreciated if read in connection with the history of that remarkable uprising'.[32] The Crusade, also known as the 'Whisky War', refers to an 1873–74 phenomenon of American women's protest against the use of alcohol and saloon culture. The Crusade had a strong evangelical character, and often took the form of mass marches and prayer meetings outside saloons, however these protests could turn violent with women smashing windows and entering into physical confrontation with male drinkers.[33] Jack S. Blocker Jr. estimates that the Crusade enlisted between 57,000 and 143,000 women in 911 events.[34]

The readiness of Scotland's female temperance reformers to identify their organisation as a legacy of an American women's temperance crusade testifies to the deep spiritual motivation which underpinned the temperance movement. Robertson's account of the origins of the BWTASCU argues that:

> The Women's Temperance Movement has its origins in the outpouring of the Holy Spirit of God ... [the Crusade] was the women's baptism by fire. It impelled them to take a position in Temperance work, public decision ... No lesser power than the power of the Holy Spirit of God could, in a moment, have changed their traditions and forced them to the front.[35]

Women's temperance unions had developed from 'ladies' prayer meetings', and prayer remained a central feature of women's temperance unions throughout the period. In the words of Robertson, 'it was from prayer meetings on both sides of the Atlantic the work emanated, and to prayer a first place was given by branch after branch as it was formed in Scotland'.[36]

Personal networks between female temperance reformers in Scotland and North America reinforced the notion that the BWTASCU was a product of the Crusade. Of most importance was the relationship between Margaret Parker and Eliza Stewart. These two women were driving forces behind the formation of the BWTASCU. As a result of her leading role in the Crusade, Stewart, a native of Ohio, emerged as a leading figure in international temperance. Parker, an Englishwoman from Bolton, was married to Edward Parker, a member of a prominent Wesleyan Methodist manufacturing family in Dundee. Parker's public life and reforming career was most strongly connected with Scotland, however as Stewart recalled of their mutual visit to Bannockburn:

> Mrs Parker, though at this time a resident of Scotland and married to one of the bravest of Scots, is by birth and evidently by attachment, English. Her criticism of the Scots for digging the pitfalls in the boggy ground and covering carefully with sod which played such sad mischief with the English mounted soldiery, showed very plainly which side claimed her sympathies.[37]

Parker and Stewart first met in June 1875 at a meeting of the National Temperance Association in Chicago; Parker was Scotland's delegate for the International Order of Good Templars. Stewart recalls this meeting as providential: 'As she clasped my hand she exclaimed "Oh! Mother Stewart, will you not come to Scotland?" and I responded with a bounding heart, if it were the Lord's will I would'.[38] From this meeting arose a correspondence between the two women, which centred on arranging a tour of Britain by Stewart. In her history of the British women's temperance movement, Stewart confirms her intention to organise with Parker WCTUs in Britain, and she credits Parker's influence with ensuring, 'that such a wide and hospitable door was opened to me to visit that country'.[39]

The working friendship between Parker and Stewart was not an isolated case. Several high-ranking members of the BWTASCU had personal experiences of North American temperance reform. For instance, Miss Mary White of Glasgow recalled that she was inspired by the Crusade while resident in Canada: 'While there, in the winter of 1873–74, I heard rumours of the Women's Whisky Crusade, then going on in the United States, and on my return home in the summer I found that the impulse from above had reached the praying women of Glasgow'.[40] White then contacted women active in the Glaswegian temperance community such as, Mrs Wilhelmina Woyka and Miss Agnes Ann Bryson, in order to establish the Ladies Temperance Prayer Union, the forerunner of the Glasgow Prayer Union. Female temperance reformers travelling from Scotland to the United States and Canada further strengthened Scoto-American networks. For instance, within three hours of arriving in Quebec at the start of her North American tour, Mrs Mary Reid, a leader of the Glasgow Prayer Union from 1890 to 1902, attended a meeting of the WCTU, 'who asked me to tell them all about our Scottish work and our increase of membership'.[41] Furthermore, the American women's temperance movement was kept before the readers of the *SWTN* with regular reports on the work of Eliza Stewart, Frances Willard and temperance conventions in the United States. Thus, it emerges that from its beginnings in the mid-1870s until the Great War the Scoto-American connection in the women's temperance movement was a sympathetic one.

The BWTASCU's willingness to follow policies innovated by the American WCTU was further encouraged by the personal charisma of Eliza Stewart. For example, Mary White claimed that Stewart's enthusiasm and adept public persona inspired Glasgow's female temperance reformers to appear on public platforms and, 'to plead with our fellow-women to abstain from strong drink as the great enemy of the home'.[42] For her part, Stewart commented on the reticence of Scotswomen take up public speaking and affirmed her own influence in encouraging Scotswomen's public participation in temperance reform:

> Of course it is known to all the world that the ladies of the old country were much more conservative than those of America. But few ladies had

the nerve to brave public prejudice by appearing on the platform. And I understand that when it was known that I was coming to Glasgow some of the very conservative ladies thought it advisable to caution the sisters that they were not to follow Mother Stewart's example by taking to the platform or participating in public meetings. But before I left, not less than half a dozen of those devoted women felt that their souls so fired with zeal for the blessed cause, and their hearts so full of thoughts, that it was 'like fire shut up in their bones'. And I, in very innocent fashion, of course, made opportunities for them.[43]

Stewart further endeared herself to female temperance reformers in Scotland by positioning herself within the Scottish diaspora. In *The Crusader in Great Britain*, Stewart repeatedly refers to her Scottish ancestry, and, for instance, recalls a Glasgow speech in which she thanked, 'the citizens of dear old Scotland for this welcome to one in whose veins runs Scottish blood; and furthermore, one who claims to have married royal family'.[44]

The BWTASCU was a significant site of middle-class women's public lives. It enlisted a range of women in a campaign which increasingly emphasised perceived links between temperance and women's suffrage. It involved women in an international and national community of reformers, and represented an important opportunity for women's public service. In this way, middle-class women's temperance reform activities constituted a key site for women's contribution to a middle-class identity rooted in public life.

The SWLF

The SWLF was established in April 1891. The east–west or Edinburgh–Glasgow split which characterised many large Scottish associations was formally incorporated into the structure of the SWLF, and the constitution instituted a twin leadership based in eastern and western 'divisions'. The Glasgow-based western division and the Edinburgh-based eastern division each had a vice-president, honorary secretary, executive committee and monthly meetings, which were attended by representatives of both divisions, were held alternately in Edinburgh or Glasgow. The SWLF's membership was based in local branches, called Women's Liberal Associations (WLA), and by 1911 the SWLF claimed a membership of 22,000.[45] The SWLF was funded largely through annual affiliation fees levied on the local WLAs (one guinea per annum in 1891), subscriptions and donations; financial reports included in the minutes indicate that the SWLF operated with an annual budget of two to three hundred pounds. Source material for the SWLF includes minute books (1891–1918) and the periodicals the *Scottish Liberal Women's Magazine and County Reporter* (1899–1900) and the *Scottish Liberal Women's Magazine (SLWM)* (1909–14).

From 1870 to 1914 the presidents of the SWLF tended to come from aristocratic backgrounds: Lady Ishbel Countess of Aberdeen (1891–93 and 1902), Lady Trevelyan (1894–97), Lady Helen Munro-Ferguson (1898–1902) and Lady Marjorie Sinclair, later Lady Pentland (1906–12). This tendency reflected an unusual naming convention within the SWLF, as aristocratic members were generally termed 'patronesses' by other contemporary organisations such as the BWTASCU. The SWLF mirrored the male Liberal Association's hierarchy, and its presidents tended to be the wives of the Secretary for Scotland; Sir George Trevelyan, Lord John Pentland and Thomas McKinnon Wood served as Secretaries of Scotland during their wives' SWLF presidencies. Notwithstanding the role of aristocratic women in the SWLF, the chair – who had a more hands-on role than the presidents in the administration of the organisation – as well as other administrative leaders were drawn from the upper middle-classes. For instance, the first chair was Mrs Anna Lindsay (1891–99), wife of a distinguished University of Glasgow principal.

The SWLF, like the BWTASCU, was organised in a sophisticated departmental structure. Early departments included finance, parliamentary bills, literature and organising. The parliamentary bills department sought to work with Liberal parliamentarians to introduce legislation deemed beneficial to women; the literature department amassed and disseminated political literature and maintained a library of its collection; and the organisation department oversaw expansion of the SWLF. In 1899, the SWLF expanded the number of departments to more accurately reflect its multi-issue programme, and added to existing departments those dedicated to: suffrage and poor law; temperance; education and industrialism; and general legislation. It is significant for this discussion that the SWLF's departmental structure integrated temperance reform and women's suffrage.

While suffrage and temperance were prominent features of the SWLF's public activities, it should be remembered that the SWLF's *raison d'être* was to support the Liberal party's political ambitions. Female Liberals were at pains to portray members of the SWLF as agents of a wider Liberal movement, and an obituary for Western Division Vice-President Miss Jane Campbell lamented: 'Through the death of Miss Campbell Scotland has lost a true-hearted Liberal. The great political movements were her constant interest, and she upheld with ardour all

Liberal traditions, and rejoiced in all Liberal developments.[46] The epitaph of 'true-hearted Liberal' highlights the idea that while the SWLF agitated for female political rights and prohibition with the aim of creating a more moral and female-friendly society, at its core the SWLF was a party organisation designed to channel the energies of devoted female Liberals. By the early twentieth century it emerges from the *SLWM* that female Liberals considered themselves exponents of a Liberal Progressivism, and, as a letter written by SWLF Secretary Miss Alice Younger indicates, female Liberals sought the inclusion of female political rights within this ideological rubric:

> The Executive wish to assure the Prime Minister of the loyal and faithful support of the Scottish Liberal Women in the serious constitutional questions which are stirring all ranks in the Country, and of their earnest belief in the new enthusiasm which would be won for Liberalism by the inclusion of the Women's Cause in this great Progressive movement.[47]

While female Liberals understood themselves as guardians of Liberalism and advancers of Liberal ideology, many in the men's Liberal associations may have viewed the WLAs largely as regiments of highly skilled, unpaid party workers.

A practical consequence of women's party loyalty was large amounts of unpaid electioneering work. After the passage of the Corrupt Practices Act in 1883, which limited the amount of money candidates could spend on their campaigns, the unpaid canvassing of female volunteers became indispensable. 'Shamrock's' report on Liberal women's electioneering during the 1909 General Election in the *SLWM* indicates the character of female Liberals' practical assistance to their party:

> By means of house-to-house visitation and personal intercourse our women workers have striven to show the voters that this is a battle from which no man must be absent, and that no sense of confidence can justify an omission to vote. They have tried to keep the waverers from lightly flinging into the ballot-box rights they never may recover. And in distributing literature of endless variety the women have done much to enthuse and enlighten the ordinary voter. In almost every constituency there were bands of Liberal women canvassers, working with cheerfulness, resource, and tact. Their influence is not to be questioned.[48]

Liberal MPs acknowledged the work of the WLAs on their behalf and Miss M. M. Anderson states in her report of a 1911 reception for the SWLF at the Glasgow Liberal Club: 'The innumerable compliments showered on the election work of the SWLF made us feel near to being political entities as we ever shall until we are permitted to serve our country with our votes'.[49] Anderson's reference to a dissatisfaction with the lack of progress towards women's suffrage is a recurring theme in the *SLWM*, yet a loyalty to serve the ideals of Liberalism could undercut this dissatisfaction and motivate Liberal women to labour on behalf of their party. Liberal women believed that their party work served a greater good, even without the vote, and Lady Marjorie Pentland, President of the SWLF (1906–12), assured her co-workers that: 'They need not regret all the time, money, labour, and strength spent on the two elections of the last year if they remembered that they must have contributed to the spread of political education and enlightenment throughout the country.'[50]

Party loyalty was also cast in a Scottish nationalist light, and the *SLWM* tended to conflate Liberalism with Scottish national character. The tendency to celebrate ideas of a noble, educated, progressive and democratic Scottish character was particularly evident in *SLWM* reporting after the 1909 General Election victory when 'Shamrock' claimed: 'In Scotland, at least, the old democratic spirit is at work in this most interesting Election, which is brimful of interest, and will be of lasting memory in the history of our country.'[51] In her praise of the Liberal victory, Mrs Macrae claimed: 'The Scotsman is Liberal-Radical – progressive both by instinct and training.'[52] M. M. Anderson's report on the Liberal Club's 1911 reception of the SWLF claimed that: 'The stirring speeches were just what one wanted to hear, and the only regret they raised in us was the fact that Scotland had not a bigger population, so that larger contingents of Scottish members might be sent to St. Stephen's to ensure that Simon Pure principles of Liberalism shall always flourish there.'[53]

The idea of an overriding party loyalty should not be taken at face value and should not be used to disqualify the SWLF from a discussion of suffragism. Helen Waddel was a devoted member of the SWLF from 1892, and a member of the suffrage department from 1899. Waddel's public career centred on campaigning for women's suffrage within the Liberal party, and while she staunchly supported Liberalism, she was one of the most outspoken critics of Liberals' delays in enacting women's suffrage. Waddel's address at the SWLF annual meeting in 1912 reflected on the failure of the Liberal Government to successfully enfranchise women:

> one had to remember that men were legislating and had legislated for a long time without any consideration for logic. Men were not at all logical. They were extremely emotional. One had to remember that they were just as they were. They were very human. She thought the women had to thank themselves for the progress made. In many of the darkest days of Liberalism it was the women who kept the fire lit in

many a constituency, and they had therefore a great claim on the Liberal Government.[54]

Here Waddel neatly subverts commonly-held notions of feminine emotionalism versus masculine rationalism while demanding a substantial reward for the services rendered the Liberal party by the WLAs. Some months later in the *SLWM* Waddel made direct reference to the Liberal party's debt to its female supporters:

> In the September number of the *Scottish Liberal Women's Magazine*, in speaking of the work and ceaseless struggle of Liberalism, Mr. Gulland says 'Now as ever women must bring inspiration and encouragement'. What right has this Liberal Government at least to expect this from Liberal women? By its policy, or want of policy, on the question of the women's vote, the party has already lost the matured intelligence and judgement of many of its finest women, and has failed to gather into its ranks the educated forces of the young womanhood of to-day.[55]

She concludes with the warning: 'Liberal women as responsible politicians will bring to their party and their cause inspiration and encouragement, enthusiasm, and a power of quiet work such as they have never yet been able to give, and such as no party, no cause, can afford to lose.'[56] Waddel's commitment to Liberalism did not inhibit her criticism of the party's refusal to bring in women's suffrage, yet her comments represent an articulation of Liberal women's acknowledgement of a conflict of interest between party-politics and suffragism.

Participation in WLAs had clear consequences for incorporating middle-class women into a bourgeois public sphere. As partisans, female Liberals were as closely involved with the electoral process and Liberal campaigns as legal restrictions on their political status allowed. Liberal networks further incorporated female Liberals within a Liberal society, locally and in Westminster. As reforming activists, Liberal women mobilised their organisations' resources on behalf of social and political justice for women. Liberal women's publications gave entry into public debate, while like-minded women might coalesce around local WLAs to organise reforming activities. The SWLF, however, did not exist within a vacuum and its membership was linked to the BWTASCU, GWSAWS and ENSWS through inter-organisational networks.

Inter-organisational networks

The organisations investigated here existed within a rich fabric of female associationalism, and were woven together through individual women's cross-membership. Women's membership across and between associations was an important characteristic of the feminine public sphere, and work with an historical database provides new evidence of inter-organisational networks. A database of nearly 600 members was prepared using a variety of source materials from the suffrage, temperance and Liberal women's associations.[57] This investigation used a relational database managed by the MySQL Relational Database Management System. The database stores information on members (names, dates of birth and death, any known address and years of residence and years of organisational membership), members' organisational roles (departmental leadership and terms in office) and organisational structure (the creation and duration of departments).[58] Relational databases are characterised by the use of many spreadsheet-like tables, which are interrelated through 'primary keys', generally a number that uniquely identifies a particular row in a particular table. Using 'queries' it is possible to retrieve information from many different tables in complex ways.[59] Data analysis thus revealed hitherto undiscovered inter-organisational networks among the temperance, Liberal and suffrage associations in central Scotland.

The quality of the source material used to prepare the database varies over time and between organisations, and falls into three categories; handwritten minute books, printed annual reports and periodicals. This evidence has both strengths and weaknesses, and viewed as a whole represents a largely untapped collection of information which can illustrate women's varied careers in associationalism. Importantly, where the evidence has been referred to by other scholars, especially those sources related to the Glasgow and Edinburgh branches of the NUWSS, there has yet been no comparable attempt to develop a comprehensive view of the organisations' membership. While the database represents a novel historical resource, the underlying evidence is marred by inconsistencies such as significant gaps in coverage; for instance, the annual reports for the ENSWS cover only the years 1868 to 1878, 1892 and 1907. The handwritten minute books are especially problematic in terms of consistency, and while, for example, the minutes of the SWLF seem systematically to note members' names and their roles, some records such as the minutes of the Glasgow Prayer Union tend to be somewhat more haphazard in noting members' names and positions. Similarly, the terse nature of the data (usually a member's title and surname); the custom of using multiple aliases for a particular woman such as, Mrs Miller, Mrs John Miller and Mrs Grant Miller; illegible and inconsistent spellings; and the apparent omission of information on name changes after marriage complicated identification of individuals.

During construction of the database, assumptions were made on how the available dataset might reflect real-world membership, especially in terms of concluding that a name referenced in two different sets of records might refer to the same individual.[60] One method used to determine identity was to analyse a member's role in one organisation in order to make a reasonable supposition regarding her involvement in another organisation. For example, a Mrs Sutherland was listed in the records of the Edinburgh Central Branch (1897–1907) and the Glasgow Prayer Union (1892; 1896; 1900–02; 1905–06), and several factors were considered to conclude that the name listed in both sets of records referred the same individual: Sutherland is included in the records during a similar time period, local temperance leaders were given roles in the national leadership in Edinburgh, and Sutherland is associated with a similar organisational role in each set of records.[61] A similar process was used to determine that Mrs Margaret Black of the Edinburgh Central Branch's education department (1897–1902) was also the Mrs Black listed as leader of the Glasgow Prayer Union's education department from 1894 to 1897. A second method was to cross-reference membership information in the official records with information contained in contemporary periodicals. For instance, the *SWTN* and the *SLWM* provided information on women's full names, as the *SLWM* consistently printed the names and positions of executive members, and the *WSJ* provided some membership data for the GNSWS which has left no known records. Ultimately, data were entered into a database designed to evaluate membership and organisational structure.

Analysis of the database suggests that the average member in the sample was a married woman, belonging to a single organisation for six years. Close to 60% of members in the dataset were described in the source material as 'Mrs', compared with 36% as 'Miss' and a remainder of other titles such as 'Dr' or 'Lady'. The data on the number of organisations associated with a particular member show a normal distribution of 1, while data on the length of membership suggest a mean of 6, a mode of 3 and a median of 1 years. This is indicative of the fact that the sample includes a wide range in members' participation, from a minimum of 1 to a maximum of 38 years of service. The average member in the sample was not associated with a leadership position, yet 21% of the sample were listed as officers and nearly a third as heads of departments. Among those in leadership roles, the average officer maintained a single position, while department heads, on average, ran two departments.

Close to 10% of the sample has been confirmed as participants in multiple organisations.[62] The most common cross-membership was between the BWTASCU and branches of the NUWSS, followed by participation in multiple branches of the BWTASCU, then involvement with the SWLF and NUWSS and finally between the SWLF and BWTASCU. Three women – Lady Ishbel Aberdeen, Mrs Anna Lindsay and Miss Eliza Wigham – are known to have participated in all three movements. Women identified as members of multiple organisations were more likely to be among the organisational elite, with 30% recorded as officers and 51% as heads of departments. Members to multiple organisations further seem to be exceptionally keen associationalists, with twice the average number of years in associational life and a majority (66%) participating in different groups during an overlapping time frame. While a small section of the overall sample, it is apparent that members to multiple organisations were among the organisations' most influential participants and might exert a disproportionate force on the direction of their organisations' reform programmes.

Higher profile members' activities across organisations seems to have encouraged the development of reform programmes based on a set of 'women's issues' versus a more single-issue approach. A comparison of members' roles across organisations suggests that members of multiple organisations pursued complementary aims in different organisations. For instance, Mrs Janet Cockburn, a member of the GWSAWS from 1903 to 1914, had spearheaded the formation of the Glasgow Prayer Union's suffrage department in 1898. Mrs MacKay and Mrs Mill, members of the SWLF's temperance committee in the years immediately preceding the Great War, had been members of the Edinburgh Central Branch in the mid-1890s. In the early twentieth century, Mrs A. Falconer was recorded as head of the SWLF's suffrage and local government department and as a member of the ENSWS. Indeed, members' parallel reforming activities, especially as illustrated by a member's headship of an organisation's department and corresponding participation in another organisation, is a hallmark of the sample of cross-members: a third of members referenced in the records of more than one organisation provide clear evidence of pursuing complementary reforms across organisations.[63] In summary, the sample analysed here indicates that cross-membership imparted some coherence to the public activism of middle-class women. Members' broad social consciences, cultivated by a deep Christian conviction and honed through voluntary work, ensured that women's organisations in central Scotland undertook a range of work that reflected the multiple experiences and reforming passions of their membership.

Conclusion

Female associationalism was the starting point for many middle-class women's public lives. Reforming organisations such as constitutional suffrage societies, temperance unions and WLAs provided more well-to-do women with opportunities to actively engage in the important social and political issues of their day. In Glasgow and Edinburgh, cross-membership knitted together women's organisations, imparting a multi-issue reform programme to a range of women's groups. These organisations, though part of international reforming efforts to enhance women's clout in public affairs, were rooted in local civic life. While it has been shown that male associational life and civic involvement was marked by cross-membership within the local sphere, evidence from these organisations suggests a similar pattern among more elite urban women active in the feminine public sphere.[64]

Notes

1 'Scotland: Glasgow Branch of the National Society for Women's Suffrage', *WSJ* 1 (1870): 24. WL.

2 SNSWS, *Minutes* (1909). Shetland Archives D.1/32.

3 ENSWS, *Annual Report* (1868). WL 324.6230604134/18323.

4 ENSWS, *Annual Report* (1871). WL 324.62306041134/18328.

5 ENSWS, *Annual Report* (1875). WL 324.62306041134/18346.

6 GWSAWS, *Minutes* (1903). Mitchell Library [hereafter ML], 891036/1/1 SR 187.

7 GWSAWS, *Minutes* (1903). ML, 891036/1/1 SR 187.

8 GWSAWS, *Minutes* (1903). ML, 891036/1/1 SR 187.

9 SNSWS, *Minutes* (1911). Shetland Archives D.1/32.

10 'Glasgow', *WSJ* 3, no. 27 (1 May 1872): 62. WL.

11 'Scotland: Glasgow', *WSJ* 4, no. 38 (1 Apr 1873): 55. WL.

12 Leneman, *A Guid Cause*, 24.

13 'Scottish National Demonstration of Women', *WSJ* 13, no. 155 (1 Dec 1882): 182. WL.

14 Simon Morgan, '"A sort of land debatable": Female Influence, Civic Virtue and Middle-Class Identity, c.1830–c.1860', *WHR* 13, no. 2 (2004): 195–6.

15 'Scottish National Demonstration of Women', 188. WL.

16 'Scottish National Demonstration of Women', 189. WL.

17 Stewart, *The Crusader*, 279. WL 178.10942 STE.

18 Stewart, *The Crusader*, 355. WL 178.10942 STE. See also Christina E. Robertson, *BWTASCU: Its Origins and Progress* (BWTASCU, 1908), 30. BWTASCU Collection.

19 Robertson, *BWTASCU*, 48. BWTASCU Collection.

20 Robertson, *BWTASCU*, 43. BWTASCU Collection.

21 Robertson, *BWTASCU*, 45. BWTASCU Collection.

22 Robertson, *BWTASCU*, 45. BWTASCU Collection.

23 Glasgow was host to several branches of the BWTASCU, and the Glasgow Prayer Union administered the work of the Glasgow branches. The Glasgow Prayer Union

was renamed the Glasgow District Union in 1902, but to ease confusion will be referred to as the Glasgow Prayer Union throughout this discussion.

24 Robertson, *BWTASCU*, 30. BWTASCU Collection.

25 Robertson, *BWTASCU*, 45. BWTASCU Collection.

26 Robertson, *BWTASCU*, 44. BWTASCU Collection.

27 Robertson, *BWTASCU*, 29. BWTASCU Collection.

28 Ruth Bordin, *Woman and Temperance: The Quest for Power and Liberty, 1873–1900* (Philadelphia: Temple University Press, 1981), 57.

29 Aspinwall, *Portable Utopia*, 109. The idea that American temperance reform inspired and influenced the movement in Britain extends beyond the rise of female temperance reform, and American influence has also been identified in the development of organised abstainers and a prohibition lobby in Britain. See, for example, Aspinwall, *Portable Utopia*; Dingle, *The Campaign for Prohibition in Victorian England*; and Harrison, *Drink and the Victorians*.

30 Bordin, *Woman and Temperance*, 97.

31 Robertson, *BWTASCU*, 53. BWTASCU Collection.

32 Stewart, *The Crusader*, v. WL 178.10942 STE.

33 Jack S. Blocker Jr. has demonstrated that American crusaders were vulnerable to ridicule and violent attack, see '*Give to the winds thy fears': The Women's Temperance Crusade, 1873–1874* (London: Greenwood Press, 1985), 76–7.

34 Blocker, '*Give to the winds thy fears'*, 24.

35 Robertson, *BWTASCU*, 26. BWTASCU Collection.

36 Robertson, *BWTASCU*, 43. BWTASCU Collection.

37 Stewart, *The Crusader*, 311. WL 178.10942 STE.

38 Stewart, *The Crusader*, 21. WL 178.10942 STE.

39 Stewart, *The Crusader*, 226. WL 178.10942 STE.

40 White, 'Recollections', 21. BWTASCU Collection.

41 Mary M. Reid, 'Correspondence: A Visit to America', *SWTN*, 12, no. 12 (Dec 1908): 178. BWTASCU Collection.

42 White, 'Recollections', 22. BWTASCU Collection.

43 Stewart, *The Crusader*, 254. WL 178.10942 STE.

44 Stewart, *The Crusader*, 216. WL 178.10942 STE.

45 'Shamrock', 'Scottish Liberals at Dunoon, 1911', *SLWM* (Nov 1911): 213. British Library [hereafter BL] P.P.3611.tc.

46 Marion Blackie, 'Miss Jane Campbell', *SLWM* (Nov 1911): 208. BL P.P.3611.tc.

47 'Women's Suffrage: Correspondence with the Prime Minister', *SLWM* (Jan 1910): 12. BL P.P.3611.tc.

48 'Shamrock', 'The Election in Scotland', *SLWM* (Feb 1910): 35. BL P.P.3611.tc.

49 M. M. Anderson, 'A Bird's-Eye View of the SWLF Meeting', *SLWM* (Apr 1911): 70. BL P.P.3611.tc.

50 'SWLF Council Meetings', *SLWM* (Apr 1911): 82. BL P.P.3611.tc.

51 'Shamrock', 'The Election in Scotland', 34–5. BL P.P.3611.tc.

52 Mrs Macrae, 'The Election in the West of Scotland', *SLWM* (Apr 1910): 76. BL P.P.3611.tc.

53 Anderson, 'A Bird's-Eye View of SWLF Meetings', 70. BL P.P.3611.tc.

54 'Annual Meeting of the Council of the Scottish Women's Liberal Federation', *SLWM* (Apr 1912): 93. BL P.P.3611.tc.

55 Helen E. Waddel, 'Woman Suffrage and the Government Franchise Bill', *SLWM* (Oct

1912): 195. BL P.P.3611.tc.

56 Waddel, 'Woman Suffrage', 195. BL P.P.3611.tc.

57 The database includes 621 member entries, however twenty-five entries are likely duplicate references to the same individual. See Appendix 4.

58 For a fuller discussion of the modelling of the database, see Appendix 2.

59 Queries in this case where built up using the Java programming language, rather than SQL syntax: a Java application interacted with the database (using Java Database Connectivity) to retrieve data and to analyse the data set.

60 A full list of assumptions made during data entry is available in Appendix 3.

61 Sutherland served as leader of the Edinburgh Central Branch's departments of rescue (1899–1903), rescue and habitual inebriates bill (1904–06) and rescue and prisons (1907) while also heading the Glasgow Prayer Union's prison department in 1896.

62 See Appendix 5 for a full listing of women identified as members of more than one organisation.

63 See Appendix 5.

64 See Trainor, 'The Elite'.

2

The feminine public sphere

The feminine public sphere represents the discourses and activities that middle-class female activists used to pursue their socio-political reforming goals. Between 1870 and 1914, suffragists, female temperance reformers and Liberal women in central, urban Scotland entered public discourse to legitimise middle-class women's work in the public sphere. The *SWTN*, *WSJ* and the *SLWM* indicate the type of arguments middle-class women employed to justify their public roles. Separate spheres was a central discursive notion in the 1870 to 1914 period, yet middle-class women generated heterodox analyses of restrictive gender ideologies by interpreting the intersecting class and religious discourses that cut across separate spheres to accommodate, ideologically, a feminine public sphere. Women's heterodox representations of religiously inspired gender ideologies such as 'complementary natures', formed the ideological bedrock of the feminine public sphere. The feminine public sphere was further founded on middle-class women's social networks, and an historical database of membership to Edinburgh organisations indicates the importance of neighbourhood, religious and kinship networks for middle-class women's public lives. Neighbourhood networks, or local concentrations of an organisations' members, point to women's adaptation of middle-class sociability to meeting their reforming goals in the wider community. Equally, religious networks could provide material resources as well as moral support for women's public projects at home and abroad. Kinship networks were also crucial for middle-class women's reforming activities, and while male kin might provide access to formal power structures female kin were vital for introducing younger women to a lifetime of service in reforming movements.

Nineteenth-century ideologues argued that men and women manifested divinely appointed 'complementary' talents and abilities, and the ideology of 'complementary natures' could be used to justify the sexual division of labour and women's social, economic and political inequality. 'Complementary natures' ideology encouraged the notion of a 'woman's mission', or a set of special duties and tasks that were associated with women's complementary role: 'Woman's mission, as we take it, is to redeem man, and so redeem herself.'[1] 'Complementary natures' and 'woman's mission' were tightly bound up with evangelical thought and emphases on Christian mothers' moral instruction of children and husbands.[2] While 'complementary natures' ideology could be construed as a mandate for female passivity and seclusion within the home, it is apparent from women's periodicals that middle-class women represented both the evangelical duty to proselytise and 'woman's mission' to morally purify society as invitations to public life.

The tensions between a conservative religious morality and the use of religious thought to justify a feminine public sphere suggests the need to include Christian women in an understanding of 'first-wave' feminism. Sue Morgan's analysis of Ellice Hopkins offers the term 'religio-feminism' to argue that Christian feminists must be analysed in context of their faith.[3] Similarly, Lesley A. Orr MacDonald has argued that evangelical notions of the individual's duty to work for the salvation of others and of feminine moral superiority resulted a 'distinct ministry' for women.[4] While noting that a reliance on 'complementary natures' ideology could circumscribe gender roles, Eileen Janes Yeo has suggested that, 'on the intellectual level, religion can provide a belief system which is culturally powerful at a particular historical moment and yet which can be manipulated to shape gender identities different from the conventional models, legitimising them with transcendent authority.'[5] It is argued here that while religious thought might ultimately confine women to particular roles, Christian belief and fellowship were important resources underpinning women's discursive defence of and their reforming activities within the feminine public sphere.

A 'complementary' public sphere

The women of this study tended to support a heterodox interpretation of 'complementary natures' ideology, in order to carve out a place for women's public lives. These arguments could suggest that more affluent women were better equipped than their male peers for benevolent work among poorer women and children. The idea that middle-class women had a special niche in public life was used by a range of organisations in support of women's reforming activities: the SWLF might use 'complementary natures' to argue for women's distinct and valuable contribution to political life, while the BWTASCU might deploy this ideology to show women's peculiar capacity for work with female drinkers. Gender ideology also influenced the day-to-day running of the organisations studied here, and members further subverted idealised gender roles by adapting their domestic spaces to reforming activism. This is particularly evident from the practice of drawing-room meetings. In contrast to public meetings, where an organisation might publicise its yearly achievements to an audience beyond its membership, drawing-room meetings were more intimate gatherings in members' private homes. Reforming organisations' use of drawing-room meetings demonstrates how public women might overcome gendered disadvantages, such as a lack of funding for dedicated meeting rooms, in order to pursue their reforming activities. Indeed, the practice of drawing-room meetings suggests that the domestic sphere, a central site of middle-class sociability, was important for cultivating the neighbourhood networks that strengthened women's reforming activities outside the home.

The *SLWM* tended to describe women's public role as a separate and feminine public service to disadvantaged women and children, rather than as a challenge to free and equal access to all areas of public life. In an account of Mrs Edwin Gray's speech at a 1909 meeting, the *SLWM* maintained that women's participation in public life could not destroy the separateness of the sexes: 'Just as women's work in the home is different from men's work in the home, so will be their work in and for the State; and neither the higher education, or the taking part in public affairs, nor anything else, will ever do away with the distinctive qualifications and attributes of women, which have hitherto been useful and pleasing to men.'[6] Similarly, in her remembrance of the 1912 annual meeting at Dundee, Mrs Latta argued that women's special insight into problems facing poorer women suggested a distinct role for women in public life, 'at almost every moment a new point of interest appeared, or another delegate was met with, full of some special interest upon which she, by careful observation and experience was not only an authority but a representative of those in whose welfare she was so deeply interested'.[7] In this way, readers were assured that public participation would not dissolve the 'natural' and harmonious differences between men and women. While this represen-tation of the feminine public sphere is problematic and any emancipatory connotations are undercut by an acknowledgement of essentialist ideas of women's role, Liberal women such as Lady Mary Murray, Western Vice-President (1892–1900), defended the different, yet equally valuable, role of women: 'She recalled the leader in *The Scotsman* twenty years ago, which had spoken of their meeting as "the hen parliament", but she did not think that type of comment would be applied to-day. They were too important for that now.'[8] Of course, the usefulness and importance of the SWLF in the eyes of male Liberals may have related largely to the voluntary labour of the WLAs during elections, yet for female Liberals it most certainly provided evidence of their own distinctive, or complementary, contribution to public life.

For the British Women, the concept of 'complementary natures' was central to discussions of women's obligation to save Scottish women from drunkenness, the BWTASCU having claimed in its first volume of the *SWTN* the organisation's mission as, 'the protection of Scottish women from strong drink'.[9] Certainly, the wider temperance press stressed female temperance reformers' special duty to work among female drinkers, an attitude that was expressed in the *League*, the official periodical of the male-dominated, mixed-sex Scottish Temperance League (STL): '[the BWTASCU] was needed to give symmetry and completeness to the general movement. There are some kinds of temperance work for which women of tact and grace are better fitted than men.'[10] The evidence suggests that the British Women legitimated their public role, in part, by highlighting women's supposedly natural ability to work with female drinkers; the BWTASCU had used the spectre of 'the female inebriate' as a rallying cry from its early days in the 1880s: 'So long as there was one woman a victim to intemperance it was the bounden duty of every woman, who looked the question fair in the face, to do everything in her power to redeem her sisters from so awful a fate as that which drunkenness brought upon them.'[11] For the BWTASCU's reform programme this emphasis on the female drinker, as later chapters will show, encouraged the formation of female inebriate homes and departments dedicated to 'rescuing' women held in prison for drink-related offences.

The British Women's emphasis on female drinkers responded to debates on 'national efficiency', or the ability of the working classes to reproduce a racially and morally sound population. Marianna Valverde has shown that the fate of the nation was understood as tied to mothers' temperate influence; 'the drink issue was ... articulated in powerful and coercive ways with the more broadly based panic about race degeneration and female / maternal duties'.[12] The idea that mothers had the greatest responsibility for ensuring the quality of the 'race' had a long pedigree, and temperance reformers had feared the impact of drink on motherhood from the middle of the century. A fear of racial deterioration through mothers' drunkenness was apparent in the records of the BWTASCU throughout the period examined here. For instance, the 1886 minutes of the Glasgow Prayer Union recall: 'Prayer offered for several special cases. One in particular described by a lady of a woman she found lying very drunk, near Cattle Market with young infant. The lady was afraid the young infant would be killed and took it to the Police Office, where the woman was also taken.'[13] Similarly, in 1907, Mrs Milne, a member of the Edinburgh Central Branch and Superintendent of the Parliamentary Department (1901–14), wrote in the *Scottish Temperance Annual*: 'drinking among women is a portentous fact, and constitutes a great national danger. The recent sad revelations in some districts in Edinburgh of the seamy side of life, and which is but a sample of what is to be found in all our cities, may well stir us to new endeavour.'[14] While the BWTASCU's understandings of 'national efficiency' and women's complementary role to labour among female drinkers worked to justify their unique and necessary role in public life, British Women's emphasis on reform of 'the female inebriate' should not be viewed purely as a calculated subversion of gender ideology. Female temperance reformers were motivated by a deep and sincere religious commitment, and it is clear from these examples that work in temperance reform created opportunities for reforming women to witness first-hand the detrimental effects of alcohol abuse on poorer women. While such reports were likely to shock British Women and to encourage fears over poorer women's ability to maintain the 'race', they might equally be expected to stir temperance reformers to action as compassionate human beings who believed in the middle classes' duty to public service. Ultimately, the British Women's internalisation of the notion of a complementary, feminine public role predicated on women's biological and familial role as mothers allowed female temperance reformers to claim responsibility for female drinkers, and to consequently negotiate a place in public life. Female temperance reformers and other reforming women further adapted domestic space, the domain most strongly associated with femininity in Victorian and Edwardian gender ideology, to their goals in the public sphere.

The widespread practise of drawing-room meetings provides some of the clearest evidence for the permeability of domestic and public spaces. Juliet Kinchin's study of the drawing-room helps to highlight the 'public' nature of the drawing-room, while Eleanor Gordon and Gwyneth Nair have cited evidence from the Claremont estate area of Glasgow to argue for the home as a centre of middle-class entertainment.[15] The drawing-room was an important site of women's sociability and while a centre of middle-class entertaining, the drawing-room might equally be employed as a key site of middle-class women's political and social activism. This is clear from the the formation of departments by the Edinburgh Central Branch and Glasgow Prayer Union to oversee drawing-room meetings as well as the *WSJ*'s regular references to drawing-room meetings organised in Glasgow and Edinburgh. Public women's gatherings in drawing-rooms were also a practical solution to providing a meeting space for small, modestly funded and newly established women's organisations, such as the SFWSS Kilmarnock Branch, which often met in members' homes until a committee room was secured in late 1913: 'By kind invitation of Mrs Brown the committee met at Roseland Kilmans for tea in the garden and afterwards the meeting was held indoors.'[16]

Suffrage and temperance periodicals often distinguish between public and drawing-room meetings. While public meetings were opportunities to communicate an organisation's reforming goals and progress to a general audience, it seems that drawing-room meetings were more important for intimate discussions of organisational interests as well as for recruitment. Smith-Rosenburg's seminal work on female rituals emphasised the importance of the domestic space for women's social lives.[17] It seems that the drawing-room, a central site of middle-class women's sociability, was used to bring together well-to-do women and encourage their reforming activism. This idea was articulated at the BWTASCU's 1882 annual meeting, where Mrs Robertson reportedly urged, 'they should hold drawing-room meetings, so that their principles might be brought in an attractive form before persons unacquainted with or indifferent about them'.[18] Thus, within this demonstrably 'feminine' space, where a family's wealth was displayed through consumption and decoration, reforming women gathered to organise and to promote their work.

Middle-class women's domestic spaces were further fundamental to the feminine public sphere as a place around which women's neighbourhood networks might coalesce. Neighbourhood networks, or localised concentrations of membership to an organisation, emerge from an analysis of members' addresses. In many cases the evidence is more strongly implied than absolute, yet the records strongly indicate the existence of these networks. For instance, Mrs McIntosh of 29 Hartington Place joined the BWTASCU in 1895, while Mrs Heron of 7 Hartington Gardens joined the following year. Hartington Place and Hartington Gardens are adjacent and parallel in the Merchiston area of Edinburgh, and it seems likely that Heron was recruited into the BWTASCU through an acquaintance with McIntosh. Whether or not this is an accurate assumption in this particular case is not of central importance, and similar patterns in the dataset suggest that women recruited their neighbours for reform. For example, incidences of women living in the same street, and working for the same organisation at similar times: Mrs Inglis from 12 Dick Place in the Grange area of Edinburgh was a member of the BWTASCU roughly between 1888 and 1898 whereas her neighbour at number 44, Mrs Jackson, was a member between approximately 1889 and 1902.

Women's neighbourhood networks were facilitated by the emergence of middle-class suburbs, such as Newington estate in Edinburgh. Newington House, the locus of Newington estate, was built by the wealthy surgeon Dr Benjamin Bell in 1805, and was purchased in 1808 by Sir George Stewart who began the process of gating off the area from the wider community.[19] During the first half of the nineteenth century, Newington became the most densely populated suburb of Edinburgh as new land and building opportunities attracted the well-to-do, and improvements in transport linked the southern suburbs with the city centre and New Town. This process was further facilitated by Duncan McLaren's purchase of Newington House in 1852. By acquiring neigh-bouring farmlands for residential development the well-known Liberal MP and husband of prominent suffragist Priscilla Bright McLaren is credited with having a profound impact on the movement of the middle classes into the area.[20] Morningside went through a similar process of settlement as local farmlands were sub-divided into large plots and trams and railways brought wealthy settlers. This movement of the wealthy into their own neighbourhoods marked a shift in the demography of Edinburgh. Where previously tenements, 'had accommodated a good social mix, with the aristocracy, the professions, merchants and working men all living together on different floors of the same tenement. The departure of the well-to-do to the New Town left the working class in flats, which quickly became overcrowded as they were sub-divided.'[21] Middle-class residents increasingly sought to guard their neighbourhoods, and, for instance, where Newington, Mayfield and the Grange bordered less prestigious sections of town, gates were constructed to protect oases of affluence.[22] Residential segregation was not isolated to Edinburgh, and historians have shown that geographical separation demarcated by social classes was a prominent feature of late nineteenth-century cities.[23] It was within these more exclusive neighbourhoods that middle-class women's collective aspirations were facilitated by daily life within a fairly homoge-neous social mix.

The reforming women of this study were likely to defend women's public lives as a facet of women's 'complementary nature'. In their organi-sations' periodicals middle-class public women subverted orthodox gender ideology to suggest women's special qualifications for public life, and so forged a discursive space for the feminine public sphere. Moreover, home-based networks drew on middle-class patterns of socia-bility to recruit women for reform, as the domestic sphere and its local environment were mobilised to serve the needs of women's reform organ-isations. While reworking the implications of 'complementary natures' for women's public lives, the reforming women of this study tended to accept the premise of a divinely appointed separation of the sexes. Indeed, their arguments for women's public lives were strongly informed by notions of Christian service. Similarly, networks of faithful appear as important for women's public careers as those of locality.

Christian service and religious networks

Middle-class women's arguments for women's access to public life were informed by a deep religious commitment, and the *SWTN* and the *WSJ* demonstrate that middle-class women considered public life a Chris-tian duty. The opportunities presented by female temperance reform for women's public Christian service were important ones; the rise of the women's temperance movement opened up an influential Christian role at a time when Protestant women in Scotland were excluded from the pulpit. Similarly, suffragists' writings sought to highlight the power of women's voting to infuse legislation with women's supposedly keener sense of Christian righteousness.

For female temperance reformers, a belief in feminine moral superi-ority was emboldened by the ascendancy of the international women's temperance movement:

> Every moment having as its aim the making of earth more like heaven, man more like God, has been much indebted to woman's labours, woman's faith, and woman's prayers. This is specially true of the present age, when woman's worth and power are being more and more realised. But for woman's heroic courage, earnest pleading, gentle persuasion, sympathetic – frequently bitterest – tears, Heaven-inspired temperance movement would not occupy the advanced position which it now does.[24]

Over a decade later, Mrs Barton, a member of the SWLF from 1900 to 1913, suggested in her memoir of an Australian and New Zealand tour: 'It is a true saying "The path of a good woman is strewn with flowers." But the flowers lie behind, not in front. To make a clean sweet path should be the desire of all true women for those who follow after her.'[25] When thanking the BWTASCU for her election as president in 1906, Miss Catherine Forrester Paton indicated an understanding of her public life as a Christian ministry:

> I gratefully thank you for the honour you have done to me, but were it not that I have also heard the voice of my Master saying, 'Go forward',

> I would not have dared to accept such a position of trust and respon-
> sibility. In utter dependence, therefore, on Him, 'Whose biddings are
> enablings', I take up the work as a gift from Him, to be used for Him.[26]

The *SWTN* upheld Forrester Paton's self-representation as a Christian
worker: 'Looking back over the past, her fellow-members cannot help
expressing their admiration for her benevolent efforts in the cause of
Christ and humanity, and their earnest prayer is that she may be long
spared to enjoy what is to her "the luxury of doing good", and to continue
her manifold works of faith and labours of love.'[27] The notion of female
temperance reformers as evangelical agents with a personal responsibility for bringing Christ into the lives of drunken sinners is prominent
in female temperance reformers' discussions of their reform work, an idea
which is evident in the *League*'s reckoning of Mrs Archibald Campbell's
address to the annual meeting of the BWTASCU: 'She had found her
temperance work a great blessing to her own soul, and besought the
Christian women present to give themselves to this work for God, and
try to save the poor drunkards by bringing them to Jesus.'[28] In her address
at the Glasgow District Union conference printed in the *SWTN* Mrs
Mary A. Reid contended: 'The reason why we women give ourselves to
the cause of temperance is that we have faith in God, and that we believe
this greatest of social evils to be alterable.'[29] Biographies and obituaries
printed in the *SWTN* were also likely to describe their subjects as servants
of Christ. In an obituary for Mrs Margaret Black, Mary White described
her fellow reformer's involvement with Gospel temperance meetings in
these terms: 'Only those engaged in this line of service can understand at
what cost of home rest and comfort and of exposure to all weathers the
busy teacher went to these meetings, but we feel sure the privilege of thus
serving God and man far out-weighed the sacrifice to her.'[30] Similarly, a
SWTN biography of Mrs McKinnon – President of the Dumfries branch,
wife of a reverend and Superintendent of the national Evangelical Department (1897–1905) – describes her as a willing Christian worker: 'Such
a record of work meant much self-denying labour, much sacrifice of
social and home life, and great physical and mental strain and were it
not for a whole-hearted consecration to the Master's service could not be
accomplished.'[31]

Suffrage publications also discussed women's public lives in terms
of a Christian duty. The *WSJ*'s 1880 report of Mrs Wellstood's speech
includes her claim:

> There were no doubt many ladies in high position who did not take
> any interest in the subject [the vote], because they knew nothing of the

degrading shackles which were put upon many women by the existing state of the law. But the more that question was becoming known, the more Christian women were beginning to see that religion and politics could not be separated.[32]

Wellstood, an early and long-standing member of the ENSWS and the wife of an Edinburgh town councillor, is further reported as arguing that women had a God-given right and duty to the parliamentary vote as a means of personal improvement and the improvement of less fortunate women; 'it was the right of every woman to raise herself to the highest point to which her Maker has given her the power to rise. And not only endeavour to raise themselves, but they must raise their sisters with them.'[33] Here, Wellstood emphasises the synergies between women's benevolent work and the opportunity of the vote to influence law-making. Of the factors common to the experiences of the women in this study, religion was perhaps the most important, and networks among the faithful helped women to expand their opportunities for public work. The organisations considered here drew members from a range of Protestant denominations, and a Christian world-view was central both to the groups and to individual members.

Considering the relatively small numbers of Quakers in Glasgow and Edinburgh in the 1870 to 1914 period, female members of the Religious Society of Friends enjoyed a disproportionately influential role in the organisations discussed here. For example, Miss Agnes Ann Bryson and Miss Mary White, described in the *Annual Monitor* as, 'maiden ladies … among the most active and zealous of our small body in Scotland', were especially distinguished among Friends and in Scotland's reforming circles.[34] Agnes Ann Bryson (1831?–1907), also known as Ann Bryson, was born in New York State but came to Scotland as a child. She lived her life in Glasgow where she was a Quaker Overseer, retiring to Ayr in her later years. Bryson was a member of the BWTASCU from 1881 to 1902, acting as vice-president of the Glasgow Prayer Union from 1895. Mary White (1827–1903) was born on the outskirts of Glasgow, the youngest child of William, a merchant, and Jane.[35] White was a leader of the BWTASCU in Glasgow, acting first as secretary of the Glasgow Prayer Union from 1881 to 1891 and later as president (1893–1902). Bryson and White were dear companions and shared a home as well as a devotion to temperance reform. The high profiles of Bryson and White in the BWTASCU reflects the conclusions of Sandra Stanley Holton and Elizabeth Isichei who have argued that the 'friendship' ethos of the Society of Friends motivated a particularly strong devotion to voluntarism.[36] Holton in particular has shown how the 'friendship' ideal could generate dependence among co-religionists, a notion borne out by Bryson and White's successful appeal to the Society of Friends for help in establishing the Whitevale Mission Shelter, a women's temperance home in Glasgow. Bryson and White proposed the female inebriate home in the Quaker journal, the *Monthly Friend*: 'For more than a year this subject has rested heavily on the mind of Agnes A. Bryson, with the belief that the Lord was calling her to devote herself to this work for Him, and open a washing-house, where such women could be welcomed to honest work and a personal influence gained over them for good.'[37] The Friends financially supported the scheme, and thereafter either White or Bryson submitted reports on the home's progress to the *Monthly Record*.

In light of the minority presence of Quakers in Scotland, it seems significant that some of the most prominent women of this study were drawn from their numbers. Thomas C. Kennedy has argued that female Friends were better equipped for a public role than, 'almost any other comparable group of females in British life.'[38] Historians of Quakerism have debated how well popular nineteenth-century perceptions of female Friends' relative liberty reflected the experiences of Quaker women. Kennedy and Isichei have argued that while Quaker women shared in the preaching of the Word, they were nonetheless largely barred from decision-making.[39] Indeed, constitutional equality of the sexes was not admitted among British Friends until 1898.[40] The Quaker women of this study, however, were exceptionally active in the public sphere and seemed to maintain an impressive profile within the Society of Friends, and in 1878 White was recorded as a minister. This is significant because while all Friends were entitled to preach, to be recorded as a minister signified the status of first among equals, and suggests that a preacher was recognised as having a special gift for the ministry.[41] Certainly, White was understood as more outspoken than Bryson: 'In our meetings Mary White held a foremost place, but was helped by the sympathy and encouragement and occasionally by the voice of her friend.'[42] So, while female Friends may have been barred from formal power within the Society of Friends, opportunities for preaching allowed women with a passion for the ministry to develop their public speaking skills, a talent that could be employed in the course of social reform as well as religious worship.

While a few Quaker women had prominent roles in the organisations, the Presbyterian denominations dominated the temperance, Liberal and suffrage groups in Scotland. In turn, Presbyterian networks were important for women's public lives and might also support middle-class women's contribution to the imperial project. Mrs Margaret Catherine Blaikie (1823–1915) was the President of the BWTASCU (1878–1905) and later Honorary President (1906–14). She was born in Banff, the daughter of an Edinburgh gentleman, Walter Biggar, and Ann née Duff, daughter of an old Banffshire family. In 1845, Margaret married William Gardner Blaikie, variously the Free Church of Scotland minister at Pilrig, Professor of Divinity, Moderator of the General Assembly of the Free Church and the President of the Pan-Presbyterian Council. The Blaikies lived first in Edinburgh, and later North Berwick. Further evidence of the strength of Scoto-American connections and religious networks is apparent in the claim that Margaret's entry into the temperance movement in the early 1870s was inspired by the American evangelical Dwight L. Moody whose visit was hosted by the Blaikies.[43]

Blaikie's faith encouraged her extensive public obligations including involvement in imperialist enterprises such as support for foreign missionary work. Near the turn of the century, Blaikie became involved with the Foreign Missionary Society. A selection of letters suggests that Blaikie led a ladies' auxiliary; from 1883 the Church of Scotland Assembly had sanctioned the establishment of ladies' auxiliaries to church reform and missionary organisations. William Stevenson wrote to Blaikie in 1898, urging her to organise a ladies' auxiliary at the Presbyterian congregation in North Berwick. This letter suggests that, like branches of the BWTASCU, the Foreign Missionary Society's ladies' auxiliaries functioned partly as prayer unions: 'The main idea is that the women of the congregation meet at least once a month for prayer on behalf of the women's mission.'[44] It is interesting to note the continuity that could run through the range of middle-class women's organisations, as 'praise and prayer' was a central feature of temperance organisations. Likewise, Blaikie's personal history reflects the experiences of the thousands of women involved in women's religious organisations who viewed 'praise and prayer' as fundamental to their work. Ladies' auxiliaries at home were an integral part of the support structure for female missionaries abroad, and MacDonald describes the work of these groups as 'work parties' to produce 'fancy goods' for sale, public speaking, and meeting with female missionaries on furlough.[45] The correspondence between Blaikie and Stevenson, who co-ordinated the efforts of ladies' auxiliaries, shows the importance both of visits from missionaries and of fund-raising to the operations of the ladies' auxiliaries.[46]

Dr Agnes McLaren (1837–1913), most often associated with Edinburgh feminist circles, the ENSWS and the campaign for women's access to medical training, was also drawn into foreign missionary work through religious networks. Excluded from medical training in Britain, McLaren studied in Montpellier, France and her decision to pursue a medical profession was attributed to her sense of Christian duty: 'From her study of the Gospels there grew up in her a deep personal love of Christ and a great desire to serve Him in the sick and poor. In order to better accomplish this, at the age of 40, she decided to become a physician, convinced that she could best serve God and her neighbour in this capacity.'[47] Certainly, her time in southern France had an important influence on her religious life. During her twenty years abroad, McLaren regularly attended Catholic retreats, and she converted to Roman Catholicism at the age of sixty.[48] At the age of seventy-two, McLaren travelled to Pakistan where she was instrumental in founding a hospital for women and children. As McLaren's health prevented her management of the hospital, and as her efforts were further confounded by Church regulations against missionary nuns from practising medicine, her biographer claims that her sense of Christian mission and the 'medical needs, misery and helplessness of the "purdah" women in the Orient' led McLaren to agitate for medically trained nuns for work in the missionary field.[49] Thus, she lobbied Rome five times for women's permission to train in medicine, work which inspired the Austrian-born Anna Dengel to study medicine, to take over the hospital in Pakistan and to found the Medical Mission Sisters in Washington DC in 1925. The later period of McLaren's life demonstrates the importance of a woman's religious community to her public life. While, a sense of national and racial superiority may have coloured McLaren's attitudes towards Indian women, her attitudes were equally influenced by a sincere interest in Asian women's health. In other words, her medical mission to Pakistan represented an aspect of the Christian life of service she embarked on when she sought medical training.

Clearly, religious networks could serve as powerful catalysts for middle-class women's public lives. Ann Bryson and Mary White's reliance on their Quaker networks demonstrates that religious communities lent important financial as well as moral support for work in the feminine public sphere. Similarly, religious networks encouraged Margaret Blaikie and Agnes McLaren's activities to enhance the capacity of women to participate in the imperial project beyond 'helpmates' to male professionals, but as missionaries and doctors. While women's worship varied among the Presbyterian, Quaker and (minor) Roman Catholic presence in the organisations discussed here, fellowship within a community of faithful fostered middle-class women's public work.

Kinship networks

Kinship networks were also fundamental to women's work in the feminine public sphere. The implications of kinship networks for women's public lives appears gendered, as male and female kin offered different opportunities for women's participation in public. Female kinship networks, especially between mothers and daughters, were vital for cultivating women's interest in and skills required for a public life, and young well-to-do women were often introduced to reforming activism by their mothers' example. Biographical evidence and membership records indicate the influence of mothers' reforming activities on the recruitment of daughters into middle-class women's organisations. Many of the affluent women of this study were linked to families prominent in professional, business, religious and manufacturing sectors. In turn, their male kin often wielded power and prestige in public life at local and national levels. Minute books and organisational periodicals suggest that middle-class women used their relationships with prominent male kin as a means of promoting their reforming goals within masculine power structures.

Kinship networks with influential men were understood as beneficial for women's public careers, and there is evidence that wives of prominent men took on equally prominent public roles. Mrs Priscilla Bright McLaren, President of the ENSWS, was one of the most distinguished British public women in the 1870 to 1914 period. She was the daughter of Jacob Bright, a well-known radical MP famous for his role in the anti-Corn Law agitation, as well as the wife of Duncan McLaren MP. McLaren's close personal connections with radical liberalism shaped her political experience and strongly influenced her own political attitudes. For instance, the *WSJ*'s report of her speech at the 1880 women's suffrage demonstration in the Manchester Free Trade Hall claims McLaren's sentiments: 'This hall was built in the cause of freedom, and some of us have learnt our political lessons within its walls many years ago, with distinguished men for our teachers, and we have learnt from them how persistent efforts leads to success in getting grievances redressed.'[50] McLaren's roots went deep into British radical society, and she was one of the most respected public women of her day in both Scottish- and British-national contexts, and the ENSWS described her as, 'the recognised public instructress in righteousness'.[51] McLaren's home was considered a centre of liberal activism, and the ENSWS described Newington House, 'as the Scottish centre and headquarters of various movements'.[52] I have discussed elsewhere Edinburgh suffragists' understanding of their central position in the women's movement, and while suffragists in others areas of Scotland may have disputed the central status associated with the Edinburgh women's movement there can be no doubt that the McLaren family was pivotal in political and social reform in Edinburgh, Scotland and Britain.[53] Priscilla's partnership with Duncan helped to ensure her respected position in public life, and the ENSWS's remembrance of its deceased leader claimed she shared a mutual set of reforming goals with her husband and that Priscilla, 'entered fully into his struggles to amend the abuses of the civic life of that time, and no less heartily into his fifteen years' representation of this city in Parliament'.[54]

Women's familial relationships further connected the interests of women in Scotland with the London political scene. Mrs Rolland Rainy of the SWLF, wife of an MP, demonstrates how some Scottish public women used the opportunities afforded by marriage to promote their causes in the centre of British politics. In the early part of the twentieth century, Rainy was often reported in the minutes as the SWLF's women's suffrage representative in London. In March 1906, Mrs Rainy and Mrs McCollum represented the SWLF at the women's suffrage conference organised by the Lancashire and Cheshire Union of WLAs, and in May Rainy was the SWLF representative in a deputation to Prime Minister Henry Campbell-Bannerman. In February 1907, Rainy again represented the SWLF at a London conference on the 'Scope of the Women's Suffrage Bill'. In February 1908, Mrs Falconer, Mrs Rolland Rainy, Mrs Watson, Mrs Dundas, Mrs White and Miss Alice Younger represented the SWLF at the Liberal parliamentary committee on women's suffrage. Scottish suffrage organisations were tirelessly engaged in organising petitions and public meetings and other events designed to extend the campaign in Scotland, yet male kinship networks provided opportunities for Scottish suffragists to present their arguments directly to the political establishment in London.

The interpenetration of middle-class women's personal and public lives is further apparent from records of the removal of Lady Helen Munro-Ferguson from the presidency of the SWLF. According to the SWLF minutes, in May 1902, Mrs Anna Lindsay and Mrs Campbell Lorimer moved to censure a circular disseminated to some of the membership by Munro-Ferguson, and to arrange for copies to be sent to all WLAs. The details of the letter are not disclosed in the minutes, only the claim that the circular was, 'calculated to nullify all the efforts for unity which were made at the last Annual Meeting' especially as regarded the election of delegates to the Council.[55] Apparently, Munro-Ferguson was alarmed by the executive's intention to distribute her circular, and a letter on her behalf was sent to the SWLF from W. S. Haldane, solicitor.

Haldane warned the SWLF, 'that those who may take part in any way in publishing such a private letter without the writer's sanction incur serious responsibility'.[56] Mrs Ada Lang Todd, Vice-Chairwoman of the SWLF, had also attained legal advice and the minutes report the opinions of James Falconer, solicitor, and J. Campbell Lorimer, advocate, which upheld the legality of the SWLF's actions. The conflict was resolved by the resignation of Munro-Ferguson and the re-election of Lady Ishbel Countess of Aberdeen. More importantly, Haldane, Falconer, and Campbell Lorimer were all related to SWLF members and this series of events reinforces the notion of a community of upper-middle-class women who operated alongside their male peers in public life.

Female kinship networks were similarly important, and the evidence suggests the influence of mothers on the public lives of their daughters. Smith-Rosenburg has stressed the importance of female kinship relationships for the 'female world', and has suggested the existence of a mother-daughter apprenticeship system.[57] Such a system is hinted at in the *Annual Monitor*'s reckoning of Mary White's experience:

> Jane White mingled in a circle of cultured and philanthropic women, in whose houses meetings were held to discuss how they could best use their influence to discourage war, slavery, and all forms of evil. Mary White often accompanied her mother, and doubtless her heart was fired with the desire to do what she could to aid the cause of suffering humanity.[58]

Thus, it appears that from her youth White was exposed both to middle-class women's reforming movements as well as women's use of networks to advance their philanthropic aims. Likewise, Eliza Wigham (1820–1899), well known for her anti-slavery activism, was also a member of the BWTASCU (1897–98), the ENSWS (1870–78, 1892) and the SWLF (1891–94). Her mother, Jane Wigham née Smeal, was a similarly renowned reformer: '[Jane Wigham] was of great service in the preparation of an address to the Queen, which is said to have given a final blow to slavery in the West Indies. 1829, is said to have signed the first temperance pledge book in Scotland.'[59] Priscilla McLaren worked with her step-daughter, Agnes McLaren, in the campaigns for women's access to medical training and for women's suffrage, while Mrs Whilemina Woyka and her daughter Dora worked together within the BWTASCU. It is difficult to know with precision how extensively mothers and daughters collaborated in the feminine public sphere: it is not always possible to identify positively women with the same surname as related. An analysis of members in the database who shared surnames and belonged to the same organisation indicates eight instances of mothers and daughters working together.[60] This data analysis also shows husbands and wives, and in one case father and daughter, working together in suffrage societies as well as sisters working alongside each other. It is difficult to gauge from the sample how extensively mothers and daughters shared their associational lives. Only a small proportion of members with shared surnames are known to be related and this method of detection is clearly flawed as it cannot account for name changes after marriage. At the very least, the database and the qualitative material strongly indicates that mothers were important factors in the public lives of their daughters. Further, middle-class women's networking suggests that the feminine public sphere was strongly defined by women's social lives in the domestic space and the local community. This seemingly contradictory idea underscores the permeability of 'public' and 'private' spheres and indicates that middle-class public women incorporated aspects of domestic life and female social customs into their pursuit of public roles.

Conclusion

Qualitative and quantitative evidence indicates that religious conviction and middle-class networks dominated the culture of Scotland's well-to-do public women. Christian faith appears as a key factor in middle-class women's determination to pursue a public life, while religious networks provided material and spiritual support for women's public work. Indeed, a range of networks contributed to women's opportunities in public life. Networks within relatively homogeneous neighbourhoods were leveraged for organisational recruitment, while social life in the local community was mobilised for reform through drawing-room meetings. Kinship networks had varied implications for middle-class women's public lives, from bringing Scotswomen's reforming concerns to a London audience to facilitating daughters' entry into public life. Yet, the feminine public sphere represents more than an arena for middle-class women's reforming activities, and it is best understood as a site of middle-class women's contribution to middle-class identity. Civic participation was a hallmark of middle-class culture in the 1870 to 1914 period. Affluent men enjoyed access to a range of formalised power structures at the local and national levels, and while women's route into civic life was largely through the informal power structures of their reforming organisations, their contributions to a middle-class culture of civic participation should be considered no less significant. Female associational life may have paralleled the structure and tenor of men's organisations, yet middle-class women's internalisation of supposed feminine moral superiority encouraged a desire to feminise middle-class public life. Thus, by contravening idealised notions of a sequestered femininity, middle-class public women sought to remould society in their own righteous image.

Notes

1 Mrs Malaprop, 'Short Essays – Woman's Mission', *The Ladies' Friend* 1, no. 2 (Oct 1886): 22.

2 Several historians have analysed the link between evangelicalism, 'woman's mission' and feminism, for example see Olive Banks, *Becoming a Feminist: The Social Origins of 'First Wave' Feminism* (Brighton: Wheatsheaf Books, 1986) and *Faces of Feminism: A Study of Feminism as a Social Movement* (Oxford: Martin Robertson, 1981); Ellen Jordan, *The Women's Movement and Women's Employment in Nineteenth Century Britain* (London: Routledge, 1999); and Barbara Taylor, *Eve and the New Jerusalem: Socialism and Feminism in the Nineteenth Century* (London: Virago Press Ltd., 1983; reprint, London: Virago Press, 1991).

3 See Sue Morgan, 'Faith, Sex and Purity: The Religio-Feminist Theory of Ellice Hopkins', *WHR* 9, no. 1 (2000), 13–34.

4 Lesley A. Orr MacDonald, *A Unique and Glorious Mission: Women and Presbyterianism in Scotland 1830–1930* (Edinburgh: John Donald Publishers Ltd., 2000), 157.

5 Eileen Janes Yeo, 'Protestant Feminists and Catholic Saints in Victorian Britain', *Radical Femininity: Women's Self-Representation in the Public Sphere*, ed. Eileen Janes Yeo (Manchester: Manchester University Press, 1998), 141.

6 'Women as Citizens', *SLWM* (Jan 1909): 16. BL P.P.3611.tc.

7 Mrs Latta, 'The SWLF at Dundee', *SLWM* (Mar 1912): 74. BL P.P.3611.tc.

8 'SWLF Council Meetings', *SLWM* (Apr 1911): 85. BL P.P.3611.tc.

9 Mary White, 'British Women's Temperance Work', *SWTN* 1, no. 3 (15 Feb 1897): 41. BWTASCU Collection.

10 'Women's Temperance Union', *League* no. 14 (Apr 1882): 209.

11 'British Women's Association: Conversazione in Edinburgh', *League* no. 49 (Dec 1882): 779.

12 Mariana Valverde, '"Racial poison": Drink, Male Vice, and Degeneration in First-Wave Feminism', *Women Suffrage in the British Empire*, eds Mayhall, Levine and Fletcher, 43.

13 Glasgow Prayer Union (GPU), *Minutes* (1886). Glasgow City Archives [hereafter GCA] TD 955/1/1.

14 Mrs Milne, 'Scotland's Women to the Rescue', *STA* (1907): 46.

15 See Juliet Kinchin, 'The Drawing Room', *The Scottish Home*, ed. Annette Carruthers (Edinburgh: National Museums of Scotland Publishing, 1996), 155–80; and Gordon and Nair, *Public Lives*.

16 SFWSS Kilmarnock Branch, *Minutes* (1913). Ayrshire Collection, Ayrshire Archives, Ayr [hereafter Ayrshire Collection].

17 See Smith-Rosenburg, 'The Female World of Love and Ritual'.

18 STL, 'Ladies Temperance Conference', *League* no. 14 (Apr 1882): 216.

19 Charles J. Smith, *Historic South Edinburgh Volume 1* (Haddington: Charles Skilton Ltd., 1978), 26. National Library of Scotland [hereafter NLS] H3. 201. 1889.

20 Smith, *Historic South Edinburgh Volume 1*, 27–8. NLS H3. 201. 1889.

21 Norma Armstrong, *Edinburgh as it Was Volume II: The People of Edinburgh* (Hendon Hill, Lancashire: Hendon Publishing Company Limited, 1977), 8. NLS 6. 2551.

22 Charles J. Smith, *Historic South Edinburgh Volume 3* (Haddington: Charles Skilton Ltd., 1978), 22. NLS H3. 201. 1889.

23 For example, see David Cannadine, 'Victorian Cities: How Different?', *Social History* 4 (1977): 457–82; H. J. Dyos, *Victorian Suburb: A Study of the Growth of Camberwell* (London: Leicester University Press, 1961); and David Ward, 'Environs and Neighbours in the "Two Nations": Residential Differentiation in Mid-Nineteenth-Century Leeds', *Journal of Historical Geography* 6, no. 2 (1980): 133–62.

24 'Mrs McKinnon, Dumfries', *SWTN* 2, no. 9 (Sep 1898): 134. BWTASCU Collection.

25 Mrs Barton, 'Impressions from the Antipodes', *SLWM* (Jun 1912): 126–7. BL P.P.3611. tc.

26 'Message from the President', *SWTN* 11, no. 2 (Feb 1907): 19. BWTASCU Collection.

27 'Miss and Mrs Forrester Paton', *SWTN* 1, no. 7 (15 Jun 1897): 99. BWTASCU Collection.

28 'British Women's Temperance Association', *League* no. 46 (Nov 1882): 723.

29 'Municipal Work', *SWTN* 8, no. 5 (May 1904): 66. BWTASCU Collection.

30 Mary White, 'The Late Mrs Black of the Glasgow School of Cookery', *SWTN* 7, no. 4 (Apr 1903): 50. BWTASCU Collection.

31 'Mrs McKinnon, Dumfries', *SWTN* 2, no. 9 (Sep 1898): 134. BWTASCU Collection.

32 'The Grand National Demonstration of Women in the Free Trade Hall, Manchester', *WSJ* 11, no. 121 (14 Feb 1880): 44. WL.

33 'The Grand National Demonstration of Women', 44. WL.

34 Society of Friends, 'Agnes Ann Bryson', *Annual Monitor* 96 (1909): 14. Library of the Society of Friends [hereafter LSF].

35 Megan Smitley, 'Mary White', *Alcohol and Temperance in Modern History: An International Encyclopedia Vol. 2*, eds Jack S. Blocker, David Fahey and Ian R. Tyrrell (Oxford: ABC-CLIO, 2003), 657.

36 Sandra Stanley Holton, 'Kinship and Friendship: Quaker Women's Networks and the Women's Movement', *WHR* 14, no. 3&4 (2005): 368; Elizabeth Isichei, *Victorian Quakers* (London: Oxford University Press, 1970), 238.

37 White, 'Proposed "Prison Gate Mission"', 172. LSF.

38 Thomas C. Kennedy, *British Quakerism 1860–1912: The Transformation of a Religious Community* (Oxford: Oxford University Press, 2001), 234.

39 See Isichei, *Victorian Quakers*; and Kennedy, *British Quakerism*.

40 Kennedy, *British Quakerism*, 227.

41 I am grateful for the insights offered by Dr Paul F. Burton. See also, Kennedy, *British Quakerism*, 211.

42 Society of Friends, 'Agnes Ann Bryson', 13. LSF.

43 Jane Darling, 'The Late Mrs Blaikie', *SWTN* 19, no. 9 (Sept 1915): 107. BWTASCU Collection.

44 Foreign Mission Society, *Letter from William Stevenson to Margaret Blaikie* (1898). NLS MSS 7922.

45 For more on Scotswomen's work for foreign missions, see MacDonald, *A Unique and Glorious Mission*, especially chapter 3.

46 Foreign Mission Society, *Letter from William Stevenson to Margaret Blaikie* (1902). NLS MSS 7926.

47 *Doctor Agnes McLaren (1837–1913) Physician Convert Pioneer* (1953), 1. NLS HP1. 86. 2696.

48 For more on the conversion of Protestant feminists, see Yeo, 'Protestant Feminists and Catholic Saints'.

49 *Doctor Agnes McLaren*, 1. NLS HP1. 86. 2696.

50 'The Grand National Demonstration of Women at the Free Trade Hall, Manchester', *WSJ* 11, no. 121 (14 Feb 1880): 38. WL.

51 ENSWS, *Report of Committee* (Edinburgh: Darien Press, 1907), 20. NLS HP1.82.1728.

52 ENSWS, *Report of Committee*, 9. NLS HP1.82.1728.

53 See Megan Smitley, 'Feminist Anglo-Saxonism?: The Representation of "Scotch" Women in the English Women's Press in the Late Nineteenth Century', *Cultural and Social History* 4, no.3 (2007): 337–55.

54 ENSWS, *Report of Committee*, 12.

55 SWLF, *Minutes* (1902). NLS Acc. 11765/23.

56 SWLF, *Minutes* (1902). NLS Acc. 11765/23.

57 Smith-Rosenburg, 'The Female World of Love and Ritual', 16.

58 Society of Friends, 'Mary White', *Annual Monitor* 63 (1905): 148. LSF.

59 Society of Friends, *Dictionary of Quaker Biography*. LSF.

60 See Appendix 6.

3

Temperance reform and the feminine public sphere

The reform programme of the BWTASCU reflected contemporary middle-class reforming goals, yet the particular contributions of the BWTASCU towards meeting these goals sought to feminise middle-class civic and public life. Through an exploration of key elements of female temperance reform such as, leisure reform, inebriate homes and the professionalisation of female associationalism this chapter seeks to provide a fresh perspective on middle-class women's contribution to a middle-class identity based on participation in public life.

The BWTASCU's representation of its leisure reform activities in the *SWTN*, minute books and annual reports highlights the British Women's loyalty to the supposed relationship between female domesticity and a happy, morally robust and 'civilised' family life. A central feature of the BWTASCU's leisure reform activities aimed at working-class recipients were 'counter-attractions to the public house', which were most prominently manifest as teetotal refreshment tents at fairs. Refreshment tents mirrored the sexual division of labour and the class relations of the middle-class home where more elite women supervised the work of domestic servants. Similarly, the BWTASCU's leisure reform among the middle classes emphasised the ability of the domestic manageress to cultivate a teetotal home environment by regulating domestic consumption. While the BWTASCU's involvement in leisure reform could reflect conventional gender ideologies, the British Women deployed administrative expertises gained in domestic management in the radical context of temperance reform in an effort to normalise their feminine values across many layers of society.

Evidence from the *SWTN* demonstrates that factors apart from a desire to normalise middle-class feminine values were essential for mobilising women's participation in the feminine public sphere, most importantly a passionate Christian faith. Female temperance reform was a central site for middle-class women's public Christian performances, and in their writings British Women characterised temperance reform as an opportunity for Christian service. This can be seen in repeated assertions in the *SWTN* to the effect that women were divinely led from other areas of benevolent work into temperance reform. This is particularly evident in the case of female inebriate homes, and the biographies and memoirs of British Women associated with these institutions highlight both the influence of philanthropic networks on female temperance reform and the mythologies surrounding women's 'inevitable' progress from philanthropy to temperance.

Middle-class women's associationalism reveals women's bona fide participation in middle-class public life. While economic dependency on male kin and access to leisure time made possible, in part, by the labour of domestic servants were vital elements in facilitating middle-class women's public lives, it is necessary to adopt a more nuanced view of middle-class women's rationale for voluntary public work. Evidence from the BWTASCU calls into question the idea that middle-class women were passively recruited into the voluntary sector by boredom. Advice in the *SWTN* on how to organise branches, and the voluntary career-histories of individual British Women indicate that female temperance reformers' investment in their public pursuits required more than the negative impetus of ennui. This analysis of the professionalisation of the BWTASCU argues that women's public lives were motivated by an internalisation of professional ideals and a dedication to Christian service.

Female temperance reform and women's philanthropic networks

Philanthropy was a training ground for middle-class women, and the skills and experiences gained in charity work were transferred to female temperance reform.[1] Female temperance reformers' implementation of methodologies tried and tested in philanthropy reveals an essential characteristic of the feminine public sphere namely an identifiable community of middle-class women active in public life who encouraged and supported one another through their extensive networks. Anglophone networks were particularly important for women's public lives in Scotland, and international reforming networks connected women in Glasgow and Edinburgh to a global community of publicly active women.[2] Reformers in Scotland tapped into these religious, kinship, friendship and pseudo-professional networks to gain experience in public life and with this experience an awareness of the latest trends in philanthropy and reform in England, the United States, Canada and elsewhere in the white settler colonies.

By the 1870s, the relationship between female philanthropy and temperance reform had an established pedigree. From the early nineteenth century, women such as Ann Biggar, mother of BWTASCU President Margaret Blaikie, had been recruited to temperance reform via philanthropic endeavour. The *SWTN* claimed that Biggar laboured, 'with singular self-denial and earnestness among the poor in Banff, where she lived, and trying hard to win to sobriety some who were much given to drinking, she became a total abstainer, in the hope that her example would have beneficial influence in her district.[3] Like their mothers and grandmothers, middle-class public women in the late nineteenth century were exposed to the living conditions of poorer women and children in the course of philanthropy, and often attributed this poverty to expenditure on alcohol. Indeed, Mrs Wilhemina Woyka, Vice-President of the Glasgow Prayer Union (1875–1902), was known to play on this theme in her temperance speeches: 'She frequently carried with her a little bag containing all the requisites for a morning meal, fuel included, at the same cost as one would pay for a glass of whisky – giving an object lesson which greatly interested her audiences.'[4]

Reports on female temperance reformers' remembrances of their entry into temperance reform often claim that experiences gained during philanthropic work were instrumental in informing the decision to join the temperance movement. For instance, the *SWTN*'s biography of Woyka records her memory of New Year's Eve in 1874 when, 'there was a barrow being wheeled along Stockwell Street in the dim evening light, and a strange sort of creature lay thereon that seemed scarcely human, so unclothed was it and so helpless.'[5] Woyka recalls asking a policeman about the 'creature':

> he said, 'Oh, it's only a WOMAN'. Mrs Woyka took off her cloak, and begged him to cover the poor creature's nakedness; but the man said, 'She is not worth your pity', and the debased woman was wheeled away … Two days after a somewhat similar sight was seen about the Broomielaw, and so impressed Mrs Woyka that the cry went up: 'Lord, help me to do something for such poor creatures!'[6]

Woyka's biographer seems to be making two points here. Firstly, that alcohol dehumanised poorer women, and secondly that female temperance reformers had primary responsibility for defending poorer women from such degradation. While the biographer is clearly seeking to heighten readers' sense of urgency with such a sensational description, the impact of her language is surely enhanced by its resonance with readers' real-life experiences with alcohol's effects on women in the slums of Glasgow and Edinburgh.

The career history of Mrs Grant A. Millar provides further evidence of British Women's broad-based experiences in charity before joining the temperance movement. Millar, the eldest daughter of Edinburgh MP Duncan McLaren, maintained an impressive public profile throughout her life. She was a founder of the BWTASCU in the mid-1870s and remained a member until 1908. In the nineteenth century her work as Secretary for the Edinburgh Central Branch led the *SWTN* to claim: 'She is in touch with every branch over the kingdom, and her influence pervades the whole organisation, which owes to Mrs. Millar not a little of the zeal and energy which have enabled it to achieve so much good and successful work in the temperance cause.'[7] In the early twentieth century, Millar continued to be a prominent member of the Edinburgh Central Branch and served as vice-president and later honorary vice-president. As a young woman, Millar taught Sabbath school for girls and launched the first Sunday services for children in Edinburgh's poor neighbourhoods. She was also known for her involvement in establishing mothers' meetings, penny savings banks and the Working Men's Mutual Improvement and Temperance Society in Edinburgh as well as for agitating against the Contagious Disease's Acts.[8] In 1877, she, 'took a house on her own responsibility, praying for help and guidance' in order to establish the Springwell House rescue home for girls who were, 'on the streets, leading a life of shame and horror'.[9] She was secretary of Springwell from its beginning, and took over as president in 1897. Millar's record as a voluntary public servant mirrors the backgrounds of many of her colleagues who were similarly incorporated into public life through benevolent work, and who complemented their commitment to temperance reform with diverse charitable obligations.

A distinguishing feature of the most committed female temperance reformers was a strong background in philanthropy, and philanthropic networks running through the Anglophone community were important for introducing female temperance reformers to the use of rescue homes. Mary White was the guest of the famous London 'child saver' Miss Annie MacPherson in 1869, an experience White would later claim convinced her of the link between poverty and intemperance: 'This month in East London opened my eyes to the sins and sorrows of great cities, and I returned to Glasgow braced in spirit and ready to engage in anything the Lord called me to do.'[10] White was a founder of the Glasgow Prayer Union, acting as leader of the Legislative and Prison departments as well as secretary (1881–91) and president (1893–1902). In her memoir published in the *SWTN*, White recalls MacPherson's role in her initiation into public life: 'I went about with her in her daily visits to these – in fact, wherever she went – to meetings and classes of all sorts among young and old, to the common lodging houses, and up many a dark and rickety stair, where dwelt poor Spitalfield weavers, Sunday scholars, widows, and sick folks among whom she worked.'[11] MacPherson was most strongly associated with child emigration, an approach to childhood poverty that viewed Empire and particularly the white settler colonies as the ideal receptacle for Britain's impoverished orphans, and in 1871 White accompanied MacPherson's sister when resettling ninety boys in Canada.[12] After returning to Glasgow, White collaborated with Agnes Anne Bryson, William Quarrier (whose legacy in 'child saving' continues to the present day) and Annie MacPherson to establish the Emigration Home for Glasgow Waifs.

Margaret Blaikie was also influenced by Annie MacPherson's work. Margaret and William Blaike met MacPherson while in Toronto, and having been persuaded by the moral righteousness of her work they established the Emigration Home in Edinburgh in 1871. Over the course of twenty years the Emigration Home in Lauriston Lane received 700 children and sent 300 to Canada. The *SWTN*'s biography of Blaikie, claims that her work in 'child saving' was key to recruiting her into the temperance movement: 'In dealing with so many destitute children Mrs Blaikie came to see more and more of the awful results of drink. She became more warmly interested in the total abstinence cause, and more thoroughly convinced that Christian people were bound to take a resolute stand against drink and the drink traffic.'[13] Here the *SWTN* upholds the idea that philanthropy exposed middle-class women to urban misery, and encouraged readers' perception of a causal link between alcohol and poverty. As Blaikie claims in the Glasgow Prayer Union's 1882 minutes: 'No Christian worker but met intemperance in every corner in which she went, and found that it was productive of the misery, poverty, lunacy, and many other evils which it was the duty of the Christian community to strive against.'[14] Blaikie's comments acknowledge readers' shared first-hand knowledge of the destructive effects of alcohol abuse, while further suggesting that an awareness of drink's role in urban misery inevitably led to a career in temperance.

The feminine public sphere's Anglophone philanthropic networks encompassed the United States, and, for instance, famed American temperance woman Eliza Stewart was a significant role model for the British Women. Mary White's memoir in the *SWTN* claims that Stewart's 1876 visit introduced the Glasgow Prayer Union to prison and police office visitation:

> At eleven o'clock, one Saturday night, in company with her, we visited the Central Police Office, and saw the wrecks of the drink traffic brought in at the closing of the public-houses, and put down like helpless sacks on

the cell floors. In one of the cells was a little dying baby, and its wretched mother lying insensibly from drink in another cell. We also saw a larger room, with an immense fire, before which those paralysed by drink were laid, lest they should die during the night from the lowering of vital heat which follows from drinking whisky.[15]

By 1878, Mary White and Anne Bryson had instituted prison and police office visiting and established the Whitevale Mission Shelter to house women persuaded to enter an inebriate home at these meetings. Inebriate homes were major undertakings for the BWTASCU, and homes operated by the Glasgow Prayer Union and Edinburgh Central Branch are considered later in the chapter. Methodologies apart from the use of rescue homes infiltrated female temperance reform from philanthropy, and district visiting was a cornerstone of the BWTASCU's everyday work.

An important element of Victorian and Edwardian women's charitable work was 'personalism', an ideology which claimed that face-to-face meetings with beneficiaries were integral to advancing social welfare.[16] For example, Wilhelmina Woyka's participation in William Quarrier's midnight suppers scheme meant walking Glasgow's streets looking for poorer, inebriated women in need of food and salvation; 'her husband with some others was an escort in case of danger, keeping at a distance, so that the women might meet their "sisters" alone'.[17] Personalism most often took the form of district visiting where women went house-to-house for purposes of inspecting a beneficiary's domestic space in order to assess a recipient's 'deservingness' as well as to dissipate class tensions in a 'neighbourly' way. Many female temperance reformers had a background in this work such as Grant Millar who had visited in four Edinburgh mission districts as a young woman.[18] In the *SWTN* Mary White argued for the central role of district visiting to the operation of women's temperance unions:

> Of not less importance than regular meetings is the visitation of members for which purpose a working committee should be formed at the outset. In this way interest and sympathy are brought to bear on those who join, notices of meetings given, and the members increased, as the visitor should always have the little pledge-book in her tract bag ... committees partly composed of working women having charge of different departments of work.[19]

White's assertion of the importance of district visiting includes a special role for working-class women. Women's temperance unions were founded on an elite membership, with local and Scottish-national leaders drawn from the upper-middle classes. Middle-class reformers did recognise the potential pitfalls arising from wealthier women's visits to poorer women's homes, and nineteenth-century organisations could enlist working-class women for district visiting such as the Biblewomen, the paid working-class visitors first organised in London by Mrs Ellen Raynard's Bible and Domestic Female Mission.

The BWTASCU sought to provide paid opportunities for female visitors, and in 1882 the Glasgow Prayer Union determined to pay a female missionary twenty-four pounds per annum to oversee district visiting. Mrs McPherson was hired, 'to labour particularly among women, by holding mothers' meetings, house to house visitation, tract distribution, &c'.[20] An 1888 report summarised McPherson's work as, 'besides addressing many women's meetings, visits the Northern Police Office twice a week, and on Wednesdays attends the Feeing Market at Graham Square, and visits the Royal Infirmary'.[21] An 1889 report gives a similar synopsis of her work, but after this date it is unclear if McPherson continued as the Home Missionary; she is listed as a member of the Glasgow Prayer Union until 1902 and it is likely that she carried on this work throughout her tenure. The employment of a full-time Home Missionary suggests an increasing professionalisation of the feminine public sphere, and the ranks of volun-tary, unpaid workers might better be understood as quasi-professional public servants rather than as bored, amateur, busy-bodies seeking to regulate the lives of poorer women.

The professionalisation of female associationalism

Middle-class women's organisations demanded a dedicated profession-alism from volunteers. Female associationalism expected a high level of commitment from participants, and as Varty has noted women's volun-tarism required, 'significant sacrifice of time and, for some, a lifelong dedication of energy, skills and resources'.[22] This is clear in part from the longevity of members' participation in women's organisations. Chapter 1 showed that the average member in the sample belonged to an organi-sation for six years, however there was a significant number active for ten or more years (20%), for fifteen or more years (10%) and twenty or more years (4%). In addition to a considerable commitment of personal time and energy, women's associations were increasingly regimented and sophisticated in structure. From its beginnings the BWTASCU was metic-ulously organised, and it became increasingly refined after implementa-tion of 'do everything' in 1893 and consequent departmentalisation. The British Women's understanding of professionalism was bound up with 'do everything', and Margaret Black argued at the 1895 annual meeting that: 'The system of departmental work shows practical wisdom, and is on the lines on which every great business firm is conducted.'[23] The *SWTN* provides evidence of the exacting standards expected of women active in the feminine public sphere, and a 1905 report of Mrs Hume's address to a meeting of branch secretaries highlights the rigour of middle-class women's unpaid associational work:

> Let us try to imagine an ideal secretary. What are some of the qualities and characteristics she should possess?:
>
> i   She must be full of interest in and well informed about her work.
> ii She must be orderly, prompt, and businesslike in dealing with her correspondence.
> iii She must spare herself no pains or trouble, down to the very smallest details, in making arrangements for meetings.
> iv She must be expert at drawing up agenda papers, and framing full but concise minutes.
> v   She must be exceedingly patient, tactful, and ingenious.
> vi She must possess enough enthusiasm in the cause not merely to carry herself through the monotony, drudgery, and disappointments inseparable from her office, but enough also to inspire others with the desire to work.[24]

Historians have tended to attribute middle-class women's participation in voluntary work to boredom, and Olive Banks has argued that: 'Women, and especially perhaps unmarried women, turned to religious and charitable exercises as a way of filling up empty time with purposeful activities.'[25] Peter Bailey has characterised middle-class women's voluntarism as leisure, rather than as a symptom of access to leisure time; fund-raising activities of bazaars and fêtes gave an outlet for the leisure energies and talents of the womenfolk'.[26] This sort of understanding of bourgeois Englishwomen's voluntarism ignores female volunteers' ardent faith and earnest commitment to Christian service. The need to recognise more meaningful motivations behind middle-class women's voluntary work is underscored by the BWTASCU's highly professionalised approach to temperance reform.

Mother–daughter apprenticeship, female networks and the pervasiveness of voluntary work among middle-class women encouraged shared, tacit understandings of the substance of public work. Minute books and annual reports can indicate the structure and policies of a group, yet these sources provide few explicit explanations of the day-to-day business of voluntary work. In the early twentieth century, the *SWTN* published several discussions of the qualities required for taking up leading positions in temperance unions. In 1905, the *SWTN* published Mrs May Morison Geddes' detailed advice for branch secretaries. Geddes – part of the national leadership from 1896, vice-president (1901–03) and honorary vice-president (1904–14) – asserted that: 'A secretary must be methodical in work, and prompt in execution, and businesslike in details. Her work mainly consists in correspondence, keeping of minutes, and making arrangements for meetings.'[27] The precision of Geddes' instructions indicates a desire to enhance the professionalism of branch officers. For instance, regarding correspondence:

> All letters would have the date and the address at the beginning and be signed at the end, putting the word (Mrs) or (Miss) in brackets before the signature. All paper printed or written must be kept by themselves either in a drawer kept sacred to BWTA, or in large envelopes marked outside with the name of the contents. Answers to communications should be sent by return post, or as soon as possible after consultation with the president.[28]

The *SWTN's* interest in a professionalised membership is evident in a 1909 description of the type of woman needed for temperance reform:

1 The woman who is willing to work, not the woman who complains of it.
2 The woman who is willing to lead, not the woman who has to be carried.
3 The woman who forgets her own individuality in her enthusiasm for the work, not the woman who is constantly sounding the personal note.
4 The woman who has courage to assume responsibility and brave criticisms, not the woman who is fearful because of possible failure and wilts under adverse opinion.
5 The woman who thinks it her duty to have opinions and offer suggestions in the discussion of ways and means, not the woman who is silent and non-committal, but after critically wonders why wiser measures were not adopted.
6 The woman who, when she makes a mistake, frankly acknowledges it, and undismayed sets about remedying it, knowing that she who never makes a mistake seldom makes anything else.
7 The woman who gives earnest thought to the business in hand, not the woman who enters the committee room airily and late, and the moment the meeting adjourns claims the attention of the ladies on some matter foreign to the subject under consideration.
8 The woman who understands that associated work will not succeed if conducted in just the way individual effort is, therefore pays due heed to Parliamentary law and practice and has regard to Parliamentary courtesy in her intercourse with her associates.

9 The woman who is steadfast and can be relied upon when difficulties arise, not the woman who gladly avails herself of some excuse for being absent when knotty problems must be solved.

10 The woman who is an inspiration to the discouraged, not the woman who is timid and yields to the councils of the faithless.[29]

This list of the qualities considered by the BWTASCU as vital for public work could be interpreted as evidence that middle-class women's associations simply aped the structure and style of elite men's organisations. Certainly, women's temperance unions echoed the hierarchical structure and operational style of men's organisations, but the work of women's organisations was informed by a uniquely feminine set of priorities and reflected middle-class female reformers' efforts to mobilise their energies on behalf of other women. Indeed, similarities between male and female associationalism are better understood as evidence of a feminine public sphere from where middle-class women contributed to the development of a robust bourgeois civic identity.

The competency of British Women in public life is evident in the records of Wilhelmina Woyka's role in the BWTASCU. Woyka was considered to be a particularly 'public-spirited' woman, and the *SWTN* and Glasgow Prayer Union minutes discuss her adept management of private and public meetings locally and throughout Scotland and England.[30] She was one of the BWTASCU's most respected public speakers, and was tireless in spreading the temperance message. For instance, in 1890 Woyka:

> addressed three meetings in Dumfries, two at Dundee, Fraserburgh, and Motherwell, and one at Aberdeen, Alexandria, Broughty-Ferry, Burnt-Island, and Perth, besides two drawing-room meetings at Ibrox, and a number of meetings in Glasgow and neighbourhood. She also addressed repeated meetings at Castle-Douglas, Dalbeattie, East Wemyss, and Peterhead, resulting in the formation of branches of the BWTA in these places.[31]

Woyka's reputation as a public speaker calls into question Shiman's insistence that female temperance reformers, 'were by training and cultural pressure ill equipped for an active public life'.[32] Woyka, though clearly exceptional, shared with many prominent British Women an impressive capacity for public life, and the BWTASCU annual reports list dozens of official speakers available for bookings at local meetings. The officers and committee members – the core of the Glasgow and Edinburgh branches – were, throughout the late nineteenth and early twentieth centuries, vigorous proponents of temperance who organised public and private meetings; participated in public debate on alcohol in the temperance and mainstream press; developed departments to systematise their temperance work; raised funds; and networked within the reforming world.

The British Women's willingness to face the challenges of a highly regimented and professionalised voluntarism was often attributed to their Christian faith. Discussions of day-to-day management of women's temperance unions were peppered with Christian imagery, and Hume's idealised portrait of the perfect secretary acknowledges that, 'striving to be a good secretary involves an amount of struggle and effort that is not in itself attractive. Indeed, I don't know how any of us can endure it, unless in it all we are consciously seeking to serve the Lord Jesus Christ.'[33] Geddes similarly reminded readers that at its core temperance reform was a vital Christian service and its demands must be born in that light: 'A spirit of earnestness, of hope, and of real belief that this work is to do real and lasting good must inspire the workers in any branch, and if they feel with all their hearts that they are doing this work for the sake of the Master, Who has called them to do it, the ultimate success of their branch is certainly assured.'[34] Wilhelmina Woyka's Christian devotion ran deep. Wilhelmina Johanna Henrietta Woyka née Elvin, a native of Hamburg and the daughter of a prominent medical family, had converted from Judaism to Protestantism. She and her Hungarian husband, John Woyka, a Roman Catholic convert to Protestantism and a timber merchant, immigrated to Glasgow to escape religious persecution. Woyka's zealous Christianity is recalled in Eliza Stewart's memoir of their visit to Aberdeen:

> As soon as the meeting was closed a young man sprang onto the platform and asked to be presented to the speakers; said he was a Jew, was the only one in the city, and was greatly delighted to meet one of his own people. He was a Good Templar and apparently a very worthy young man. He accompanied us to the hotel and Mrs Woika [sic] at once opened up the great and important question, 'What think ye of Christ?' and they continued the discussion until one o'clock, or rather she continued to present Jesus as the 'Hope of Israel', and to plead with him to accept Him as his Savior. The next morning early, with other gentlemen, he was on hand, as we had to leave on the early train for Glasgow, and at once Mrs W. again took up the theme of the previous evening. At length she arose and as she went to the organ where Mr Brown was playing, said, 'I am praying for you', and with Mr B.'s assistance sang the sweet song of which the above words are the refrain. As the song ended she knelt and offered a very touching prayer for our young friend, I and Mr Brown following, Mr Smith the while standing with bowed head and solemn mien.[35]

This extraordinary testimony provides a unique glimpse of the religiosity of female temperance reformers, and emphasises that temperance reform was a site for middle-class women's Christian performances.

Evidence of the public profiles of Blaikie, Millar, White and Woyka alongside the *SWTN*'s discussions of the professionalism expected of female temperance reformers suggests that voluntary work was very much professionalised for upper-middle-class women. The emergence of professional society has been linked to the late nineteenth and early twentieth centuries, and has been characterised as a society 'made up of career hierarchies of specialized occupations selected by merit and based on trained expertise'.[36] The increased systematisation of work associated with professional society has been mapped onto women's unpaid domestic work, and more recently integrated onto an analysis of female missionaries.[37] These studies share an emphasis on Victorian and Edwardian trends toward the provision of quality services and individual advancement (and exclusion) through a hierarchy of qualifications. Middle-class women's endeavours in the feminine public sphere existed largely outside the sphere of formal qualifications, yet the British Women mirrored and reinforced the legitimacy of professional ideals by consciously seeking to systematise the structure and operation of their temperance unions. The British Women's professional ethic pervaded all the BWTASCU's endeavours, and is visible in discussions of its leisure reform activities.

Counter-attractions to the public house

Victorian and Edwardian middle-class reformers sought to 'rationalise' working-class leisure, and the BWTASCU joined the push to develop teetotal alternatives to working-class pub-based recreation. Initiatives in 'counter-attractions to the public house' were early elements of the reform programmes of both the Edinburgh Central Branch and Glasgow Prayer Union. British Women's contributions to the 'rational recreation' movement could reflect an idealised middle-class femininity, such as refreshment tents at fairs, equally their leisure reform measures could diverge from an affirmation of domesticity, as in the female Mizpah band.

A hallmark of the BWTASCU's counter-attractions was the provision of teetotal refreshment, and the most elaborate undertakings in this vein were refreshment tents at fairs. One of the richer descriptions of a 'tent' comes from an account of the Stirling Branch's tent at the Highland and Agricultural Society show in a 1900 annual report. The tent was a long wooden shed, 108 feet by twenty feet, enclosed on one side and divided into a luncheon section, a kitchen in the middle and a take-away counter.[38] Miss Nellie Harvie, Superintendent of Stirling's Decorative Committee, organised to have the wood inside and outside the shed covered in panels of blue and white sateen with dark blue paper thistles hung between these panels. A Scottish flag, BWTASCU flag and a large white banner with 'BWTA' printed in dark blue completed the decorations outside the tent, while flower baskets were hung within. The Waiting Committee was composed of women from the Young Ladies' Committee who were asked, 'to wear white dresses, and, if possible, sailor hats, and we provided them with [blue] bands for their hats, and badges of the same ribbon, which were worn across the front of the bodice from shoulder to waist'.[39] The British Women and their young protégé waitresses did not get their hands too dirty: 'The staff of workers in the Kitchen (who were, of course, all paid hands) consisted of an experienced waiter who did all the carving, a staff of seven women and two servants who, with pretty caps and aprons, served the food through the "hutches".[40] Pricing was based on the rates charged by the temperance restaurants in Stirling, except for the last day of the fair when farm-servants and other manual labourers were served and the prices modified. The tent raised £343–8s, a successful taking which the Stirling British Women attributed to the *a la carte* pricing versus the fixed price menus offered by rival caterers.

The description of the Stirling tent highlights two important ideas associated with the BWTASCU's refreshment tents namely, the monumental effort required for these enterprises and the apparent parallels between the operation of the tents and the running of the middle-class home. Similar accounts of refreshment tents emphasise the meticulousness of female temperance reformers, and the exhaustive attention to detail required by these undertakings. The *SWTN*'s coverage of the Glasgow Prayer Union's 1905 tent claims: 'a staff of about 150 lady helpers had been secured, and three distinct departments (restaurant, buffet, and pantry) were equipped with double staffs, each giving from four to eight hours' service daily. The heads were present from early mourn till dewy eve, as early breakfasts were served to the drovers and stall-keepers, etc.'[41] The British Women's thoroughness may be attributed in part to the professionalisation of domestic work that is associated with the nineteenth century. Historians such as Jeanne Boydston and Deborah Simonton have argued that nineteenth-century female domesticity was subject to increasingly exacting standards.[42] Refreshment tents replicated both contemporary standards for domestic work as well as the class relations of the middle-class home, where the lady of the house administered the work of domestic servants. Cooking and cleaning in the tents was undertaken by paid staff, but food service was done by young middle-class women, often the daughters and young relations of the British Women. While the tents were discussed by the BWTASCU as a means of providing fair-goers and fair-workers with teetotal food and drink, a majority of the clientele were drawn from more well-to-do fair-goers. The more elite background of the diners in the tents is evident in the *SWTN's* description of Glasgow's 1905 tent:

> The restaurant was draped in blue and white; a tasteful setting in which the white-robed waitresses looked so winsome that some of the onlookers enquired if they were all angels inside. It was known as the 'Bachelor's Tent' on the show-ground, so popular was it with the young men, who seemed to breakfast, dine, tea and sup daily under its canvas roof. Often the would-be diners had to form a queue at the door and wait their turn for admission.[43]

Thus, for young middle-class women refreshment tents represented an opportunity to socialise and to launch a public career, while British Women's supervisory roles echoed the mature middle-class woman's role as household manageress.

Refreshment tents may have conformed to the sexual division of labour, yet British Women deployed their domestic skills in the radical context of temperance reform on the public stage of the fairground. While the British Women's methods may not have opposed gender stereotypes, temperance reform was itself a courageous rejection of a cornerstone of Victorian and Edwardian social life. Alcohol was central to working- and middle-class sociability, and Mark James has argued that while temperance was intertwined with more conservative forces in society, the 'radicalism of its ideas, and its example should not be underestimated'. Clearly, initiatives in counter-attractions provided an opportunity for women's participation in middle-class public life; refreshment tents allowed more experienced women to exercise and publicly demonstrate their organisational and administrative expertises, while younger women might announce their interest in public life. From this perspective, the BWTASCU's counter-attractions challenged the ideal of a cloistered femininity, and asserted women's place in bourgeois public life.

The BWTASCU's counter-attractions could take forms less easily equated with female domesticity. The British Women were well known in temperance circles for organising two female Mizpah bands in Glasgow. Mizpah bands were first conceived by the American evangelical Dwight L. Moody, and were inspired by the Mizpah benediction, 'the Lord watch between me and thee, when we are absent one from another'.[45] As the allusion to the Mizpah benediction suggests, the bands were designed to foster working-class teetotal support networks. In October 1886, Anne Bryson proposed that the Glasgow Prayer Union form a female Mizpah band, and in December she pressed her case with the claim: 'Great desire for a female Mizpah band, the husbands willing to stay at home one night in the week, to let the women attend.'[46] By 1887, the Glasgow Prayer Union had established the first two female Mizpah bands in Britain. The bands provided entertainment at teetotal gatherings and often performed in the Glasgow Prayer Union's refreshment tents.

Middle-class female temperance reformers, through counter-attractions, endeavoured to normalise middle-class social ideals. In so doing, female temperance reformers asserted the social value of the home and family, the realms most strongly associated with middle-class femininity. As Jane Rendall has rightly suggested: 'For women ... the temperance movement had a deeper dimension: it was about the use and control of family resources and leisure time, an assertion of domestic priorities.'[47] By developing alternatives to the pub, the British Women hoped to stimulate sobriety among working men and women with the aim of making their own 'domestic priorities' central to the daily lives of a broader section of society.

Female temperance reformers were motivated as much by internal religious feeling as a desire to regulate working-class family life, and counter-attractions should be understood in light of the millenarianism of temperance reform. William M. Walker has shown that the Scottish temperance movement was deeply informed by millennialist beliefs, or a belief in a prophesied thousand-year reign of saints before the Last Judgement.[48] From this point of view, temperance reformers, who believed themselves to be the pure and righteous of society, took personal responsibility for clearing the way for the Kingdom of God on Earth: 'By their "purity" the Prohibitionists demonstrated the viability of a future paradise by exemplifying their present fitness for it.'[49] The British Women's efforts to remove alcohol from leisure, whether among labourers or professionals, should be seen in part as an attempt to prepare society for an expected time of Earthly bliss. There is no doubt that female temperance reformers were more comfortable labouring among the working rather than the middle classes, yet the British Women did agitate for a shift in the social practices of their peers.

Leisure reform among the middle classes

Perhaps a more unexpected aspect of the British Women's leisure reform activities was agitation for total abstinence among their social equals.

In the middle-class home, wine, beer and spirits were key features of entertaining, and Gordon and Nair have demonstrated the prominence of alcohol in the inventories of middle-class estates.[50] The prevalence of drink at well-heeled dinner parties led the Scottish temperance movement to encourage middle-class women to leverage their domestic role to create a teetotal home environment. Margaret Black was a chief exponent of drives to convince, especially middle-class, women to exile alcohol from their tables. Black, a lecturer in Domestic Economy, used her celebrity as a cookery instructor to disseminate alcohol-free recipes. In 1897, she admonished those female temperance reformers who, while taking no alcohol themselves, continued to offer drink to their guests:

> Many persons are personal abstainers, and yet continue to have alcohol on their table – for the use of their friends, they say. This is not a strong position, for if our convictions tell us that alcohol is not desirable or right for our personal use it is certainly neither kind nor wise to present it to our friends. The courage of conviction is sadly wanted. Every table on which wine is set and presented to personal abstainers' guests is an undesirable object-lesson to servants and young people. We cannot say how far the influence of the lesson may radiate. Would the British Women prayerfully consider the propriety of banishing alcohol from their homes where this has not already been done?[51]

Black reminds her readers of middle-class women's duty to uplift morally the young people and working-class girls in their charge as guests, children or servants, and she demands that all female temperance reformers exploit their role in domestic management to stop the use of alcohol in their homes.

There is evidence that British Women expelled drink from their homes. The *SWTN*'s obituary for Grant Millar reported, 'it was not long after their marriage when wine was absolutely banished from their table and house, both Mr and Mrs Millar feeling that the use of what was such a curse to the nation could never be blest in their home'.[52] Eliza Stewart claimed in *The Crusader* that after meeting Anglo-American temperance reformer, John Bartholomew Gough, and taking the total abstinence pledge Margaret and Edward Parker of Dundee, 'brought forth their wine decanters and goblets, emptied wine into the sink and smashed bottles and glasses. They did not propose to have half way measures in their teetotalism.'[53]

Alcohol was also an important feature of public dinners. To the extent that the upper-middle classes dominated local civic and political life, the British Women's agitation against the use of alcohol at public dinners was a significant aspect of reform directed at their peers. An address to the

Glasgow Prayer Union's annual conference in November 1888 articulated the temperance movement's disapproval of alcohol in public life: 'There is scarcely a public dinner but there must be toasting with alcoholic liquor.'[54] The BWTASCU lobbied against such practices, and three years later the *SWTN* reported that: 'On learning that a motion for discontinuing the use of intoxicants at the public entertainments of the [Edinburgh] Town Council had been proposed by one of its members, we at once united with other Temperance Organisations and sent a petition in his favour.'[55] By co-operating with sympathetic local politicians, British Women sought to infiltrate public sociability and regulate its rituals in the same way that they endeavoured to regulate domestic sociability.

Attempts to excise alcohol from middle-class sociability and civic life reflected the temperance movement's increased emphasis on total abstinence, rather than moderation, from the mid-nineteenth century.[56] The rise of total abstinence from the 1850s led the temperance movement to mobilise the sexual division of labour in order to eliminate drink from the home. As the STL's *Scottish Temperance Review* (1846–58) reminded its female readers in 1851: 'The presentation of the beverage falls to your lot.'[57] The ascendancy of teetotalism was well established by the 1870s, and the British Women dismissed moderation, or abstinence from 'spirituous liquors' and the avoidance of drunkenness, as inadequate in the battle against the sin and vice that they associated with alcohol. Thus, in 1882 the *League*, the STL's official journal from the 1860s, reported Margaret Blaikie's assertion that: 'Every woman has her own special place. Let not one say "I have so little influence", for every one affects to a certain extent the circle in which she moves ... Mothers should put the drink out of their homes for the sake of their own families and those of their acquaintances and friends.'[58] Blaikie's appeal effectively used 'complementary natures' ideology and the practical circumstances of the sexual division of labour to integrate female domesticity into temperance agitation. The reverence for female domesticity evident in the BWTASCU's representations of efforts to eliminate alcohol from middle-class and working-class social life was also an important influence on the BWTASCU's female inebriate homes.

Female inebriate homes

The BWTASCU's inebriate homes were informed by a fidelity to female domesticity and a desire to curb female criminality. The Edinburgh Central Branch's Brownsland Temperance Home for Women and the Glasgow Prayer Union's Whitevale Mission Shelter aimed to convert poorer women to total abstinence, develop their domestic and maternal skills and prepare them for life as a wife and mother or domestic servant. Similar institutions used to house orphans, prostitutes and – in the case of settlement houses – middle-class reformers themselves, inspired the operation of the inebriate homes.

Female inebriate homes were some of the first major undertakings of the Glasgow and Edinburgh branches, which established the Brownsland Temperance Home for Women in 1876 and Whitevale Mission Shelter in 1877, respectively.[59] Inmates at Brownsland were required to be, 'women who, having fallen into habits of intemperance, have the desire to reform, and are willing to go into such a home'.[60] The Whitevale Mission Shelter housed an average of seventy inmates who might be cajoled into residency through the efforts of the Police Office and/or Prison Visiting Committees led by Mary White and Anne Bryson or by Wilhelmina Woyka's 'Free Breakfast' scheme. Between 1886 and 1887, Woyka organised a programme whereby: 'A "Free Breakfast" is provided each morning for the women prisoners on being liberated. Ladies meet them within the prison gates, and bring those who accept the invitation to the breakfast room, whence those who desire to do better are taken to one of the homes. Eleven have already been added from it to the inmates of Whitevale Mission Shelter.'[61] Entry into the homes was voluntary and applications for admission were collected annually, yet both homes had difficulty in retaining their charges. Brownsland recommended a year's stay as the minimum period for successful treatment, however: 'Mrs Lockhart spoke of the great difficulty those in charge of Brownsland Temperance Home had to deal with, from the fact that they had no legal power to detain women patients in the Home, and the patients, finding that out, left the home when they pleased.'[62] In Glasgow, women who volunteered to enter Whitevale were prevented from leaving; the grounds were walled and the home's authorities retained inmates' clothes. Notwithstanding these precautions the determined escaped, and the Glasgow Prayer Union's minutes from 1890 record Mary White's claim that one inmate, 'got over the wall with all her good clothes on and her rags left behind'.[63]

The inebriate homes were organised to reflect the ideals of the sexual division of labour, and it was hoped that the institutions would operate as self-supporting laundries. It was difficult to meet the financial ambitions of these projects and the laundry at Whitevale was unsustainable. Anne Bryson and her successors relied on donations from sister temperance unions, and Bryson frequently issued pleas, 'for more washing, common sewing, and dorcas work, that more poor women may be housed employed, and an opportunity for reformation given them'.[64] Brownsland mirrored

Whitevale's approach, and aimed to occupy inmates' time with instruction in washing, sewing, gardening, 'moral education' and literacy classes
for purposes of reading Scripture. The day-to-day running of the inebriate
homes reflects what Patrick M. McLaughlin has termed Victorian 'institutional ideology', which responded to the needs of an industrial capitalist
society by stressing routine, discipline and constant employment.[65] The
centrality of laundry work to the BWTASCU's inebriate homes suggests
that the 'regime of prayers and piecework' prescribed by institutional
ideology was further shaped by gender.[66] McLaughlin's argument for
an institutional ideology is persuasive, yet from the British Women's
perspective the importance of total abstinence and Christian influence
was taken at face value: 'The experience of sixteen years proves that the
methods adopted in the conduct of the [Brownsland Temperance] Home
are admirably fitted to secure the ends desired: these are, entire abstinence
from drink, strict regularity of life, constant and cheerful employment,
personal sympathy and religious influence.'[67] The BWTASCU's notion of
what constituted successful treatment provides evidence of the British
Women's loyalty to the ideal of female domesticity. Brownsland's annual
reports regularly published testimonials from reformed inmates, which
upheld the importance of female domesticity, such as the letter from a
former inmate's husband reproduced in the 1889 annual report: 'Mrs —
has kept all right since she came home, and has got the house very nice
indeed, and we are very comfortable ... I assure you, it is many years since
our home was as comfortable as it now is.'[68] British Women referred to
work in the homes as 'rescue' or 'reclamation' work. This language reveals
that the British Women sought to 'reclaim' women for motherhood and
domesticity, and a woman's rehabilitation was assessed in terms of her
dedication to maternal and domestic duties. This attitude is clear from
Brownsland's reports on rehabilitated women, for example:

> Eight women have left since January, and of these six are doing well.
> Two went to situations, three returned to their own homes or went
> to live with relatives, and another, after sixteen months' residence in
> the Home, sailed for Australia in the beginning of December, and was
> looking forward with great pleasure to joining her husband, a Christian
> man, from whom she had been separated because of her habits.[69]

The Glasgow Prayer Union also defined rehabilitation as an inmate's
allegiance to domesticity. At an 1888 discussion of rescue work, the
speaker recalled the case of, 'a girl brought up in a workhouse, then sent
out to a situation and between the ages of 14 and 26 (or 28) she had been
in prison 140 times, each time for being "drunk and disorderly", at last she

was saved and got married and for five years has been conducting herself admirably'.[70] Linda Mahood has argued that rescue homes' emphasis on domesticity was motivated by middle-class women's desire to generate a class of reliable and well-trained domestic staff.[71] Without doubt, industrial capitalist values informed the work of inebriate homes in so far as they prized sober, regular and constant employment. Certainly, poorer women who internalised these values would make better workers for wealthier women, yet this analysis tends to caricature the British Women – and all middle-class female reformers – as cynical agents of capitalist oppression. While their approach to 'the female inebriate' was highly problematic and hinged on their privileged social position, female temperance reformers were self-consciously fulfilling their duty as good Christians to uplift morally their proverbial neighbours. The British Women's interest in rehabilitating 'the female inebriate' further sought to break the perceived links between alcohol use and criminality.

Female temperance reformers viewed alcohol as the root of female criminality, and the British Women hoped to curb women's crimes by rehabilitation in the inebriate homes. The British Women shared the temperance movement's somewhat shallow view of social problems, which tended to distil the source of crime down to the 'evil of intemperance'. At the annual meeting of the Glasgow Prayer Union in 1889, Anne Bryson alleged alcohol was responsible for female criminality: 'Bryson spoke of the large new prison at Duke Street, which is being erected for women at the public expense. Would it not be more sensible to shut up the public houses that make the drunkards?'[72] Rehabilitation in inebriate homes sought to sever the links between alcohol and female criminality, and evidence from the Glasgow Prayer Union indicates that some women were diverted from prison to the Whitevale Mission Shelter: 'Reports were given of girls let off by the Magistrate on promising to go to a home, and when the ladies took them away from the police office the girls made their escape. Miss White said that notwithstanding the number that did this, yet there were many cases of girls so let off, who had gone to <u>Home</u> and had turned out well'.[73] The court's use of Whitevale for the rehabilitation of women accused of alcohol-related offences represents a formal recognition of middle-class women's contribution to the public sphere. This is significant for demonstrating that women's role in public life was not merely symbolic, but might be formally incorporated into middle-class public life.

Conclusion

Female temperance reformers were integrated into and integral to middle-class public life both through their reforming interests and their inter-nalisation of a professional ideal. The BWTASCU was heavily invested in middle-class endeavours to 'rationalise recreation' along respectable, teetotal lines. For female temperance reformers, this meant work among 'travelling showpeople' as well as the fair-going public. Refreshment tents at fairs allowed female temperance reformers to make an active contribu-tion to initiatives in leisure reform while simultaneously contributing to middle-class public identity within the public spaces of fairs. Refresh-ment tents largely conformed to the sexual division of labour and middle-class woman's role as domestic manageress, however tents were organised in the radical context of temperance and represented a public spectacle of middle-class women's moral authority. Leisure reform might take forms less overtly associated with conventional femininity such as the Mizpah band. Moreover, the British Women and the temperance movement more widely did agitate (albeit to a more limited extent) for leisure reform among the middle classes. This agitation tended to represent the middle-class domestic manageress as the arbiter of domestic consumption and entertainment, and thus in the responsible position of influencing guests, servants and family members by enforcing teetotal leisure within the home. Nonetheless, evidence from the BWTASCU suggests that the British Women's reforming energies were overwhelmingly trained on poorer women. The spectre of 'the female inebriate' alternately fascinated and repulsed the men and women of the middle classes, and an important aspect of the British Women's complementary role within the temperance movement to work particularly with women and girls was manifest in the creation and maintenance of female inebriate homes. These homes were informed by a Victorian institutional ideology and a desire to train a sober and reliable class of domestic servants. Equally they were articulations of female temperance reformers' commitment both to Christian service and to the spiritual power of total abstinence. Methodologies for temper-ance reform such as rescue homes were integrated into the BWTASCU by the philanthropic experiences of the British Women. These experi-ences included extensive charitable obligations locally and co-operation with female reformers internationally, especially within the Anglophone community. Finally, the public lives of the women discussed here and in earlier chapters demonstrate the influence of a professional social ideal on the feminine public sphere. Professionalisation's emphasis on the provision of a valuable though esoteric service and on the development of expertise through a system of qualifications was layered onto women's reforming careers. Leading members of women's temperance unions were expected to live up to rigorous standards of organisational and administrative skill, and key members of the BWTASCU came to temperance reform with impressive human capital gained through a lifetime of public service in their local communities. In sum, female temperance reform should be viewed as a fundamental realm of women's active participation in middle-class identity construction rather than simply as a religiously inspired movement bogged down in a conservative understanding of women's social role.

Notes

1 The importance of philanthropy for developing women's skills for public life has been recognised by many others, see, for example, Martin Gorsky, *Patterns of Philanthropy: Charity and Society in Nineteenth-Century Bristol* (Woodbridge, Suffolk: Royal Historical Society and The Boydell Press, 1999); John L. Duthie, 'Philanthropy and Evangelism among Aberdeen Seamen, 1814–1924', *The Scottish Historical Review* 63, no. 2 (1984): 155–73; Seth Koven, 'Borderlands: Women, Voluntary Action and Child Welfare in Britain 1840 to 1914', *Mothers of a New World: Maternalist Politics and the Creation of Welfare States*, eds Seth Koven and Sonya Michel (London: Routledge, 1993), 94–135; F. K. Prochaska, *Women and Philanthropy in Nineteenth-Century England* (Oxford: Oxford University Press, 1980); and Jane Rendall, *The Origins of Modern Feminism: Women in Britain, France and the United States, 1780–1860* (London: MacMillan Press Ltd., 1985).

2 I have argued elsewhere for the importance of Anglophone networks for the policies of the BWTASCU, see Megan Smitley, '"Inebriates", "Heathens", Templars and Suffragists: Scotland and Imperial Feminism', *WHR* 11, no. 3 (2002): 455–80.

3 'Mrs Margaret Blaikie. President of the Scottish Christian Union (British Women's Temperance Association)', *SWTN* 2, no. 1 (Jan 1898): 5. BWTASCU Collection.

4 Robertson, *BWTASCU*, 36. BWTASCU Collection.

5 'An Interview with Mrs Woyka', *SWTN* 2, no. 2 (Nov 1898): 165. BWTASCU Collection.

6 'An Interview with Mrs Woyka', 165–6. BWTASCU Collection.

7 'Sketch of Mrs Grant A. Millar's Life', *SWTN* 2, no. 4 (Apr 1898): 52. BWTASCU Collection.

8 'Sketch of Mrs Grant A. Millar's Life', 52–3. BWTASCU Collection.

9 'Sketch of Mrs Grant A. Millar's Life', 53. BWTASCU Collection.

10 White, 'Recollections of My Temperance Work', 21. BWTASCU Collection.

11 White, 'Recollections of My Temperance Work', 21. BWTASCU Collection.

12 For a detailed analysis of child emigration from Scotland see Lynn Abrams, *The Orphan Country: Children of Scotland's Broken Homes from 1845 to the Present Day* (Edinburgh: John Donald Press Ltd., 1998).

13 'Mrs Margaret Blaikie', 5. BWTASCU Collection.

14 GPU, *Minutes* (1882). GCA TD 955/1/1.

15 White, 'Recollections of My Temperance Work', 2. BWTASCU Collection.
16 The importance of personalism in philanthropy has been discussed elsewhere, see, for example, Olive Checkland, *Philanthropy in Scotland: Social Welfare and the Voluntary Principle* (Edinburgh: John Donald Publishers, 1980); Prochaska, *Women and Philanthropy*; Bonnie G. Smith, *Ladies of the Leisure Class: The Bourgeoisies of Northern France in the Nineteenth Century* (Princeton: Princeton University Press, 1981); Martha Vicinus, *Independent Women: Work and Community for Single Women, 1850–1920* (London: Virago Press, 1985); and Howard M. Wach, 'Unitarian Philanthropy and Cultural Hegemony in Comparative Perspective: Manchester and Boston, 1827–1848', *Journal of Social History*, 26, no. 3 (1993): 539–57.
17 'An Interview with Mrs Woyka', 165. BWTASCU Collection.
18 'Sketch of Mrs Grant Millar's Life and Work', 52. BWTASCU Collection.
19 Mary White, 'British Women's Temperance Work', *SWTN* 1, no. 3 (Feb 1897): 41. BWTASCU Collection.
20 GPU, *Minutes* (1883). GCA TD 955/1/1.
21 BWTASCU, *Annual Report for 1888*, 31. BWTASCU Collection.
22 Varty, '"A career in Christian charity"', 248.
23 BWTASCU, *Annual Report for 1895*, 23. BWTASCU Collection.
24 Mrs Hume, 'The Duties of a Secretary', *SWTN* 9, no. 2 (Feb 1905): 18. BWTASCU Collection.
25 Banks, *Faces of Feminism*, 15.
26 Peter Bailey, *Leisure and Class in Victorian England: Rational Recreation and the Contest for Control* (London: Methuen & Co. Ltd., 1978; Reprint, London: Methuen & Co. Ltd., 1987), 73.
27 May Morison Geddes, 'The Duties of a Secretary and the Successful Working of a BWTA Branch', *SWTN* 9, no. 1 (Jan 1905): 3. BWTASCU Collection.
28 Geddes, 'The Duties of a Secretary', 3. BWTASCU Collection.
29 'Women Who Should Compose Committees', *SWTN* 13, no. 12 (Dec 1909): 178. BWTASCU Collection.
30 'An Interview with Mrs Woyka', 165. BWTASCU Collection.
31 GPU, *Minutes* (1890). GCA TD 955/1/1.
32 Shiman, *Crusade Against Drink*, 186.
33 Hume, 'The Duties of a Secretary', 18. BWTASCU Collection.
34 Geddes, 'The Duties of a Secretary', 3. BWTASCU Collection.
35 Stewart, *The Crusader*, 315–16. WL 178.10942 STE.
36 Harold Perkin, *The Rise of Professional Society: England Since 1880* (London: Routledge, 1989), 2.
37 See Jeanne Boydston, *Home and Work: Housework, Wages, and the Ideology of Labor in the Early Republic* (Oxford: Oxford University Press, 1990); Deborah Simonton, *European Women's Work: 1700 to the Present* (London: Routledge, 1998); and Rhonda Anne Semple, *Missionary Women: Gender, Professionalism and the Victorian Idea of Christian Mission* (Woodbridge, Suffolk: The Boydell Press, 2003), 190.
38 BWTASCU, *Annual Report for 1900*, 28. BWTASCU Collection.
39 BWTASCU, *Annual Report for 1900*, 29. BWTASCU Collection.
40 BWTASCU, *Annual Report for 1900*, 30. BWTASCU Collection.
41 'Glasgow BWTA Tent', *SWTN* 9, no. 8 (Aug 1905): 115. BWTASCU Collection.
42 See Boydston, *Home and Work*; and Simonton, *European Women's Work*, 92.

43 'Glasgow BWTA Tent', 115. BWTASCU Collection.

44 Mark James, 'Temperance', *The Oxford Companion to Scottish History*, ed. Michael Lynch (Oxford: Oxford University Press, 2001), 596.

45 Gen. 31:49.

46 GPU, *Minutes* (1886). GCA TD 955/1/1.

47 Rendall, *The Origins of Feminism*, 255.

48 See William M. Walker, 'The Scottish Prohibition Party and the Millennium', *International Review of Social History* 18 (1973): 353–79.

49 Walker, 'The Scottish Prohibition Party', 364.

50 Gordon and Nair, *Public Lives*, 120.

51 Margaret Black, 'The Drink Problem', *SWTN* 1, no. 7 (Jun 1897): 110. BWTASCU Collection.

52 'The Late Mrs John Millar – Portrait and Obituary Notice', *SWTN* 14, no. 4 (Apr 1910): 49. BWTASCU Collection.

53 Stewart, *The Crusader*, 229. WL 178.10942 STE.

54 GPU, *Minutes* (1888). GCA TD 955/1/1.

55 BWTASCU, *Annual Report for 1890*, 11. BWTASCU Collection.

56 For more on the debate over total abstinence versus moderation, see Aspinwall, *Portable Utopia*; Dingle, *The Campaign for Prohibition in Victorian England*; and Shiman, *Crusade Against Drink*.

57 'Woman's Duty Towards the Temperance Reform', *Scottish Temperance Review*, 12.

58 'Ladies Temperance Conference', *League* no. 14 (Apr 1882): 216.

59 The Brownsland Temperance Home for Women was moved to Blairadam, Fifeshire in 1903 and re-named the Navitie Home. To ease confusion the home will be referred to throughout as 'Brownsland Temperance Home'.

60 BWTASCU, *Annual Report of Brownsland Temperance Home for Women, 1888*, 17. BWTASCU Collection.

61 GPU, *Minutes* (1887). GCA TD 955/1/1.

62 BWTASCU, *Annual Report for 1891*, 17. BWTASCU Collection.

63 GPU, *Minutes* (1890). GCA TD 955/1/1.

64 GPU, *Minutes* (1887). GCA TD 955/1/1.

65 See Patrick M. McLaughlin, 'Inebriate Reformatories in Scotland: An Institutional History', *Drinking: Behaviour and Belief in Modern History*, eds Susanna Barrows and Robin Room (Oxford: University of California Press, 1991), 287–314.

66 McLaughlin, 'Inebriate Reformatories in Scotland', 293.

67 BWTASCU, *Annual Report of Brownsland Temperance Home for Women, 1892*, 20. BWTASCU Collection.

68 BWTASCU, *Annual Report of Brownsland Temperance Home for Women, 1889*, 19. BWTASCU Collection.

69 BWTASCU, *Annual Report of Brownsland Temperance Home for Women, 1889*, 21. BWTASCU Collection.

70 GPU, *Minutes* (1888). GCA TD 955/1/1.

71 See Linda Mahood, *The Magdalenes: Prostitution in the Nineteenth Century* (London: Routledge, 1990).

72 GPU, *Minutes* (1889). GCA TD 955/1/1.

73 GPU, *Minutes* (1889). GCA TD 955/1/1.

4

The women's movement and female temperance reform

Female temperance reform in Scotland is most strongly differentiated from sister movements in the rest of the United Kingdom by its role in the women's suffrage campaign. In contrast to women's temperance societies in England and Wales, the BWTASCU officially supported women's parliamentary enfranchisement, and the BWTASCU prosecuted its own constitutional-style campaign for women's right to vote.[1] The BWTASCU's distinctive position in British suffragism can be attributed to two main factors; temperance reform ideology and the timing of women's municipal enfranchisement in Scotland. Late nineteenth-century temperance reform ideology was informed by two main strands, moral suasion and legal suasion. Moral suasion sought the personal salvation of individual drunkards, whereas legal suasion, also known as prohibition, sought legislative means of stopping trade in alcohol. The BWTASCU's temperance reform activities encompassed both moral and legal suasion, but agitation for prohibition most politicised British Women. The politicising influence of prohibition was given greater impetus by the municipal enfranchisement of female ratepayers in Scotland in 1881. The ascendancy of prohibitionist ideology in the BWTASCU coincided with women's limited access to the local electorate, and the nexus of these two factors galvanised British Women's support for female political rights.

The BWTASCU's pro-suffrage majority ensured that campaigns for women's political rights – at the local and parliamentary levels – were included in the organisation's reform programme. Structurally, the BWTASCU's agitation for female political rights was guided by the principles of the 'do everything' policy, which advocated the use of departments to oversee the different aspects of work undertaken by women's temperance unions. Thus, municipal and suffrage departments were organised by local branches as well as at the national level by the Edinburgh Central Branch to agitate among female voters during local elections and to campaign for women's equal enfranchisement. While the BWTASCU was formally pro-suffrage, there is evidence that the suffrage issue was contentious for British Women, and 'Correspondence' columns in the *SWTN* demonstrate debate on women's suffrage. British Women's discourse on suffrage reveals both the complicated positioning of the BWTASCU in the British women's movement and the inter-national character of the BWTASCU. Contemporaries credited the New Zealand WCTU with leading the world's first successful women's suffrage campaign, which culminated in women's enfranchisement in 1893.[2] In Scotland, women's suffrage groups had demanded the vote since the late 1860s, and the rise of the BWTASCU during the mid-1870s and 1880s helped to broaden the appeal of the movement. In New Zealand, however, the Women's Franchise League developed after the New Zealand WCTU began agitating for women's suffrage in 1887. The prominence of the New Zealand WCTU in the suffrage campaign and the received knowledge that legislation for prohibition increased after women's enfranchisement greatly influenced the BWTASCU's decision to incorporate agitation for women's suffrage into its reform programme.

Temperance reform ideology in the BWTASCU

This research suggests that the BWTASCU's temperance ideology drew on moral and legal suasion, and integrated both approaches into its reforming activities. The passage of the 'Maine Law' in 1851 is often viewed as a water-shed moment in temperance reform, after which temperance societies organised around either moral suasion or prohibition.[3] In turn, histories of the temperance movement tend to characterise the early nineteenth-century movement as led by moral suasion, while the presenting the later nineteenth-century movement as more strongly prohibitionist.[4] This body of literature tends to marginalise moral suasionist aspects of temperance reform in the later period, and this discussion seeks to demonstrate the continued importance of moral means of reform for the BWTASCU's reforming ideology.[5]

Moral suasion conformed to evangelical notions regarding an individ-ual's capacity for personal redemption. Moral suasionists viewed the drinker as a morally responsible individual, whose conscious choosing of total abstinence was vital to a sustained rejection of alcohol.[6] In the words of John Stuart Mill: 'People could only progress morally if their freedom of choice remained unfettered, so drunkenness should only be punished when it was contrary to the public interest.'[7] For this reason, moral suasion focused on educating individuals with the aim of promoting a teetotal lifestyle.[8] Echoes of the evangelical conversion experience reverberate in moral suasion in which the drunkard's choice of total abstinence mirrored the redemptive path of personal salvation and self-help. Moral suasionists opposed prohibition using two main arguments: firstly, that legislative means of reform interfered with personal liberty; and secondly, that legislation alone was insufficient to end the 'evil of intemperance', and a fundamental shift was needed in (especially working-class) attitudes towards drink and drunkenness.

Reforming activities guided by moral suasion in the BWTASCU were directed by evangelistic departments. The Scottish-national Evangelistic Department was established in 1895 under the leadership of Mrs McKinnon née Miller, the daughter of a Rothesay harbourmaster and wife of John D. McKinnon, reverend of the Dumfries South Free Church.[9] Evangelistic work had two main purposes: firstly, to win souls for temperance by promoting the temperance pledge; and secondly, to counter antagonism to the temperance movement within the Christian community. McKinnon's Evangelistic Department aimed to accomplish these goals by organising Gospel Missions to be taken over by local BWTASCU branches.[10] McKinnon described these missions as a means:

> First to break down the prejudices which still exist in the minds of many Christian people in regard to the Temperance movement, and the methods employed by Temperance workers. Even at this advanced stage of the movement there are still those who say we put Temperance before the Gospel, and so make it supersede God's way of salvation. That is if we would get men and women converted we would have no need of Temperance Associations, forgetting the fact that drunkenness is a *physical* as well as *moral disease*.[11] (emphasis is original???)

The tensions between some sections of the evangelical Protestant community and the temperance movement have been discussed elsewhere, and as McKinnon's comments indicate, these tensions centred on the perception that temperance reformers tended to treat the symptoms of moral corruption rather than the cause by focusing on the temperance pledge rather than on a more wide-ranging religious conversion.[12] McKinnon further argued that Gospel Missions reached a different section of the population than conventional temperance meetings: 'We aim also at the reclamation of the drunkard by the direct power of the Gospel. Many people may be inclined to attend a Mission meeting that would not enter a Temperance meeting, and in this way the truth may be brought home to them, and it may be some who have been secretly drinking arrested by the word spoken.'[13] The theme of evangelical soul-winning was further applied to evangelistic work by Mrs Veronica Allan Gardiner, Superintendent of the Evangelistic Department from 1906: 'Perhaps the most encouraging feature in connection with this Department is the fact that in quite a number of Branches the work is carried on by those who are not only interested in the great cause of Temperance but who are also earnest and experienced soul-winners.'[14] A 1907 report by Gardiner claimed the pervasiveness of evangelistic work among local women's temperance unions, 'most of the Branches carry on their work on evangelistic lines.'[15] The use of departments to carry on evangelistic activities further testifies to the importance of the 'do everything' policy for broadening and systematising the BWTASCU's reforming activities.

The BWTASCU's broad reform programme, which was formally incorporated into the organisation's structure after 'do everything', facilitated the intermingling of evangelical desires to convert drinkers to total abstinence with a campaign for prohibition. This is evident from the 1893 annual report, the year in which 'do everything' was implemented, which lists departments motivated by both moral and legal suasion: 'The means to be employed may embrace any or all of the following:- (1) Individual Effort, (2) Organised Demonstrations, (3) Evangelistic Meetings, (4) Preventive Schemes, (5) Social Work, (6) Educational Plans, (7) Legislative Supervision – Licensing Boards and Town and County Councils, (8) Political Methods.'[16] Moral suasion was often discussed as a complement to prohibition activities. For instance, at the BWTASCU's 1890 Spring Conference in Glasgow – during which a variety of prohibition issues were considered such as, grocers' licences, alcohol selling at rail stations, the Sunday Closing (Ireland) Bill and the Local Veto (Scotland) Bill – delegates, 'proposed a day of humiliation and prayer on account of the liquor traffic.'[17] There followed a day of prayer on 9 June: 'On that day we amalgamated with the Noon-day Prayer-meeting and had a large gathering of Temperance friends of all denominations.'[18] In this way, the British Women sought to mobilise the prayers of many Christians in support of legislation for prohibition. The mixed temperance reform ideology of the BWTASCU led to a mapping of religious language onto prohibition agitation: 'Prayer was asked for cases visited in prison and police office also that a licence might not be granted in Byres Road, Partick. Ladies were asked to be present tomorrow at the Justice's Court in Brunswick Street, so that if possible the licence might be refused.'[19] After the passage of the Temperance (Scotland) Act in 1913, Gardiner's report on the measure used a providential language: 'God has answered prayer in giving us as a nation, through the Temperance Act, the opportunity of rising shortly, and, with a strong hand, putting down this great evil.'[20] The Temperance (Scotland) Act instituted a form of local veto, which allowed local authorities to poll electors on whether to allow alcohol selling. In sum, it emerges from British Women's discussions of prohibition that an evangelical moral mission, which had underpinned the temperance movement from the early 1800s, having been adapted to new emphasises on prohibition, remained a significant force in late nineteenth-century female temperance reform.

The mixed reform ideology of the BWTASCU supports Joseph Gusfield's assertion that both moral suasion and prohibition were elements of the temperance movement – perhaps with different degrees of emphasis – throughout the nineteenth century.[21] Gusfield's analysis of the American temperance movement as a 'symbolic crusade' argues that because the temperance movement was largely aimed at maintaining and extending the social values of the white, Protestant middle classes, moral suasion and prohibition are best viewed as attempts to normalise one group's set of social values, rather than as two mutually exclusive reform ideologies.[22] Gusfield argues that 'assimilative' temperance reform, or moral suasion, is feasible as long as reform takes place within a shared society where the reformer's values are dominant.[23] In contrast, 'coercive' temperance reform, or prohibition, is marked by social conflict and a hostile approach to the drinker.[24] So, while moral suasion and prohibition have different views on the role of the state and the individual's ability for self-help, the two ideologies share a reliance on a dominant middle-class Protestant morality.

By interweaving moral suasion and prohibition, the BWTASCU reflected wider trends in the Scottish temperance movement. The STL, a key mixed-sex temperance organisation from the mid-nineteenth century, was deeply concerned to advocate the teetotal lifestyle, yet the STL's heterogeneous reform ideology accommodated support for prohibition. The STL argued that prohibition, without a fundamental shift in attitudes towards drink and drunkenness, could not generate a sustainably temperate society. The STL endeavoured to morally transform society with a massive media onslaught, and from its publishing base in Glasgow, the STL circulated masses of tracts and several periodicals such as, the *League*, a weekly discussion of local, national and global temperance reform and *The Adviser* a monthly journal for children. The intensity of the STL's propaganda offensive is indicated by its claim to have undertaken 2,300 lectures and to have sold an estimated 16,000 temperance 'volumes' and 430,000 tracts in 1898.[25] While seeking to convert individual drinkers the STL also pursued prohibition, and in the late nineteenth century the STL was part of successful campaigns for the Public Houses (Amendment) (Scotland) Act, the Publican's Certificate (Scotland) Act, the Passenger Vessels Licensing (Scotland) Act, and after the passage of the 1913 Temperance Act the STL vigorously canvassed on behalf of local veto. The capacity of both the BWTASCU and the STL to accommodate two potentially competing temperance ideologies suggests that British Women's temperance reform ideology was well within the mainstream of the Scottish movement.

While driven in many ways by evangelical belief, conservative gender ideologies and the politics of class, temperance reform and especially prohibition was a key and highly debated political issue of the day. In other words, participation in Scottish temperance reform was a significant site of middle-class women's experiences of public protest and campaign. While female temperance reformers' sense of Christian duty was intrinsic to their reforming activities, and can clearly be correlated to the continued relevance of moral suasion for their late nineteenth-century campaign, the British Women further embraced contemporary enthusiasm for prohibition. The relationship between electors' roles in supporting candidates keen to pass prohibition legislation and women's right to vote were not lost on the British Women, and the 1881 municipal enfranchisement of female ratepayers in Scotland gave increased momentum to female temperance reformers' demands for women's political rights.

Prohibition, local government and the politicisation of the British Women

The BWTASCU enthusiastically supported prohibition, and in 1888 the BWTASCU, 'unanimously resolve[d] to agitate for the legislative suppression of the manufacture and sale of intoxicating liquor as a beverage.'[26] A legislative ban on alcohol was deemed essential for British Women's efforts to morally purify society, and the Glasgow Prayer Union demonstrates this attitude in its 1907 annual report: 'We have reminded Parliament that we look to them for help in this great work of ridding our country of a traffic that is deteriorating and demoralising to our womanhood.'[27] The appeal of prohibition for British Women was enhanced by the municipal enfranchisement of women in Scotland in 1881; reciprocally, prohibition encouraged British Women's desire for a formal stake in representative politics. The ascendancy of prohibition in the international temperance movement coincided with the emergence of the WWCTU, and the role of prohibition in politicising female temperance reformers has been recognised for Anglophone communities outside the United Kingdom.[28] The evidence suggests that during the 1880s and 1890s the BWTASCU reflected international trends towards prohibition, and the 1888 constitution stated:

> The object of this Association is to form a union of all the Women's Temperance Societies in Scotland, in the belief that, by combined effort and hearty co-operation, much greater work may be done, by the blessing of God, in the extension of the Temperance cause, *the control of the liquor traffic*, and the moral and religious elevation of the people.[29]

Prohibition's emphasis on the state's role in regulating vice heightened the political expectations of British Women, and the idea that moral reforms required legislative action implied that feminine moral superiority required formal political expression. Thus, it seems that prohibition provided the impetus, and the 1881 municipal enfranchisement of women provided the opportunity for British Women's participation in electoral politics. Further, female temperance reformers' voting took on evermore importance after the enacting of local veto by the Temperance (Scotland) Act, 1913.

Prohibition was a vital political issue in Victorian and Edwardian Scotland, and was frequently equated with local veto. Local veto refers to the ability of local authorities to poll the electorate on the issue of licences for alcohol selling. In order for a no-licence resolution to pass and thus end all local alcohol selling, 55% of the vote must be in favour and 35% of the electorate must vote. Crucially, when local veto was passed for Scotland in 1913 electors included those qualified for town and parish council elections, which by this time included female ratepayers.[30] Local veto enjoyed widespread support among local electors and temperance societies. This is somewhat apparent from the turnout associated with a Glasgow plebiscite held in March 1887 in order to determine public opinion on local veto. Newspaper reports claimed that 76% of those polled in the plebiscite responded. The intensity of interest in local veto emerges from a comparison of the number of respondents in the local veto plebiscite versus other polls taken during the political calendar: 77% from seven districts during the 1886 parliamentary election; 48% for the Free Libraries Act; and 47% for the 1885 school board elections.[31] The BWTASCU's prohibition activities were organised by legislative departments, and the Edinburgh Central Branch and Glasgow Prayer Union established legislative departments in 1890 and 1892, respectively. The Edinburgh and Glasgow temperance unions had conducted legislative work from the 1880s, but this work was systematised after 'do everything', and the legislative, legal and vigilance departments monitored advances towards Scottish- and British-national prohibition. These departments were charged with persuading all British Women of the necessity of political activism by, '[bringing] before the various branches the advisableness of influencing all Members of Parliament regarding any Bill which may come before Parliament bearing on the liquor traffic.[32] The BWTASCU deployed traditional extra-parliamentary methods to campaign for prohibition, and legislative departments drafted memorials and petitions, which demanded an end to trade in alcohol. Using these methods, British Women in 1890 lobbied against grocers' licenses, confectioners' licences, the sale of alcohol in rail stations and compensation for publicans put out of business by local veto; simultaneously they petitioned in support of legislation for local veto and the Sunday Closing (Ireland) Bill.[33] Throughout the period studied here, the BWTASCU's prohibition activities emphasised local veto, and efforts to enforce prohibition at the local level were important for integrating British Women into the sphere of electoral politics.

The BWTASCU fulfilled a similar role for local temperance candidates as the SWFL fulfilled on behalf of Liberals, i.e. large amounts of unpaid canvassing work. For example, the Glasgow Prayer Union's canvassing for the 1887 plebiscite was linked to support for a local temperance politician. The Glasgow Prayer Union's participation is described as primarily 'moral', and entries in the minutes from January to March 1887 do not reveal the extent of British Women's practical support, yet it is reasonable to suspect that volunteers were drawn from the ranks of the Glasgow BWTASCU:

> 14th March, Prayer was asked for the plebiscite to be taken early next week, Mr Oatts having now secured 2,500 voluntary workers.

> 21st March, Much prayer was asked for all the 2,500 workers to be engaged tonight and tomorrow taking the Plebiscite on the drink question.

> 28th March, Mr Oatts came in and spoke for a few minutes, he thanked the Meeting for having upheld him by prayer while the work was being arranged for the Plebiscite. The results of this have been fully up to our expectations, and we thanked the Lord for His goodness in regard to this matter.[34]

The Glasgow Prayer Union's annual report for 1889 explicitly claimed British Women's practical support for temperance candidates; 'at the Municipal Elections several members of our Union have rendered assistance to Temperance candidates by meeting with and canvassing women electors'.[35] Whatever the extent of individual British Women's practical support for local veto and temperance candidates, evidence from the BWTASCU highlights the idea that prohibition involved increasing numbers of women in the public world of electoral politics. This is especially evident after women's municipal enfranchisement.

The Municipal Elections Act (1881) immediately invigorated the British Women's interest in local veto and female political rights. The 1882 minutes from the Glasgow Prayer Union record Mrs Robertson's enthusiasm for women's municipal voting; Robertson urged that British Women, 'should also take means to induce female rate-payers, who were to have the privilege of voting at municipal elections in November, to vote only for those who opposed the granting of licences'.[36] Evidence from the SWTN further indicates British Women's interest in women's status in local politics. From its beginning in 1896, the SWTN ran a series of articles entitled 'Guide to Women Voters – Scotland', which aimed to keep readers informed about women's access to the many local boards. The SWTN further outlined the qualifications for the household, lodger, occupancy and ownership franchises as well as when and where women could register for the various rolls. The BWTASCU further organised municipal departments to support local veto, canvass for local temperance politicians, encourage women's voting and plan demonstrations against licences. The Glasgow Prayer Union established its municipal department under Mrs Marion A. Reid in 1893, while the Edinburgh Central Branch formed its municipal department in 1899 under the supervision of Edinburgh parish councillor Miss Mary Carr Lees.

Reid sought to encourage more conservative British Women to accept the value and respectability of temperance women's political agitation by representing participation in formal politics as a Christian duty. Many of Reid's contemporaries associated electoral politics with masculine prerogatives in the public sphere, and reports of Reid's discussions of municipal work in the SWTN suggest an effort to counter these gendered assumptions by stressing the Christian merit of this work. For instance, the SWTN's report of Reid's address at a 1904 conference in Glasgow reminded British Women of the importance of electing local politicians committed to temperance: 'Women can do much in returning candidates to the Town Council who are loyal and true to the temperance cause. This work is most valuable when we remember that the Councillors we return may one day become licensing magistrates'.[37] The SWTN claims that Reid pressed her point with the suggestion that women's local voting constituted a Christian duty: 'The reason why we women give ourselves to the cause of temperance is that we have faith in God, and that we believe this greatest of social evils to be alterable. What we need as a people is to be impressed with a sense of our social duty, so that from us can emanate a hearty and pronounced public opinion'.[38] Reid further submitted a piece to the SWTN which urged readers to understand women's local voting as a powerful tool to be used in purifying the local community:

'Women no longer shrink from election work as suitable for men only, but are realising the responsibility of Christian citizenship, and feeling that a burden is upon them to secure the best possible local government in order to promote the wellbeing and dignity of the city or town with which they are connected.'[39] Reid's notion of 'Christian citizenship' encompassed women's participation in voting and electioneering: 'In supporting the candidature of a good man, we to some extent contribute to making our city or town healthy, happy, and holy.'[40] Reid's vigorous defence of women's role in local politics reflected the Glasgow Prayer Union's support for women's political inclusion.

There is some evidence that the Glasgow Prayer Union was more committed to municipal work than the Edinburgh Central Branch. At the very least, the Glasgow Prayer Union was more concerned with demonstrating its commitment to this area of temperance reform, and the Glasgow branch more frequently submitted reports on its municipal work to the BWTASCU's annual report. For example, the 1890 annual report from the Glasgow Prayer Union claimed: 'At the recent municipal elections we assisted the Temperance candidates by calling on lady electors and inducing them to vote.'[41] Similarly, in 1893 the Glasgow Prayer Union reported: 'Members of our Committee have addressed a number of meetings of Lady householders, while the municipal elections have been going on with a view to securing the return of Temperance candidates.'[42] M. Neill, head of the Glasgow Prayer Union's Municipal Department in 1905, reported that: 'Greenock ... had only one contest, and their arrangements were so complete that every woman elector in the ward was canvassed, and a number of women recorded their vote, who hitherto had never been inside a polling booth.'[43] The 1903 report of the national municipal department in Edinburgh claimed: 'The returns from Municipal Associations are rather scanty this year, only Dumfries, Glasgow and Dunfermline having responded. But in those places, as well as at Greenock and other towns not reported, our members worked heartily, and in many cases to good purposes.'[44] This is not to suggest that the Edinburgh Central Branch neglected to canvass among female voters locally, and the head of the national Municipal Department, Mary Lees, was an outspoken advocate of women's participation in local government, and in 1898 she prepared a three-part series for the *SWTN* detailing her experiences as a parish council candidate.[45]

One of Lees' most visible contributions to the BWTASCU's municipal work was her detailed account of canvassing in the poorer areas of Edinburgh, which was published in the *SWTN*. It is unusual to find such an exhaustive articulation of a woman's experiences in late nineteenth-century local politics, and it is therefore worth quoting at length from her article:

> Many of the voters had to work during the night or to go out early in the morning. I generally started to work about five in the afternoon, a kind friend accompanying me carrying a small lantern, whilst I carried the roll of names. And now you can see us start. We light the lamp at the foot of a long stair, and are at once joined by a crowd of children with profuse offers of help. We make some enquiries as to the various names on the roll, and get ready answers, 'Aye, Smith he's on the top landing', 'McCallum, he's in the area', 'Where does Mrs Jones live?' we ask, 'Oh, she's a weedow, her man was kilt on the railway'. So we go through the list, then proceed to mount the stair. The crowd surges round us, big boys in front, older sisters dragging little brothers, girls carrying babies, driven against the wall, and with shouts of 'Vote for Conolly' (the labour candidate opposed to myself), up we go. Now the lantern comes into play, and with its aid we decipher our list and read the names on the bells or doors. Four or five little red knuckles knock at the door or have the joy of ringing the bell, and while we go in to do the canvassing the ratepayers of the future proceed in a scattered way to knock up the inmates of the floor above. Up and up we go, climbing perhaps a hundred steps, coming upon poverty and comfort, cleanliness and the opposite, miserable crowded dens, and rooms lofty and spacious, decorations that once had delighted the eyes of our old nobility and views of an illuminated Edinburgh that were worth climbing to see even if we did not secure a single vote, and never an uncivil word in the six weeks' work. Now the hour grows late and we descend, carried along by the small tumultuous throng, and soon girls, boys, babies, and would-be Parish Councillors, regain what an official promoted from the ranks called 'terra cotta'.[46]

Here Lees is clearly attempting to present local government work as befitting and safe for women. In her narrative she is not confronted by violent or threatening men, rather the emphasis is on her contact with local children. In so doing, Lees may have hoped to calm her readers' fears over canvassing in poorer neighbourhoods. Moreover, in the context of the late nineteenth century, surely Lees' readers would have recognised the implication that through the simple act of canvassing, much less as a councillor, a respectable middle-class woman might exert her 'civilising' and 'moralising' influence through physical proximity with poorer women, children and men. In the words of renowned educator Louisa Lumsden as reported in the *SLWM*, 'they as individuals could not help teaching and influencing one another. They had to realise what a tremendous responsibility rested upon them, for each unconsciously diffused a moral atmosphere around them'.[47]

It emerges from the *SWTN* that many temperance women in Scotland believed that local and national, Scottish and British governments had the power to enact temperance reform. A letter sent from 'B. B.' in Aberdeen to the 'Correspondence' column of the *SWTN* spelled out the case for local boards as avenues for temperance: 'The stir of School Board Elections is beginning to make itself heard all over the land. These triennial periods are golden opportunities not only for Temperance reformers, so called, but for all who have any interest whatever in the sobriety and conse-quent well-being of the coming generation.'[48] In addition to asserting the importance of local boards for prohibition, 'B. B.' uses the language of citizenship to encourage women's pursuit of positions on school boards: 'We do wish that women everywhere would rouse themselves and take up their responsibilities as citizens, whether the call comes to them to serve in the more prominent capacity, or to work for the return of true men and women, or simply to record their votes on the side of purity and righteousness.'[49] Temperance women did successfully enter political life, and, for example, Glasgow School Board members Mrs Margaret Black (1891–1903) and Mrs Mary Mason (1911–14) were also prominent members of the BWTASCU.[50]

The timing of the municipal enfranchisement of women in Scotland, and the rise of a strongly prohibitionist women's temperance movement created a unique climate for the politicisation of British Women. Murdock has suggested that prohibition's ability to force women to confront the limits of their citizenship made it the greatest single issue motivating American women's demands for formal political rights; 'alcohol, more than slavery or suffrage or any other single cause, effected American women's politicization.'[51] Similarly, in Scotland, the pursuit of local veto integrated British Women into the democratic processes of canvassing, voting and in some cases candidature, while simultaneously gathering women together under the auspices of the BWTASCU to discuss local, Scottish- and British-national political issues, giving rise to a political dialogue between female temperance reformers, prohibitionist politicians and their opponents. Political confidence gained through these prohibi-tion activities had far-reaching implications for the political expectations of British Women, and helped to ensure the BWTASCU's role in the campaign for women's parliamentary enfranchisement.

Women's suffrage in the BWTASCU

In 1898, the Glasgow Prayer Union claimed: 'The association has also done much by writing to members of Parliament on the burning questions of the day. They wanted female suffrage – even were it only to help on the temperance cause – they wished for better lives for their children and protection for their homes.'[52] The BWTASCU was unique among women's temperance organisations in the United Kingdom for using its branches to campaign for women's suffrage. Scotland's distinctiveness was influenced by the sum of many factors: female temperance reformers' sense of Christian mission to uplift the nation morally; the contemporaneous expansion of the WWCTU and the municipal enfranchisement of women in Scotland in 1881; and understandings in Scotland (and Britain more widely) of women's role in passing legislation for social reform in New Zealand after women's enfranchisement in 1893. The idea that political participation was a Christian duty was applied to both local and parliamentary voting, and an 1884 report of Anna Lindsay's speech, 'Christian Women as Citizens', claims:

> Christian women of late years had been showing their responsibility, and she wished to impress upon them the fact that in the votes they already possessed they had an engine of which they did not yet know the full power, and which they had hardly yet begun to use … In one of the wards a publican's candidate – who was a publican himself – was started and when that came to the knowledge of their local Women's Suffrage Association they felt that it was a case in which every effort should be put forth to bring women voters to the poll … The temperance reformers were of opinion … that some means must be found to regulate the drink traffic. Women felt this as much as men, but that question could only be decided by Parliament, and in Imperial politics no woman was allowed to have a voice. She trusted, however, that the time would soon come when they would have the Parliamentary as well as the municipal franchise.[53]

Lindsay's remarks regarding Parliament's supposed role in regulating the 'drink traffic' highlights the importance of prohibition for the politicisation of female temperance reformers, while her reference to 'Christian women' surely alludes to the emergence of an organised and increasingly politicised international women's temperance movement. The account of her speech further asserts the galvanising effect of prohibition and women's municipal enfranchisement, which here is linked to co-operation during local elections between the BWTASCU and the 'local Women's Suffrage Association', in this case the GNSWS. Indeed, the BWTASCU's own suffrage campaign may well have broadened women's support for female political rights. Women's public service as a Christian duty was a core belief among female temperance reformers, and more conservative British Women may have come to see the vote as an essential tool for the moral health of the national. For instance, Margaret Blaikie, President of the BWTASCU, claimed that, 'she had listened to Mrs Lindsay's paper with so much interest that she was almost converted to woman suffrage, which she had never gone in for'.[54] Blaikie's suggestion of a more accommodating view of women's suffrage indicates the potent combination of religious duty, prohibition and women's access to the local electorate in fostering female temperance reformers' demand for women's parliamentary enfranchisement. While it is unclear from the primary source material how many women may have come to support women's suffrage through involvement in temperance reform, it is clear that as an organisation the BWTASCU increasingly supported women's parliamentary enfranchisement and used its resources to actively pursue women's equal enfranchisement.

The BWTASCU's participation in the women's suffrage campaign should be considered in an international context. The American and New Zealand WCTUs acted as role models for the BWTASCU, and their example encouraged the Scottish organisation to mobilise its resources on behalf of British women's political emancipation. The influence of the American WCTU on the BWTASCU is evident from the formation of a national Suffrage Department in 1906. Local temperance unions had campaigned for women's suffrage from the 1890s, and the Glasgow Prayer Union had co-ordinated its efforts through a suffrage department from 1898.[55] The use of suffrage departments at national and local levels indicates that the BWTASCU accepted the American WCTU's 'do everything' policy and the associated idea that the work of women's temperance unions should be diversified through departmentalisation. An adherence to a prohibitionist temperance reform ideology underlay 'do everything', departmentalisation and the BWTASCU's suffrage activities, yet prohibition and women's suffrage incited controversy within the BWTASCU, and while suffrage departments operated at local and Scottish-national levels, there was no consensus on the role of women's temperance unions in the campaign for women's suffrage. Support for active participation in the suffrage campaign was concentrated in the Glasgow, Edinburgh and Stirling branches, while opposition to incorporating suffragism into women's temperance unions was based in the St Andrews BWTASCU.

The President of the St Andrews BWTASCU, Lady Griselda Cheape, led the challenge to the BWTASCU's intention to campaign for women's suffrage. Cheape was a zealous and respected temperance reformer as well as a prominent anti-suffragist: she was President of the St Andrews Scottish National Anti-Suffrage League (1909–12) and formed the St Andrews 'Beehive' anti-suffrage society in 1913. During the BWTASCU's

1913 annual meeting in Dundee, the St Andrews branch moved a resolution to discontinue the national Suffrage Department. The St Andrews British Women argued that local branches should decide their own stance on women's suffrage, and not be forced to affiliate with a pro-suffrage policy at the Scottish-national level. Pro-suffrage delegates from Glasgow opposed the St Andrews resolution, and the anti-suffragists were defeated: 'After a lively discussion, in which several members took part, the amendment and then the resolution were voted on, with the result that the former was carried by a large majority.'[56] Controversy over women's suffrage further made its way into the *SWTN*.

In 1913, Griselda Cheape submitted inflammatory anti-suffrage letters to the *SWTN*. In April, Cheape asked her readers, 'Is Woman's Suffrage Progress?': 'If you give a woman a vote, do you give her more influence? I contend that you do not.'[57] Cheape's comments reveal her belief in moral versus legal suasion: 'I contend the law can only punish crime, and in that way punish vice. You cannot make people good by Acts of Parliament.'[58] Cheape further argues that human law, such as prohibition, is fundamentally flawed, and therefore only moral means of temperance reform can fulfil the mission of British Women: 'Laws are not bad because they are made by men; but because they are made by humans. Women stand where they are good higher than men [*sic*], because they seek their laws from God's Word, and so prove that they, by His grace, are beacons.'[59] Here Cheape alludes to the idea of feminine 'disinterestedness', or the notion that women were above partisan feelings and that feminine moral superiority was predicated on a certain distance from the hoi polloi of public life. In this way Cheape draws on a more conservative and orthodox understanding of feminine virtue as in danger of corruption by the public-political sphere. While Cheape's comments are driven by a commitment to an orthodox interpretation of middle-class woman's domestic role, her analysis is further motivated by a complex understanding of gender and a fear of socialism. On the one hand, Cheape asserts that the home 'must not be neglected' by women's public obligations.[60] On the other hand, Cheape upholds women's right to higher education – 'We rejoice that the University doors are open' – and to service in social work and municipal government.[61] Indeed, she incorporates these civic and professional pursuits into women's mothering: 'And a true woman is a mother – not only her own child [*sic*] – but nurses and teachers are little ones' mothers too.'[62] Nonetheless, Cheape betrays a fear that female enfranchisement would benefit socialism: 'If woman's franchise is granted, it will be Revolution! … The Socialist will gain, and he alone.'[63] Thus, Cheape, the BWTASCU's most outspoken anti-suffragist, demonstrates that a variety of factors may have prevented female temperance reformers from backing the British Women's suffrage campaign: a belief in moral rather than legal means of reform; the idea that women had many existing opportunities for public service and further obligations might undermine their capacity for domestic work; and a fear that change in the parliamentary electorate might shift politics to the Left.

Debate in the *SWTN* suggests that women's political status in New Zealand was the single most important factor in persuading a majority of British Women that the campaign for women's suffrage was a cause appropriate to the work of women's temperance unions. Griselda Cheape was clearly aware of the force of this argument and took it as a theme for a June letter to the *SWTN*: 'We hear so much of how the country will be dry when women get the vote, and New Zealand and Australia are often quoted as to what the women have done for Temperance by legislation. Let us see what the facts are.'[64] Cheape goes on to posit that: 'Women got the vote in 1893–1894, so that the Temperance legislation was before they had a voice in the State.'[65] In other words, Cheape denies the influence of women's suffrage on prohibition in New Zealand, and claims that anti-vice legislation was in place prior to the extension of the franchise. The received wisdom in this period supposed that New Zealand women's enfranchisement resulted in a raft of legislation for social reform. Raewyn Dalziel has shown that understandings of New Zealand women's suffrage, from within and without, perpetuated the notion that the female vote resulted in legislation aimed at social reform.[66] Cheape ends her discussion by reiterating her belief in moral suasion versus prohibition:

> We must educate individually, as we are trying to do in the BWTA, by God's grace. It is not legislation from without but the love of God from within which will keep us temperate in all things.[67]

Cheape reasserts that temperance reform is not a matter for state intervention but rather an opportunity for the steady and concerted application of a feminine moralising influence: 'It is not legislation which will make people good; it can at most deter them from sin, but it is the loving individual, Christ-like man or woman thirsting for souls will bring redemption to our land.'[68]

Cheape's assertions on women's suffrage and prohibition in New Zealand provoked a fierce reaction from fellow readers, and the following issue of the *SWTN* carried two responses to Cheape's comments. A letter signed Jeanie F. Fraser countered Cheape's claims by insisting that New Zealand women's suffrage was indeed a force for prohibition: 'What your correspondent evidently does not know is that when women voted from the first time in 1893, New Zealand gained its first Prohibition electorate, and since 1893 the "No License" vote increased at each poll, twelve electorates now being under Prohibition.'[69] Fraser further quoted from an article written by Fanny Cole, President of the New Zealand WCTU, which insisted on the value of women's suffrage for prohibition: 'Its effect on Temperance Reform is undeniable, the "No-License" movement receives much of its impetus from the woman's vote.'[70] Fraser further attacked Cheape's contention that female temperance reformers had no place in parliamentary politics, and that moral suasion was the only viable approach to temperance reform:

> all women who lead in the Temperance movement are Suffragists. Frances Willard was a life-long Suffragist; Lady Henry Somerset, formerly the leader of the Women's Temperance party in England, is also Vice-President of the National Union of Suffrage Societies. This is also the reason why, at our last Council Meeting, the delegates agreed to petition Parliament to introduce, with the least possible delay, a Government measure for Women's Suffrage. Will Women's Suffrage Advance Temperance? Surely, every British Woman who has thought intelligently on the subject has only one answer to this question.[71]

A second letter signed J. D. Smalley, who claimed to have been resident in New Zealand for thirty years, further suggested Cheape's misrepresentation of the facts: 'Let me say that the Local Option Act, now in operation was not passed until 1893, so that there has only been 19 years in which the Act has been at work. In that time, 12 electorates have voted out the liquor traffic, and that by a three-fifths majority, and many others are just bordering on the required large majority.'[72] Smalley then ascribes success of prohibition to women's voting: 'This desirable result could never have been obtained but by the vote of women. The women's vote is largely in favour of Prohibition.'[73]

The legitimacy of prohibition, rather than women's voting per se, was certainly at play in the BWTASCU's suffrage debate. On the one hand, Cheape's arguments represent a celebration of female temperance reformers' evangelical mission to 'convert' drinkers to total abstinence. On the other hand, Fraser and Smalley represent the prohibitionist point of view, which accepted the state's role in coercing drinkers into sobriety. Clearly, then, an individual's temperance reform ideology had important implications for her stance on the suffrage question. This is not to suggest that pro-suffrage British Women rejected female temperance reformers' evangelical mission to 'convert' drinkers to total abstinence, and Smalley articulated the combined temperance reform ideology prevalent in the BWTASCU: 'It is both legislation from without, as well as the grace of God from within, that is to effect the great change in our drinking customs.'[74] The suffrage debate in the *SWTN* further indicates the role of gender ideology in shaping women's approaches to public life. Where Cheape associates the feminine public sphere with women's roles in the local community – as Christian-minded benevolent workers, local electors and representatives, mothers and professionals – Fraser, Smalley and other pro-suffrage women saw this sphere as extending into the region of parliamentary politics. Finally, the reliance of Cheape, Fraser and Smalley on their understandings of events in New Zealand, along with Fraser's reference to American and English temperance women's interest in suffrage, further demonstrates the Anglophone perspective of the BWTASCU.

New Zealand's importance for British Women in Scotland was cultivated by immigration networks. New Zealand was a particularly attractive destination for nineteenth-century Scots, an idea which Marjory Harper suggests was encouraged by the, 'promise of land and the reassurance of an acceptable Scottish-based society which retained valued religious and educational institutions'.[75] One Scotswomen immigrant is particularly important for this discussion: Mrs Isabel Napier, Superintendent of the BWTASCU's national Suffrage Department. Opportunities for mobility presented by Empire resulted in a cosmopolitan society at home, and returning emigrants, such as Isabel Napier, brought fresh perspectives to Scotland from their experiences abroad. Napier was born in Scotland, but spent much of her life in Australia and New Zealand. She married and had a child in New Zealand, but when her family duties expired with the death of her husband and son, 'she threw herself heart and soul into the battle for Women's Suffrage and the advance of Temperance'.[76] Napier's remembrances of her path to temperance reform reflected female temperance reformers' tendency to attribute their interest in temperance to first-hand experience of the hardships faced by the urban poor. Napier's professed rationale for joining the temperance movement further linked women's suffrage to prohibition, and Napier recalled in her interview with the *SWTN*:

> It was my first visit to Scotland and the state of the slums in Edinburgh that awakened me to the necessity for Women's Suffrage, and that first made me start to work in earnest for the same. When Suffrage (Women's) became law in New Zealand all their influence was thrown on the side of Temperance Reform, and so you have the advanced laws that now obtain.[77]

Here Napier juxtaposes two major themes of nineteenth- and early twentieth-century female temperance reform: the perceived causal link between alcohol and urban poverty and the notion – supposedly borne out by events in New Zealand – that women's parliamentary enfranchisement would result in legislation for prohibition. In 1898, Napier returned to Edinburgh, and Margaret Blaikie proposed her as a member of the BWTASCU executive leadership. A year later, she acted as Financial Secretary and helped to organise the 1900 WWCTU Conference held in Edinburgh. In 1906, in response to widespread support for women's parliamentary enfranchisement within the BWTASCU, Napier accepted the office of Superintendent of the newly created national Suffrage Department, thus undertaking, 'lecturing and speaking on this subject as connected with Temperance'.[78] It is perhaps unsurprising that the first leader of the national Suffrage Department had personal knowledge of the close ties between temperance reform and women's suffrage in New Zealand.

While an international perspective is important for understanding the BWTASCU's support for women's suffrage, the BWTASCU suffrage campaign should also be understood in a British context. The BWTASCU's adoption of 'do everything' and consequent formal support for women's parliamentary enfranchisement distinguishes Scotland from female temperance reform in England, Wales and Ireland. In Scotland, local branches such as the Glasgow Prayer Union had organised suffrage departments from the 1890s, with the formation of a national Suffrage Department in 1906. Barrow's work on the leadership of the BWTA in England shows that the suffrage issue drove the English BWTA's rejection of 'do everything' and its refusal to agitate for women's suffrage.[79] Controversy over the suffrage issue split the BWTA in England, and resulted in the formation of the breakaway British Temperance League in 1893. The British Temperance League restricted itself to traditional areas of women's public work such as house-to-house visiting, and shunned the integration of female political rights into temperance reforming activities. The lack of work on the British women's temperance movement makes comparative work on the BWTA in England and Scotland difficult, yet it seems clear that the BWTASCU took a distinctly more radical approach to female temperance reform than its English counterpart. Logan supports this view and suggests that the conservatism that marked the BWTA in England was largely absent from the BWTASCU.[80] Certainly, no BWTASCU branches joined the British Temperance League in the 1890s, preferring instead to prosecute their work in line with 'do everything'. For Wales, where female temperance reform was organised outside of the WCTU, Lloyd-Morgan argues that while individual female temperance reformers supported women's parliamentary enfranchisement, the major Welshwomen's temperance organisations did not officially join the suffrage campaign. Cliona Murphy has suggested that Irish women's suffrage organisations such as the Irish Women's Franchise League garnered clerical support due to their interest in prohibition, and that a similar coupling of temperance and suffrage is evident for Ireland as for other parts of the Anglophone world.[81] While Irish suffrage may have enjoyed clerical sympathy over its support for prohibition, Elizabeth Malcolm has argued that Irish women did not 'play an active independent role in the temperance movement, as was to be the case in the United States'.[82] The current state of research indicates that the BWTASCU was the largest and most internationally significant British women's temperance organisation to campaign formally for women's parliamentary enfranchisement.[83] More regional studies on, for example, the provincial branches of the English BWTA, may yet reveal women's temperance union's work for women's suffrage at the grass roots.

The BWTASCU's willingness to support the suffrage campaign gives further weight to the importance of women's temperance associations as sites of outside suffrage in analyses of British constitutional suffragism. Indeed, Priscilla McLaren supported the BWTASCU's adoption of 'do everything', and while recognising the suffrage controversy within the English BWTA McLaren pressed the importance of the female vote for the temperance movement:

> Each contingent of the army of women is knocking separately at the door of the House of Commons, asking that the good they are seeking may be granted. Only a vote can gain an entrance to them, and they have no vote. I would affectionately ask all those women who refrain from stretching forth their hand to ask for this vote, how far they are retarding the good each and all have so long laboriously worked to attain?[84]

McLaren's comments reveal that in Scotland the impulse towards 'do everything' was further reinforced by support from the main body of constitutional suffrage societies.

Conclusion

Prohibitionist temperance reform ideology and women's municipal enfranchisement in the early 1880s worked to incorporate acts of democratic citizenship into the feminine public sphere. Temperance reform, and more specifically prohibition, created space for British Women in local electoral democracy. Moreover, the BWTASCU sought to persuade women, who might otherwise have preferred informal expressions of women's social and political influence, of the legitimacy of women's participation in electoral politics. Female temperance reformers' involvement in prohibition presented a greater challenge to gender roles than moral suasion. While moral suasion could be related in a fairly straightforward way to the idea of women's 'complementary nature', prohibition's stress on a legislative means of temperance reform highlighted the limits of women's public role. If women's moralising influence was insufficient to end the 'evil of intemperance', then, reasoned many British Women, middle-class women's complementary moral role needed a formal recognition in order to ensure the passage of prohibition.

The paucity of work on both female temperance reform and the women's movement in Scotland makes it difficult to evaluate the relative importance of prohibition for the politicisation of middle-class women in Scotland. While Barrow's work offers a starting point for a discussion on divergent attitudes towards suffrage between English and Scottish women's temperance reform, more work is needed on the grass roots in England and Scotland, and crucially on women in Irish temperance reform, before any considered conclusions may be drawn. The existing literature, albeit limited, does suggest that the temperance movement was more important for constitutional suffragism in Scotland than for other areas of Britain. At the very least, the apparently unique importance of women's temperance reform in the Scottish women's suffrage campaign highlights the necessity of regional perspectives to a balanced and sophisticated body of British historiography. Nevertheless, cross-membership between the BWTASCU, the SWLF and women's suffrage organisations identified in Chapter 1, indicate – at least – that Scotland's public-minded and politically active women maintained, in large part, a consensus on the importance of the temperance movement and prohibition. This consensus was driven in part by the BWTASCU's understanding of international women's temperance reform.

The BWTASCU believed itself to be a partner in an international temperance movement. This is clear, in part, from its decision to incorporate suffrage into its reforming activities. By implementing the American WCTU's 'do everything' policy, and diversifying the BWTASCU through a series of departments, the BWTASCU demonstrated a willingness to follow an international policy of female temperance reform. While 'do everything', and especially consequent action for women's suffrage, was controversial within the BWTASCU, justifications for an intermingling of temperance and suffragism often relied on British Women's understandings of the suffrage activities of female temperance reformers in New Zealand. This understanding was cultivated in part by the immigration networks which were particularly strong between Scotland and New Zealand. Thus, an Anglophone perspective can help to explain Scotland's unique position in the United Kingdom. Finally, an examination of the BWTASCU's participation in the suffrage campaign demonstrates that constitutional suffragism was composed of a more diverse range of organisations than has been acknowledged.

Notes

1 Work by Barrow and Lloyd-Morgan suggests that while individual female temperance reformers in England and Wales supported women's suffrage, women's temperance societies in these countries did not officially join the campaign for women's right to vote. See Barrow, 'Teetotal Feminists'; and Lloyd-Morgan, 'From Temperance to Suffrage?'.

2 See Patricia Grimshaw, *Women's Suffrage in New Zealand* (Auckland: Auckland University Press, 1987); and Claire Wood, 'Campaigning Women and Bad, Bad Men: Otago's Campaign for Women's Suffrage', *Mrs Hocken Requests ... Women's Contributions to the Hocken Collection*, ed. Rosemary Entwisle (Otago: Otago University Press, 1993), 11–18.

3 In 1851, the 'Maine Law', the first successful piece of prohibition legislation, was enacted to criminalise alcohol in the American state of Maine. For a comprehensive discussion of the influence of the 'Maine Law' on demands for prohibition in the United Kingdom see Dingle, *The Campaign for Prohibition*.

4 This is evident from work on the British and American temperance movements. See, for example, Jack S. Blocker Jr., *Retreat from Reform: The Prohibition Movement in the United States 1890–1913* (London: Greenwood Press, 1976); Dingle, *The Campaign for Prohibition*; Harrison, *Drink and the Victorians*; Kneale, 'The Place of Drink'; Norma Davis Logan, 'Drink and Society: Scotland 1870–1914', unpublished Ph.D. thesis Faculty of Arts, University of Glasgow, 1983; Shiman, *Crusade Against Drink*; and Andrew Sinclair, *Prohibition: The Era of Excess* (London: Faber and Faber, 1962).

5 A notable exception is Logan's 'Drink and Society', which includes a multi-faceted discussion of moral suasion.

6 See Blocker, *American Temperance Movements: Cycles of Reform* (Boston: Twayne Publishers, 1989) and *'Give to the winds thy fears'*; and Logan, 'Drink and Society'.

7 Citied in Dingle, *The Campaign for Prohibition*, 21.

8 By the 1870 to 1914 period, total abstinence from all alcoholic drinks was generally accepted as the way forward among temperance reformers. Earlier in the century, the temperance pledge often demanded abstinence only from 'spirituous liquors'. This moderationist pledge reflected an elite temperance movement that wished to disallow the use of the cheap spirits associated with working-class leisure, while allowing use of fine wines in more affluent circles. For this reason, teetotalism, or total abstinence from all alcohol, can be seen as a more radical challenge to the social hierarchy. For more on the class dimensions of moderation versus total abstinence see Blocker, *American Temperance Movements*, and Ian Tyrrell, *Sobering Up: From Temperance to Prohibition in Antebellum in America, 1800–1860* (London: Greenwood Press, 1979).

9 'Obituary – Mrs McKinnon', *SWTN* 10, no. 7 (Jul 1906): 98. BWTASCU Collection.

10 BWTASCU, *Annual Report for 1895*, 23. BWTASCU Collection.

11 BWTASCU, *Annual Report for 1895*, 23. BWTASCU Collection.

12 Most recently, Simon Morgan has suggested that women were actively recruited into the mid-century temperance movement in an effort to counter claims that the temperance movement was erecting a 'false idol' out of teetotalism and the pledge. See *A Victorian Woman's Place*, 97.

13 BWTASCU, *Annual Report for 1895*, 24. BWTASCU Collection.

14 BWTASCU, *Annual Report for 1910*, 43. BWTASCU Collection.

15 BWTASCU, *Annual Report for 1907*, 40. BWTASCU Collection.

16 BWTASCU, *Annual Report for 1893*, 8. BWTASCU Collection.

17 BWTASCU, *Annual Report for 1890*, 12. BWTASCU Collection.

18 BWTASCU, *Annual Report for 1890*, 13. BWTASCU Collection.

19 GPU, *Minutes* (1887). GCA TD 955/1/1.

20 BWTASCU, *Annual Report for 1913*, 49. BWTASCU Collection.

21 There is a tendency in studies of temperance to suggest a dichotomy between moral suasion and prohibition, for example see Shiman, *Crusade Against Drink*.

22 See Joseph Gusfield, *Symbolic Crusade: Status Politics and the American Temperance Movement* (London: University of Illinois Press, 1970).

23 Gusfield, *Symbolic Crusade*, 69.

24 Gusfield, *Symbolic Crusade*, 70.

25 William Johnston, 'The Scottish Temperance League', *STA* (1899): 60.

26 BWTASCU, *Annual Report for 1888*, 14. BWTASCU Collection.

27 BWTASCU, *Annual Report for 1907*, 60. BWTASCU Collection.

28 For the US, see Bordin, *Woman and Temperance*; Epstein, *The Politics of Domesticity*; Janet Zollinger Giele, *Two Paths to Women's Equality: Temperance, Suffrage, and the Origins of Modern Feminism* (London: Twayne Publishers, 1995); and Catherine Gilbert Murdock, *Domesticating Drink: Women, Men, and Alcohol in America 1870–1940* (London: Johns Hopkins University Press, 1998). For Australia and New Zealand see, Grimshaw, *Women's Suffrage in New Zealand*; and Audrey Oldfield, *Woman Suffrage in Australia: A Gift or a Struggle?* (Cambridge: Cambridge University Press, 1992).

29 BWTASCU, *Annual Report for 1888*, 5. BWTASCU Collection. Emphasis is author's own.

30 See Public General Statutes Affecting Scotland, *Temperance (Scotland) Act, 1913*, 3 & 4 George, c. 33.

31 'Plebiscite of Glasgow and Suburbs, 21 March 1887, Analysis of Voting Papers', in *Book of Compiled Newsclippings, Glasgow*. GCA TD 912.

32 BWTASCU, *Annual Report for 1891*, 18. BWTASCU Collection.

33 BWTASCU, *Annual Report for 1890*, 33. BWTASCU Collection.

34 GPU, *Minutes* (1887). GCA TD 955/1/1.

35 BWTASCU, *Annual Report for 1889*, 35. BWTASCU Collection.

36 GPU, *Minutes* (1882). GCA TD 955/1/1.

37 'Municipal Work', *SWTN* 8, no. 5 (May 1904): 66. BWTASCU Collection.

38 'Municipal Work', *SWTN* 8, no. 5 (May 1904): 66. BWTASCU Collection.

39 Marion Reid, 'Municipal Superintendent', *SWTN* 8, no. 10 (Oct 1904): 153. BWTASCU Collection.

40 Reid, 'Municipal Superintendent', 153. BWTASCU Collection.

41 BWTASCU, *Annual Report for 1890*, 34. BWTASCU Collection.
42 BWTASCU, *Annual Report for 1893*, 37. BWTASCU Collection.
43 GDU, *BWTA, Scottish Christian Branch, Third Annual Report, Glasgow District Union* (Glasgow, 1905), 17. GCA TD 955/1/1.
44 BWTASCU, *Annual Report for 1903*, 31. BWTASCU Collection.
45 See Mary Carr Lees, 'Parish Council Work', *SWTN* 2, no. 1 (Jan 1898): 9; 'Parish Council Work', *SWTN* 2, no. 2 (Feb 1898): 26–7; and 'Parish Council Work', *SWTN* 2, no. 3 (Mar 1898): 37. BWTASCU Collection.
46 Lees, 'Parish Council Work', 9. BWTASCU Collection.
47 'The Obligation and Benefit of Work', *SLWM* (Feb 1909): 42. BL P.P.3611.tc.
48 'B. B.', Letter, *SWTN* 7, no. 4 (Apr 1903): 54. BWTASCU Collection.
49 'B. B.', Letter, 55. BWTASCU Collection.
50 Details of the terms and roles of Black and Mason on the Glasgow School Board can be found in: Minutes of the Monthly Public Meetings of the Glasgow School Board. *Minutes* (1884–1913). GCA D-ED 1.1.1.3–1.1.1.16.
51 Murdock, *Domesticating Drink*, 9.
52 GPU, *Minutes* (1898). GCA TD 955/1/1.
53 STL, 'Christian Women's Union', *League* no. 151 (Jan 1884): 747.
54 STL, 'Christian Women's Union', 747.
55 GPU, *Minutes* (1898). GCA TD 955/1/1.
56 BWTASCU, *Thirty-Sixth Annual Report for the Year 1912-13* (Edinburgh, 1913), 41. BWTASCU Collection.
57 Griselda Cheape, 'Is Woman's Suffrage Progress?', *SWTN* 17, no. 4 (Apr 1913): 75. BWTASCU Collection.
58 Cheape, 'Is Woman's Suffrage Progress?', 75. BWTASCU Collection.
59 Cheape, 'Is Woman's Suffrage Progress?', 75. BWTASCU Collection.
60 Cheape, 'Is Woman's Suffrage Progress?', 75. BWTASCU Collection.
61 Cheape, 'Is Woman's Suffrage Progress?', 75. BWTASCU Collection.
62 Cheape, 'Is Woman's Suffrage Progress?', 75. BWTASCU Collection.
63 Cheape, 'Is Woman's Suffrage Progress?', 75. BWTASCU Collection.
64 Griselda Cheape, 'Will Women's Suffrage Advance Temperance?', *SWTN* 17, no. 6 (Jun 1913): 84. BWTASCU Collection.
65 Cheape, 'Will Women's Suffrage Advance Temperance?', 84. BWTASCU Collection.
66 Raewyn Dalziel, 'Presenting the Enfranchisement of New Zealand Women Abroad', *Suffrage and Beyond*, eds Nolan and Daley, 56.
67 Cheape, 'Will Women's Suffrage Advance Temperance?', 84. BWTASCU Collection.
68 Cheape, 'Will Women's Suffrage Advance Temperance?', 84. BWTASCU Collection.
69 Jeanie F. Fraser, 'Will Women's Suffrage Advance Temperance?', *SWTN* 17, no. 7 (Jul 1913): 101. BWTASCU Collection.
70 Fraser, 'Will Women's Suffrage Advance Temperance?', 101. BWTASCU Collection.
71 Fraser, 'Will Women's Suffrage Advance Temperance?', 101. BWTASCU Collection.
72 J. D. Smalley, 'Women's Suffrage Has Advanced Temperance in New Zealand', *SWTN* 17, no. 7 (Jul 1913): 101. BWTASCU Collection.
73 Smalley, 'Women's Suffrage Has Advanced Temperance in New Zealand', 101. BWTASCU Collection.
74 Smalley, 'Women's Suffrage Has Advanced Temperance in New Zealand', 101. BWTASCU Collection.

75 Harper, *Emigration from North-East Scotland*, 303.

76 'Mrs Napier', 51. BWTASCU Collection.

77 'Mrs Napier', 51. BWTASCU Collection.

78 'Mrs Napier', 51. BWTASCU Collection.

79 See Barrow, 'Teetotal Feminists'.

80 Logan, 'Drink and Society', 475.

81 Cliona Murphy, 'The Religious Context of the Women's Suffrage Campaign in Ireland', *WHR* 6, no. 4 (1997): 561; and *The Women's Suffrage Movement and Irish Society in the Early Twentieth Century* (London: Harvester Wheatsheaf, 1989) 157–8.

82 Elizabeth Malcolm, *'Ireland Sober, Ireland Free': Drink and Temperance in Nineteenth-Century Ireland* (Syracuse: Syracuse University Press, 1986), 176.

83 See Barrow, 'Teetotal Feminists'; and Lloyd-Morgan, 'From Temperance to Suffrage?'.

84 Priscilla McLaren, 'A Retrospect and a Welcome', *WH* (23 Feb 1893): 20. WL.

5

New views of the women' suffrage campaign: Liberal women and regional perspectives

This chapter seeks to reveal hitherto hidden facets of the British women's movement by focusing on Glasgow suffragists' view of a London-led campaign and the contribution of the SWLF to constitutional suffragism. An analysis of the minute books of the GWSAWS reveals the influence of early twentieth-century trends towards Scottish Home Rule on the relationship of suffragists in Glasgow and London and on the character of the women's movement in Scotland. The GWSAWS was established in 1902 as the successor to the GNSWS, which had earlier been established as a branch of the NUWSS in the 1870s. The GWSAWS was keen to assert its independence from the NUWSS and a London-based campaign, and this is most clearly seen in its struggle to establish an autonomous SFWSS. Similarly, the records of the SWLF's work for female political rights – in minute books and the *SLWM* – reveal the organisation's position in the Scottish and British suffrage campaigns and highlights the importance of regional perspectives to developing a fuller account of the British women's movement.

The SWLF's campaign for women's suffrage reflected Liberal perspectives on citizenship. The SWLF's agitation for women's suffrage could parallel the activities of dedicated constitutional suffrage organisations: the SWLF endeavoured to use its Liberal party networks to encourage the introduction of women's suffrage bills in parliament; and the SWLF engaged in public suffrage debates such as the controversies associated with the Conciliation Bills. Nevertheless, the SWLF's approach to women's suffrage did have special characteristics, and Liberal women incorporated activities for women's parliamentary enfranchisement into a wider campaign for women's political participation. Official records and contemporary periodicals demonstrate that the SWLF understood itself as a major site of women's 'political education', and the organisation sought to encourage women's involvement in local politics, as electors and representatives. The SWLF vigorously supported married women's right to fully participate in local government, and attempted to expand women's access to local government while encouraging women to make full use of their existing rights.

While the SWLF has received only passing interest in studies of the British women's suffrage movement, women's suffrage was included as a prime objective of the SWLF when it was established in 1891, and this research suggests that the SWLF played a central role in campaigns for women's enfranchisement. In fact, the SWLF's role in suffragism was very similar to that of the BWTASCU; the SWLF minute books and the *SLWM* suggest that the two organisations shared several common themes with regards to suffragism. Firstly, Liberal women's discussions of suffrage mirrored those of female temperance reformers by stressing the inter-relatedness of these issues. The SWLF's understanding of the interconnectedness of temperance reform and women's suffrage was influenced by notions prevalent within the wider Anglophone reforming community, namely that women's voting would naturally lead to a more temperate society through prohibition. Next, in the early twentieth century, the SWLF tended to link temperance with Scottish Home Rule; the *SLWM* does not hesitate to accuse English interests in Westminster of obstructing prohibition legislation for Scotland, and thereby justify calls for Scottish independence. Lastly, while both the SWLF and the BWTASCU included pro-suffrage majorities, both organisations accommodated a degree of anti-suffragism among their members. In the case of the SWLF, Liberal women's periodicals sought to represent Liberal women's anti-suffragism as misguided and antithetical to the SWLF's mission. While the SWLF's discussions of suffrage and temperance echoed those of the BWTASCU, a situation no doubt encouraged by cross-membership between the organisations, the SWLF also reveals a particularly Liberal approach to the problems of temperance and suffrage.

Suffrage, temperance and women's Liberalism

The SWLF was conceived with the understanding that women's suffrage represented a cornerstone of the organisation's reforming activities, and the 1891 constitution declared the objective: 'To secure just and equal legislation and representation for women, especially with reference to the Parliamentary Franchise, and the removal of all legal disabilities on account of sex, and to protect the interests of children.'[1] By clearly aligning itself with women's suffrage, the SWLF took the lead in British Liberal women's advocacy of women's equal enfranchisement. The WLF in England did determine to campaign for women's suffrage in 1892, but this issue split the organisation and resulted in the emergence of the Women's National Liberal Association, which did not support agitation for suffrage by Liberal women's organisations.[2] Evidence from the *SLWM* suggests that the SWLF believed itself to be a more resolute supporter of women's suffrage than the WFL in England. For instance, a 1911 report describes the SWLF's correction of the NUWSS's misapprehension of the Scottish organisation's stance on the second Conciliation Bill:

> A letter was submitted which had been sent by instruction of the Convenor to the London office of the NUWSS calling their attention to the error in asking their Scottish members to protest against the action of the WLF Executive in withholding support from the Conciliation Bill, the WLF having no jurisdiction in Scotland, and the SWLF having consistently worked for the Bill.[3]

While a dedicated women's suffrage department was not formed until 1899, a 'suffrage appeal committee' operated from 1893, and, as the constitution indicates, suffrage was fundamental to the SWLF's mission from its inception.[4]

While the SWLF was established as pro-suffrage and included a suffragist majority, the SWLF's position in suffrage is complicated by the presence of a minority of anti-suffragists. The most striking evidence of anti-suffragism comes from the *SLWM*'s report of the Midlothian WLA's suggestion that the SWLF proclaim itself, 'opposed to the enfranchisement of women'.[5] The Midlothian anti-suffrage resolution was moved in response to a resolution proposed on behalf of several WLAs, including Glasgow and Edinburgh, to urge the Government's support of women's suffrage.[6] According to the *SLWM*, Mrs Durham, the representative for Midlothian, justified her position with the idea that: 'Women had no need for the franchise. Their Members of Parliament would attend to any demand which the women might have put before them. "One man one vote" would mean, if the franchise were extended to women on the same basis, "one woman one vote," and it would simply result in petticoat government.'[7] Durham's opposition to women's suffrage was treated with some ridicule, and a correspondent to the *SLWM* recalled the incident: 'The anti-Suffrage lady who so pluckily stood up for her own views made a delightful episode.'[8] Certainly, the *SLWM*'s reporting suggests that the Midlothian WLA's proposal represented a minority view, and the periodical carried the facetious response of Mrs Helen Barton, leader of the suffrage (1908–09) and temperance (1908–09, 1913) departments; 'on the fear of petticoat government … they had had trouser government for many years, and she did not think they had made too good a job of it'.[9] The *SLWM* further shared with its readers the astonishment of Mrs Anderson of Kilmarnock who, it was claimed, 'remarked that this was the first occasion on which she had seen an anti-Suffragist in the flesh, and she admired her courage in coming before an audience of women and saying that she was content to remain in the hands of men in the matter of legislation'.[10] A more earnest rebuke was attributed to Mary Crosthwaite who admonished that, 'there was an opportunity for women to do battle against poverty and destitution, and secure an equal opportunity for every man and every woman in seeking self-development. The country required the help of women as well as men in these matters'.[11] Ultimately, the pro-suffrage resolution passed with a vast majority, while Durham's anti-suffrage resolution was dismissed after receiving only two votes. The *SLWM*'s coverage of this episode highlights the notion that while outside suffragists in the SWLF might work in some tension with anti-suffragist colleagues, the *SLWM*'s description of the derision and censure with which this position was greeted reveals that the SWLF sought to demonstrate its commitment to women's parliamentary enfranchisement in spite of the 'misguided' views of a few wayward members.

A less controversial element of the SWLF's reform programme was the pursuit of prohibition. Interest in temperance reform was as integral to the SWLF's founding principles as suffrage, and Mrs Anna Lindsay, chair of the SWLF, proposed in 1893 that, 'all Associations take into consideration the question of Legislative Control of the Liquor Traffic'.[12] From this time prohibition was monitored by the bills department until the formation of a dedicated temperance department in 1899. The SWLF's discussions of temperance mirrored the BWTASCU's tendency to highlight the inter-connectedness of women's suffrage and prohibition, and these issues were often discussed concurrently in the *SLWM*. For example, 'Shamrock's' 1909 report on the SWLF's annual meeting states: 'The resolutions on Temperance, a subject very near the hearts of women, were, needless to say, carried unanimously. On Women's Suffrage, also a subject of paramount interest to women, there were a large number of resolutions presented for consideration'.[13] In 1909, the Edinburgh South WLA reported of its drawing-room meeting:

> A resolution regretting the action of the House of Lords in rejecting the Licensing Bill, and trusting that the Government would have an early opportunity of bringing it forward again was unanimously passed … Miss Goodfellow moved, and Miss McIntosh seconded, that a telegram of greeting and good wishes be sent to the Women's Suffrage Demonstration in the Albert Hall, London, on the 5th.[14]

Similarly, in 1911 it was reported: 'It was cheering to realise that the numerous speakers who supported the resolutions dealing with Local Veto were convinced prohibitionists at heart; and in the discussion on Women's Suffrage one felt that many present were really in favour of Adult Suffrage.'[15]

In Scotland prohibition was uniquely entangled not only with women's political rights, but also with Scottish nationalism. The lifespan of the *SLWM*, 1909 to 1914, coincided with the ascendancy of Scottish national-ism's stress on Home Rule.[16] The *SLWM* supported Scottish Home Rule, and this issue was interwoven with the *SLWM*'s discussion of the temper-ance question. By the early twentieth century, moves towards Scottish local veto had gained momentum, and local veto – a form of prohibition which allowed local voters to determine the fate of local alcohol-selling – was enacted for Scotland by the Temperance (Scotland) Act, 1913. In the years immediately preceding the Temperance Act, the *SLWM* claimed that Scotland's lack of national autonomy was a barrier to local veto. For instance, the *SLWM*'s account of the 1910 annual meeting noted: 'That this Council re-affirms its belief in the necessity for Devolution or Home Rule for Scotland, Ireland, and Wales. It in particular, protests against the delay in dealing with Scottish affairs in Parliament, and against the preponderating and often adverse influence of English members which is brought to bear on Scottish measures.'[17] This resolution was passed to protest blockage of the 1909 Temperance (Scotland) Bill. In 1910, the *SLWM* reported that Charles Roberts, MP for Lincoln, introduced a bill for local veto, 'to make some amends to Scotland for the action of the English members who had blocked it before'.[18] As Westminster continued to frustrate the passage of a Scottish temperance bill, the *SLWM* reported in 1911 that:

> They [the SWLF] wanted legislation according to the needs and condi-tions of the Scottish people. Of course this was really an argument for Home Rule for Scotland, because they found that measures dealing especially with liquor and land when framed by English people from the English standpoint did not apply satisfactorily to Scotland at all.[19]

The *SLWM* reported that the bill was headed to the Scottish Grand Committee for consideration, but added: 'We are only sorry to see that the usual band of pertinacious and obstructive English members ... have been added again to the committee.'[20] The synergy of temperance and Scottish Home Rule was further elucidated in the *SLWM*'s report of the SWLF's 1912 annual meeting, when it was claimed Mrs A. Falconer, Eastern Division Vice-President (1908–14), argued: 'The Federation came into existence on the Home Rule question, but the Temperance question had brought in the members, and it had been a burning question among earnest-minded people, among urban and rural workers.'[21] This view of temperance and Scottish Home Rule was not confined to the SWLF, and the BWTASCU, whose membership overlapped with the SWLF, also discussed temperance reform in patriotic terms. For instance, in 1905 Louise Gulland somewhat sensationally described football and ice cream shops in the *SWTN* as, 'where the cigarette or the cold sweet mouthful are not the deadliest evils', and further claimed that the 'glass of grog' was undermining Scotland's noble past of 'spiritual independence'. Gulland's solution: 'By gathering into our hearts the force of our fealty to national traditions, and bringing them to bear upon these evils with combined effort, with might and power, and earnest endeavour of every servant of Christ.'[22] Gulland's call to arms against all that would degrade Scotland finds antecedents in Margaret Blaikie's 1899 open letter in the *SWTN*: 'We are a UNION, first Scottish, and that implies that we are patriotic, that we have a common country, that we deplore every evil thing that hurts it, and would resist every enemy that would destroy it.'[23]

It is, perhaps, unsurprising that Scottish Liberal women were such keen advocates of temperance, and it is apparent that nineteenth-century contemporaries recognised the connections between Liberalism and temperance. This is illustrated by the changing fortunes of the English women's periodical, the *Women's Penny Paper* (*WPP*). The *WPP*, which was established in 1888 under the editorship of Mrs Henrietta Muller, reported on a wide range of topics including news from the suffrage, Liberal and Conservative women's associations. In April 1892, the *WPP* transferred ownership to the *Women's Herald* Co. and was henceforth a Liberal women's publication. The range of subjects discussed in the *Women's Herald* (*WH*) was less diverse than in the *WPP*, but temperance and women's suffrage remained prominent. In February 1893, the *WH* became the official organ of the WWCTU in Britain, co-edited by Lady Henry Somerset, President of the English BWTA, and Edwin Stout. The new *WH* made plain the union of temperance and female Liberalism in a statement of its policy:

> The *Women's Herald* will in future be as much identified with the cause of Temperance, and other social reforms advocated by the World Women's Christian Temperance Union, as it is with the cause of the Women's Liberal Federation. Henceforth, there will be no division of forces. The two great sections of public-spirited women will march under one banner against the common foe, to the ringing watchword 'For God, Home, and Humanity'.[24]

Thus, prominent Liberal women's periodicals, such as the *SLWM* and *WH*, highlight Liberal women's understanding of temperance and suffrage as two elements in a diverse web of 'women's issues'.

The Anglophone community was important for encouraging the SWLF's conflation of women's suffrage and prohibition. As was the case for the BWTASCU, New Zealand was especially influential. The SWLF accepted the conventional wisdom regarding the relationship between female temperance reform and suffrage in New Zealand, and the *SLWM* reproduced a letter from the Wellington *Morning Post*, which suggested that the women's suffrage campaign was, 'mostly organised by the Women's Christian Temperance Union'.[25] Similarly, the *SLWM* echoed claims that prohibition was a natural consequence of women's enfranchisement: 'The most noteworthy point about the countries where women exercise the vote is that practically everywhere women have not begun by asserting their own personal claims. Their first act has been to declare war on alcohol ... In New Zealand ... feminine direct influence has had excellent results in the cause of temperance'.[26] Thus, the SWLF could argue that women's enfranchisement was not sought out of self-interest, but rather as a means of empowering supposed feminine moral superiority with a formal political expression.

This perception of the New Zealand women's vote as purifying was reinforced by individual women's testimonies. Mrs Helen Barton, a member of the SWLF from 1900 and connected with the Glasgow Prayer Union from 1898, undertook a tour of Australia and New Zealand in 1910–12. Her letters to the *SLWM* provided Liberal women at home with an eyewitness account of the good work done by Antipodean women's suffrage. Barton claims to have voted in the Australian Federal Election, the State Election of New South Wales and the Dominion Election in New Zealand, experiences which led her to assert the improving influence of female electors:

> There is no doubt whatever regarding the women's vote; they are always on the side of progress and the uplift of the people. The presence of women on polling day at the polling booth has elevated the polling stations; vulgarisms and rowdyism are altogether extinct. Men and women, with their children come together to vote, the husband taking charge of the children while the woman records her vote.[27]

Barton's cosy, familial imagery was certainly designed both to reassure Liberal suffragists and to persuade the sceptical of the propriety of women's voting. Barton's report implies that feminine influence 'civilised' the voting process by encouraging men's self-control, and that harmonious martial relations were little disturbed by female voting. Her comments on the serenity and sobriety of Australian and New Zealand elections were further juxtaposed with female voters' influence for prohibition, and the notion that women voted 'straight' for local veto.[28] Barton gives women's voting in Australia and New Zealand special relevance for her Scottish readers by repeatedly emphasising the cultural, and even geographical, similarities between the antipodes and Scotland:

> I have had the honour of being asked by the Caledonian Society of Bendigo to meet the Scotch Commissioners on St. Andrew's Night in Bendigo ... Really the Scotch residents here keep up the traditions of their land, and everywhere one goes the excellences of character and the stability of the Scottish race are in evidence, and really the people of Australia love the Scotch. They seem to me to be a favoured people, for wherever you go you find the Scotch are in place and power.[29]

The 'special relationship' between these white settler colonies and Scotland is further cultivated by Barton's rather sentimental notion that New Zealand, 'is a beautiful country, something like Scotland', as well as her claim to have, 'interviewed a large number of people who have gone from Scotland'.[30] In this way Liberal women such as Barton sought to mobilise the example of the Anglophone world to justify female political rights at home.

The SWLF's interest in temperance and suffrage reveals the need to understand these two issues as fundamental and intertwined in the British women's movement. The structure of the SWLF was designed with the pursuit of suffrage and temperance in mind, and while a minority dissented against the SWLF's pro-suffrage policy, the SWLF encouraged activities on behalf of these two movements in its public discussions and reforming work. The SWLF's stance on the temperance and suffrage issues further highlights the unique position of Scotland in the British women's movement, and this is especially so regarding the SWLF's understanding of the intimate relationship between temperance and Home Rule for Scotland.

The SWLF in constitutional suffragism

The SWLF contributed to the constitutional suffrage campaign through its campaigning activities and public debates on women's suffrage. In 1899, the SWLF established a suffrage department to manage its campaigning activities. The suffrage department further reported on the suffrage agitation of SWLF members in Westminster through the Liberal women's press and local WLA meetings. The SWLF's support for suffrage may best be understood as part of a broader interest in women's active citizenship, and

Liberal women rallied on behalf of female representatives and electors in the local arena.

The SWLF used its networks with Liberals in Westminster to lobby for women's equal enfranchisement. In February 1910, Mrs McCallum represented the SWLF at a Liberal Suffrage Committee meeting in London, while Mrs Wood attended the meetings of the Parliamentary Joint Suffrage Committee in 1912.[31] McCallum and Wood further attended a meeting of the Parliamentary Committee of Liberal MPs for the further-ance of Women's Suffrage which resolved: 'That this meeting urges the members of the Committee to ballot for a Women's Suffrage Bill, and to pledge itself to do its utmost during this session to secure the enfranchise-ment of women on a broad and democratic basis.'[32] Exploiting Liberal party networks in order to infiltrate and perhaps influence parliamentary debates on women's suffrage represented one aspect of SWLF suffrage agitation. Liberal women further used the public forum of their period-ical publications to contribute to contemporary suffrage debates with the aim of women's enfranchisement.

The SWLF's willingness to enter public debate on suffrage is particu-larly evident from its discussions of the second Conciliation Bill. After the 1910 General Election, which returned a Liberal Government, the Liberal Party initiated a cross-party committee to draft a women's suffrage bill; in 1910, 1911 and 1912 this committee produced the so-called Concilia-tion Bills. The Conciliation Bills were very limited in scope and sought to enfranchise approximately one million wealthier women. The less than democratic character of the Conciliation Bills made them controversial among suffragists, and reports on the second Conciliation Bill contained in the Liberal women's press show that similar concerns and debates were present within the SWLF. A resolution – supported by the Glasgow and Edinburgh WLAs – in favour of the second Conciliation Bill was passed at the 1911 annual meeting. The *SLWM* reported Mary R. Crosthwaite's defence of the bills as, 'a thoroughly democratic measure'.[33] Crosthwaite was a member of the west of Scotland leadership (1910–14) and the Suffrage and Local Government Department (1911–13) and a leading apologist for the SWLF's support for the bill. In contrast, Miss A. Milne of the Helensburgh WLA moved a resolution against the SWLF's support for the bill based on the argument that:

> It was conferring a vote as a privilege on a selected number of women. As a Liberal and a Democrat she did not believe in privilege. She thought that what was right for a number was right for all … The householding woman had many privileges and rights and a certain status which the lodger woman had not, and she thought it was the lodger woman who

needed the vote most. The Conciliation Bill was something thrown to them to keep them quiet. Instead of being leverage for a better bill she thought it would be used as a hindrance.[34]

At the highest level, the SWLF did support the second Conciliation Bill, but the organisation had to continually defend its position against members' criticisms that it was an undemocratic measure. In addressing the men's Scottish Liberal Association in October 1911, 'Shamrock' reports Crosthwaite's argument:

> She then described the Conciliation Bill, which, she said, contained a common basis of assent, and that was that women who pay rates and taxes should have a vote. It had been said that the Bill gave preference to propertied women, but to say that only showed ignorance. Only so far as a woman owned and occupied a house is she to have a vote. The woman who owned one small house had therefore the same right to vote as the woman who owned a castle. The promoters had made it their business to find out how the Bill would work, and they had found that 80 per cent of the women who would be enfranchised were wage-earning women. It was therefore a democratic measure.[35]

Crosthwaite's support for the Conciliation Bill received a mixed reaction from Scottish male Liberals. Andrew Bannatyne and J. Grant Davies from Glasgow and Professor Paterson from Edinburgh moved a resolution in favour of the Conciliation Bill, 'as the best solution of the question meantime'.[36] Bannatyne and Paterson were closely linked to the GWSAWS and ENSWS, respectively, and Banantyne's daughter, Kathleen V. Bannatyne, was a suffragist and member of the Glasgow School Board (1906–14).[37] H. J. Darnton Fraser from Edinburgh argued that a women's suffrage measure be subordinated to a redistribution of seats and franchise reform and at any rate, 'said that there was no clear evidence that the women wanted the Bill, and he challenged anyone to say there was any decided movement in the country for it'.[38] The lack of consensus among female suffragists was reflected by their male supporters and Fraser was seconded by Pringle MP, husband of ENSWS and Edinburgh Central Branch member Mrs Robert Pringle who, claimed the *SLWM*, 'regarded the Bill as a spurious reform. It narrowed down democratic government. For one thing the treatment of married women under the Bill was not such as would commend it to Liberals.'[39] Ultimately, the SWLF and the Scottish Liberal Association endorsed the 1911 Conciliation Bill. The response to the bill of male and female Liberals in Scotland reflected debates among constitutional suffragists around the UK: some saw the bill as an inherently flawed measure, while others argued for its expediency as setting a precedent for more wide-ranging future reforms. What is most significant here, is the SWLF's participation in public debate around suffrage. That is, by arguing the merits or otherwise of the Conciliation Bills, the SWLF behaved more like a constitutional suffrage society than a party organisation slavishly supporting Liberal men's political ambitions.

While the SWLF was a major player in constitutional suffrage, Liberal women's interest in parliamentary suffrage should be read in light of a wider commitment to female citizenship. Activities to enhance women's presence in local politics were as vigorous as those regarding access to parliamentary democracy. Activities on behalf of women's rights in local politics included support for female politicians. In order to support the candidacy of female politicians, the SWLF regularly compiled lists of female councillors and school board members. In 1899, the SWLF asked secretaries in the local WLAs to supply the names and addresses of female parish councillors in their regions, and in the twentieth century the SWLF organised several 'postcard campaigns' whereby post cards were sent to local boards requesting that they be returned with information on female representatives in order to mobilise support for these women at election time.[40] Electioneering on behalf of female politicians was often co-ordinated with the Women's Local Government Society and the Association for the Return of Women to Public Boards; because the records from these organisations in Scotland do not survive it is difficult to gauge the extent of this co-operation. The SWLF minutes do give an indication of inter-organisational efforts, and, for instance, the 1903 minutes describe co-operation with the Glasgow Society for the Return of Women to Local Boards' postcard campaign.[41] Support for women's candidacy was one aspect of the SWLF's interest in women's participation in local politics; Liberal women further sought to encourage female electors' participation.

The SWLF considered itself an important force in the political education of women: 'The work which the SWLF has done during the years of its existence in building up the political education of women cannot be too highly appreciated.'[42] This instruction consisted largely of the creation and distribution of pamphlet literature, and following new legislation the SWLF prepared and print leaflets describing women's status under the law. In 1900, the SWLF Executive distributed 3,000 copies of 'Women's Franchise and Local Government (Scotland)' and 5,000 copies of 'School Board Elections' to the local WLAs for dissemination in the regions.[43] Similarly, following the passage of the Local Government (Scotland) Act, 1894 the SWLF published a supplementary leaflet on the new position of women in local politics to complement the pamphlet produced by the (men's) Scottish Liberal Association.[44] In this way evidence from the

SWLF mirrors Linda Walker's assertion that the English WLF pursued four main objectives: women's political education; women's exercise of existing rights in local voting; women's candidacy for local boards; and parliamentary enfranchisement.[45] While supporting women's participation in local politics the SWLF further sought to expand women's access to local franchises and boards. Agitation for women's local political rights relied on similar methods as used in the campaign for parliamentary suffrage, and Liberal women made use of their networks with sympathetic male Liberal MPs both locally and in Westminster. Lady Isobel Martin, the wife of Carlaw Martin MP and member of the SWLF from 1891 to 1910, championed women's increased access to local government and vigorously lobbied prominent male Liberals in pursuit of electoral reform. In 1895, she consulted with male Liberals on alternative property qualifications for the 1894 Local Government Act in order to draft a proposal to Sir Trevelyan, the Secretary for Scotland.[46] In early 1897, in the run-up to the creation of county councils, Martin worked with Mr Shaw MP to draft a bill to admit women as county councillors; this bill was introduced by MPs Munro-Ferguson, Sir John Leng and Haldane, relatives of prominent SWLF members Lady Helen Munro-Ferguson, Miss and Lady Leng and Miss E. Haldane, and though the bill did not do well, the SWLF resolved that if the bill gained a second reading the organisation would write immediately to all Liberal MPs and send a Whip to Scottish Liberals.[47] Co-operation with Liberal MPs was augmented by other means of extra-parliamentary agitation, and the SWLF's campaigns relating to the Local Government (Qualifications of Women) (Scotland) Acts from 1903 to 1914 included demonstrations, deputations to MPs, and memorials and petitions to Scottish Liberal MPs, the secretary for Scotland and the prime minister.

The SWLF emphasised the rights of married women in local politics. In the period preceding the 1894 Act, the SWLF sent several memorials to the Government asking that the Local Government (Scotland) Bill include provisions for the political rights of women regardless of marital status:

> This Memorial shewth that no scheme for the formation of District or Parish Councils will be satisfactory which does not secure to women, married or single, the right of electing and of being elected as members and officers to all governing bodies ... your Memorialists ... pray that you will, on behalf of Her Majesty's Government, introduce and support such legislation only with regard to Local Government in Scotland as shall recognise and establish the equal rights of Women, married and unmarried alike, with men.[48]

Similarly, Isobel Martin thanked Scottish Liberals for the addition of clauses to the Local Government Bill that empowered single and married women to elect and be elected parish councillors, but she called their attention to the proviso, 'that there shall be two registers for registering married women – one for the Parish Council, for which marriage is no disqualification, the other for the County Council and Municipal Register, under which no married woman living in family with her husband can be registered, only absentee wives being qualified'.[49]

The early years of the suffrage campaign in the 1860s and 1870s generally focused on the need for the equal enfranchisement of single women. This approach reflected suffragists' refusal to contest the notion that married women's voting would result in marital discord or that married women were already represented by their husbands. This attitude is evident in the first decade of the ENSWS's campaign. Between 1868 and 1878, the ENSWS stressed the political rights of single women 'breadwinners' who lacked the representation of a husband; 'if a woman be unmarried, and has a house that is her own house, or lands that are her own lands, this Committee thinks that that woman has as good a right as a taxpayer, and as an intelligent inhabitant of this country, to give a vote in the election of Members of Parliament as any man placed in the same circumstances'.[50] The place of married women in politics was controversial, and as Harrison has shown, anti-suffragists often warned that if the vote was as valuable as suffragists claimed, 'one could not be sure that women would ever marry: or that once they lost their vote through marriage, they would not immediately seek to regain it through divorce'.[51] Support for single women's suffrage, then, responded to the ENSWS's concentration on propertied women's enfranchisement and the strategic decision to avoid a debate on the possible 'dangers' of wives' voting. While by the 1890s the SWLF had made the rights of married women in local government central to its programme, the SWLF's advocacy for the equal rights of married and single women was pursued less fiercely with regard to demands for the parliamentary franchise. The SWLF argued that married women's parliamentary enfranchisement should echo the local government franchise in which married women were qualified if they were registered under a different property than their husbands, this form of property qualification enfranchising only the richest married women or those who were separated from their husbands.[52] While it is clear that the SWLF as a whole considered itself a force in the political emancipation of women, the potential conflict of interest arising from links with a Liberal party slow to introduce women's suffrage led some to question Liberal women's efficacy in the women's movement.

Contemporary critics of the SWLF – as well as historians of suffragism – challenged Liberal women's commitment to suffrage principles. For example, Priscilla McLaren submitted a letter to the *WH* in 1892, which congratulated fellow member of the ENSWS, Miss Louisa Stevenson, on her resignation as Vice-President of the Edinburgh West End WLA. Stevenson had left on the grounds that without the parliamentary franchise no just legislation was possible for women and children. In her letter, McLaren referred to her own distrust of the Liberal party, and recalled an invitation to act as President of the Edinburgh South WLA: 'I said I would only consent to be its President on condition that we should make justice to women the first consideration – as I believe this would be doing good to the nation. His countenance fell at once. He replied, "That is not what we want; we want to help the Liberal Party." What a confusion of ideas! I thought, to confound Liberalism with helping men only.'[53] There is evidence that female Liberals' suffrage activities were tempered by party loyalty, and for instance, the high levels of Liberal membership to the GWSAWS led to that organisation's rejection of the NUWSS's Election Fighting Fund policy. In 1912, the NUWSS sought to channel local suffrage societies' resources towards the election of Labour candidates. The GWSAWS joined with the Cardiff society in refusing to implement such a policy.[54] In the same year, when Miss Grace Paterson of the Glasgow College WLA proposed the resolution that, 'this Council desires to state that it will regard as unacceptable any measure relating to the Franchise which does not provide for the extension of the suffrage to women', she was over-ruled in favour of a more moderately worded resolution.[55] Nonetheless, this discussion of the SWLF's support for women's right to formal participation in local and British-national politics chimes with existing analyses of Liberal women's pro-active feminism, political autonomy (from the men's Liberal groups) and suffragism.[56] So, while the SWLF's stance on women's suffrage could generate tension within the organisation, women's right to formal political participation was a central tenet of the organisation. In this way, the SWLF's reforming efforts represent an important, though often overlooked, aspect of the British women's movement. The SWLF's marginal place in accounts of British suffragism further reflects a lack of regional analyses, and an exploration of regional suffrage campaigns might expose fission within British constitutional suffragism.

The GWSAWS and the SFWSS

Evidence for antagonism between the 'core' and the 'periphery' of the British suffrage campaign comes from the early twentieth-century minutes of the GWSAWS. From its beginnings, the GWSAWS exhibited an independent character and the organisation's minute books reveal its turbulent relationship with the NUWSS, the London-based umbrella organisation for constitutional societies. As was the case for the Liberal and temperance societies, it appears that twentieth-century demands for Scottish Home Rule encouraged the GWSAWS to seek autonomy from a campaign organised under a London headship. This is most clearly evident from records of disagreements between Glasgow and London suffragists over the formation of an independent SFWSS.

The GWSAWS first attempted to establish an independent SFWSS when the NUWSS underwent re-organisation in 1906:

> The Secretary submitted a letter from Miss Hardcastle enclosing a Draft Constitution for the re-forming of the National Union of Women's Suffrage Societies. After discussion the Secretary was instructed to reply that whilst sympathizing with the objects of the scheme we feel that the distance from England is so great that it annuls in great measure the benefit to be derived by joining the Union and that in the opinion of this Committee a Scottish Union would be more effective for extending the work in Scotland.[57]

The GWSAWS's desire to break from the London-based campaign was thwarted by the ENSWS's refusal to unite with the Glasgow policy.[58] The GWSAWS therefore determined to rejoin the NUWSS, but asked that the NUWSS make its meetings more accessible to women working at great distances from London. The expense of travel was a frequent cause of friction between the GWSAWS and the NUWSS, and geographical isolation from the London campaign was an issue for all Scottish suffrage societies, and for example, in 1909 the SNSWS 'decided that it was impossible for the society to send a delegate' to a special NUWSS meeting in London.[59] Relations continued to sour between the Glasgow suffragists and London headquarters: 'A letter was submitted from the NU saying it had been decided to have a demonstration on 13 June in London and hoping that 15 representatives would go from the Association. This was felt to be quite out of the question as the expense would be quite prohibitive.'[60] Three years later, the GWSAWS again sought to form an independent Scottish organisation, a move which was precipitated by a clash with NUWSS over a Glasgow by-election. In 1909, the NUWSS reprimanded the GWSAWS for publishing its by-election policy in the *Women's Franchise* without first gaining NUWSS consent: 'The Secretary submitted a letter from Miss Sterling, Hon. Sec. to the NU saying her Committee would be glad to know on whose authority the Glasgow Secretary had sent the report to *Women's Franchise*. That the NU would do propaganda work only.'[61] The minutes recalled the association's nterviews with parliamentary candidates Bowles and Dickson: the GWSAWS reports Bowles' opposition to suffrage, while Dickson was described as in favour of the principle but reluctant to support a suffrage measure.[62] The GWSAWS claimed to have, 'at once sent a report of the two interviews to London and no reply was received and it was necessary to declare our policy she announced on the 19th that as Mr Dickson's attitude was so unsatisfactory we would do propaganda work only.'[63] The minutes then report that the GWSAWS received word from the NUWSS on the 23rd to begin work on behalf of Dickson, 'but under the circumstances it was felt to be impossible, and we wrote to the NU explaining this and no further communications referring to this were received.'[64] The NUWSS's response to the Glasgow society's decisions suggests that as the GWSAWS struggled for self-determination, equally, the NUWSS struggled to maintain control over affiliates' policy. The NUWSS's reaction to the GWSAWS's policy demonstrates the London organisation's mistrust of the competency and understanding of women in the local sphere of action:

> Two letters were submitted from the NU regarding the Central by-election. One addressed to the Chairman dated March 22nd stated that this Committee had defied the policy laid down by the NU and that the delay of the NU in declaring their policy was entirely due to the action of Glasgow in withholding information about Mr Scott Dickson's views although the NU had asked for it both by letter and telegram. The letter further asked for a copy of the resolutions passed by the Glasgow Committee embodying their decision to adopt a policy other than that of the NU. The Chairman reported that no such telegram and letter had been received by Glasgow. In reply to this letter he [Andrew Ballantyne] asked for copies of the letter and telegram referred to in order that he might look into the whole matter. He received no acknowledgement of his letter.[65]

The tensions between the Glasgow and London leadership moved towards a resolution in June 1909, when the Birmingham National Society for Women's Suffrage proposed a scheme for re-organisation of the NUWSS, which included a Scottish Federation. In October, the GWSAWS hosted a meeting of Scottish societies in order to, 'draw up a letter of motivation and a scheme for organising a Scottish Federation.'[66] A Scottish Federation was created out of these initiatives, but it was not the independent body desired by the Glasgow suffragists; all local branches within the SFWSS had to affiliate directly to the NUWSS, rather than via the SFWSS. A final insult marks the conclusion of the GWSAWS's pursuit of an autonomous Scottish national organisation: 'Letters and the NU minutes of 7 April were submitted and from these it appeared that the NU was under the impression that the Scottish Federation had been initiated and organised by the Edinburgh Society'.[67] The NUWSS agreed to correct its records but failed to credit the Glasgow suffragists as the progenitors of the Scottish Federation.

The GWSAWS's minute books expose a divisiveness within the NUWSS which calls into question Garner's assertion that, 'the democratic structure of the National Union [was] aided by the reorganisation of 1909, [which] allowed the voice of many more women to be heard'.[68] On the contrary, the records of the GWSAWS indicate that Glasgow suffragists had hoped for independence from London, and continued to feel marginalised, rather than represented, within the NUWSS even after the 1909 reorganisation. In this way, this analysis supports Ursula Masson's challenge to the notion of greater democracy in the constitutional versus militant suffrage organisations.[69] While the supposed autocracy of the WSPU has been well-documented, the NUWSS's disregard for local opinion and administrative autonomy has been largely overlooked. Likewise, Leneman underestimates the importance of the GWSAWS's failed pursuit of an independent SFWSS: 'There was a *contretemps* when the NUWSS initially refused to recognise the Scottish Federation on the lines proposed by Scotland. However, not long after, the National Union passed new rules recognising federation of local societies, as long as all the societies were affiliated to the NUWSS'.[70] While I have shown that the disagreement over the by-election strengthened the GWSAWS's resolve to establish an independent Scottish Federation, Leneman concludes that: 'The relationship between the NUWSS ... and local societies was often difficult, though there was enough mutual respect for it to right itself eventually'.[71]

As the only major monograph on the Scottish suffrage campaign, Leneman's study has coloured subsequent analyses of the relationship between the GWSAWS and the NUWSS. For instance, June Hannam's reliance on Leneman leads her to claim that the GWSAWS's refusal either to join or advertise the NUWSS's June 1908 suffrage demonstration in London was motivated purely by pragmatism, rather than a deep irritation at the insensitivity of London suffragists to the difficulty of travel.[72] In terms of the formation of the SFWSS, Hannam's work fails to appreciate the GWSAWS's efforts in 1906 and states only that: 'After 1909 more effort was made to set up branches throughout Scotland and in November a Scottish Federation was formed'.[73] *A Guid Cause* was a vital step in working towards a recognition of the contribution of Scotland to British suffragism, yet Leneman's study is not the final word. As this discussion has shown, an analysis of the Scottish suffrage campaign has yet more to offer in exposing the depth and breadth of constitutional suffragism as well as the local dynamics that characterised the British women's movement.

Conclusion

This investigation's analysis of the GWSAWS's relationship with the NUWSS suggests the need to re-evaluate the supposedly superior democratic character of constitutional versus militant suffragism. The NUWSS's apparent resistance to the Glasgow suffragists' desire for a fully autonomous Scottish organisation betrays an interest in consolidating control of the constitutional movement in London. Similarly, the SWLF's consistent support for women's equal enfranchisement further demonstrates the need to broaden understandings of suffragism to incorporate the efforts of organisations such as the SWLF and BWTASCU. The work of Liberal women – and female temperance reformers – for women's suffrage could parallel that of organisations more often associated with suffragism, but equally the SWLF made a distinct contribution to the campaign. Criticisms of Liberal women's loyalty to the women's movement need to be contextualised in female Liberals' positioning of themselves as 'practical politicians' engaged in the gamut of Liberal concerns, and female Liberals agitated among men and women in support of the Liberal party, and demanded temperance and electoral reform in order to generate a more female-friendly society. Finally, as women's organisations, the SWLF and GWSAWS were key sites of upper-middle-class women's participation in public life: these organisations aimed to encourage women's involvement in formal politics, while bringing their members into the public sphere of debate and reforming activities.

Notes

1 SWLF, *Minutes*, 1891. NLS Acc. 11765/20.
2 Linda Walker, 'Party Political Women: A Comparative Study of Liberal Women and the Primrose League, 1890–1914', *Equal or Different*, ed. Rendall.
3 'Meeting of Executive', *SLWM* (Dec 1911): 231. BL P.P.3611.tc.
4 SWLF, *Minutes*, 1893. NLS Acc. 11765/20.
5 'Annual Meeting of the Council of the Scottish Women's Liberal Federation', *SLWM*

(Apr 1912): 94. BL P.P.3611.tc.

6 'Annual Meeting of the Council of the Scottish Women's Liberal Federation', 94. BL P.P.3611.tc.

7 'Annual Meeting of the Council of the Scottish Women's Liberal Federation', 94. BL P.P.3611.tc.

8 Mrs Latta, 'The SWLF at Dundee', *SLWM* (Apr 1912): 74. BL P.P.3611.tc.

9 'Annual Meeting of the Council of the Scottish Women's Liberal Federation', 94. BL P.P.3611.tc.

10 'Annual Meeting of the Council of the Scottish Women's Liberal Federation', 94. BL P.P.3611.tc.

11 'Annual Meeting of the Council of the Scottish Women's Liberal Federation', 94. BL P.P.3611.tc.

12 SWLF, *Minutes*, 1893. NLS Acc. 11765/20.

13 'Shamrock', 'SWLF Meetings, 1909', *SLWM* (May 1909): 105. BL P.P.3611.tc.

14 'WLA News: Edinburgh (South)', *SLWM* (Jan 1909): 21. BL P.P.3611.tc.

15 Anderson, 'A Bird's-Eye View of the SWLF Meetings', 70. BL P.P.3611.tc.

16 'Scottish nationalism' was interpreted in a variety of ways in the nineteenth century, such as a demand for an equal recognition of Scotland's role in a British imperial project. See Morton *Unionist Nationalism* for a discussion of the shifting meanings of Scottish nationalism.

17 'Annual Meetings of the Council of the SWLF', *SLWM* (Apr 1910): 93. BL P.P.3611.tc.

18 'Scottish Temperance Bill', *SLWM* (May 1910): 113. BL P.P.3611.tc.

19 'SWLF Council Meetings', *SLWM* (Apr 1911): 91. BL P.P.3611.tc.

20 'Scottish Temperance Bill', 114. BL P.P.3611.tc.

21 'Annual Meeting of the Council of the Scottish Women's Liberal Federation', *SLWM* (Apr 1912): 85. BL P.P.3611.tc.

22 Louise Gulland, 'How Can I Help Scotland?', *SWTN* 9, no. 1 (Jan 1905): 5. BWTASCU Collection.

23 Margaret Blaikie, 'President's Letter', *SWTN* 3, no. 2 (Feb 1899): 24. BWTASCU Collection.

24 'Our Policy', *WH* (23 Feb 1893): 1. WL.

25 'Women's Suffrage in New Zealand', *SLWM* (Oct 1910): 231. BL P.P.3611.tc.

26 'What the Women's Vote Has Done', *SLWM* (Nov 1912): 220. BL P.P.3611.tc.

27 Helen Barton, 'Impressions from the Antipodes', *SLWM* (Jun 1912): 125–6. BL P.P.3611.tc.

28 'Mrs Barton in Australia', *SLWM* (Mar 1911): 60. BL P.P.3611.tc.

29 'Mrs Barton in Australia', 59. BL P.P.3611.tc.

30 Barton, 'Impressions', 126. BL P.P.3611.tc.

31 'Editorial Notes', *SLWM* (Mar 1911): 48; 'Meeting of SWLF Executive', *SLWM* (Jun 1912): 134. BL P.P.3611.tc.

32 'Notes of a Special Meeting of Executive', *SLWM* (Mar 1912): 58. BL P.P.3611.tc.

33 'SWLF Council Meetings', *SLWM* (Apr 1911): 86. BL P.P.3611.tc.

34 'SWLF Council Meetings', 86. BL P.P.3611.tc.

35 'Shamrock', 'Scottish Liberals at Dunoon, 1911', *SLWM* (Nov 1911): 212. BL P.P.3611.tc.

36 'Shamrock', 'Scottish Liberals at Dunoon', 213. BL P.P.3611.tc.

37 See Glasgow School Board, *Minutes* (1906–14). GCA D-ED 1.1.1.3–1.1.1.16.

38 'Shamrock', 'Scottish Liberals at Dunoon', 214. BL P.P.3611.tc.

39 'Shamrock', 'Scottish Liberals at Dunoon', 214. BL P.P.3611.tc.
40 Post Card Campaigns were undertaken for School Boards in 1902 and 1903, and for Parish Councils in 1904. NLS Acc. 11765/23;/24.
41 The SWLF contributed £3 to the campaign and the WLA secretary addressed half of the postcards. SWLF, *Minutes* (1903) NLS Acc. 11765/24.
42 'Shamrock', 'SWLF Meetings, 1909', *SLWM* (May 1909): 105. BL P.P.3611.tc.
43 SWLF, *Minutes* (1900) NLS Acc. 11765/22.
44 SWLF, *Minutes* (1894) NLS Acc. 11765/20.
45 Walker, 'Party Political Women', 182.
46 SWLF, *Minutes* (1895). NLS Acc. 11765/21.
47 SWLF, *Minutes* (1897). NLS Acc. 11765/21.
48 SWLF, *Minutes* (1894). NLS Acc. 11765/20.
49 SWLF, *Minutes* (1894). NLS Acc. 11765/20.
50 ENSWS, *Annual Report for the Year 1869* (Edinburgh, 1870), 5. WL 324.6230604134/18325.
51 Harrison, *Separate Spheres*, 52.
52 SWLF, *Minutes* (1911). NLS Acc. 11765/27.
53 Priscilla McLaren, 'The Edinburgh West End Women's Liberal Association', *WH* 7, no. 218 (31 Dec 1892): 9. WL.
54 GWSAWS, *Minutes* (1912). ML 891036/1/2.
55 'Annual Meeting of the Council of the Scottish Women's Liberal Federation', *SLWM* (Apr 1912): 95. BL P.P.3611.tc.
56 For Cornwall Bradley has demonstrated the central role of Liberal women in suffragism,while Hollis has asserted the importance of WLAs for English women's political education. See Bradley, '"If the vote is good for Jack; why not for Jill?": The Women's Suffrage Movement in Cornwall, 1870–1914', Publication of the Institute of Cornish Studies, ed. Philip Payton, Cornish Studies, no. 8. (Exeter: University of Exeter Press, 2000): 127, 134; Hollis, *Ladies Elect*, 61; and Walker, 'Party Political Women' and 'Gender, Suffrage and Party'.
57 GWSAWS, *Executive Committee Minutes* (1906). ML 891036/1/2.
58 GWSAWS, *Minutes* (1906). ML 891036/1/2.
59 SNSWS, *Minute Book* (1909). Shetland Archives D.1/32.
60 GWSAWS, *Minutes* (1908). ML 891036/1/2.
61 GWSAWS, *Minutes* (1909). ML 891036/1/2.
62 GWSAWS, *Minutes* (1909). ML 891036/1/2.
63 GWSAWS, *Minutes* (1909). ML 891036/1/2.
64 GWSAWS, *Minutes* (1909). ML 891036/1/2.
65 GWSAWS, *Minutes* (1909). ML 891036/1/2.
66 GWSAWS, *Minutes* (1909). ML 891036/1/2.
67 GWSAWS, *Minutes* (1910). ML 891036/1/2.
68 Garner, *Stepping Stone to Women's Liberty*, 15.
69 See Masson, '"Political conditions in Wales are quite different…"'.
70 Leneman, *A Guid Cause*, 93.
71 Leneman, *A Guid Cause*, 76.
72 Hannam, '"I had not been to London"', 227.
73 Hannam, '"I had not been to London"', 232.

Conclusion

The feminine public sphere represents a locus of middle-class women's public lives and elite women's contribution to a middle-class identity rooted in public service. Late Victorian and Edwardian middle-class women's participation in the feminine public sphere was underpinned by a shared evangelical Protestantism and a fidelity to middle-class notions of domesticity. Indeed, the cultural and social values derived from evangelical religion, which in turn supported idealised notions of women's domesticity, further supported middle-class women's sense of duty to public service. In other words, notions of women's 'complementary nature', feminine moral superiority and an evangelical interest in actively pursuing the conversion of others – ideas which might be mobilised to justify the sexual division of labour and an idealised female domesticity – could be subverted by middle-class public women to encourage the formation and expansion of women's reforming associations in the 1870 to 1914 period. So, while female involvement in civic life and public service was in some sense an extension of the feminine nurturing role, it was also a site of political participation and social activism. Female associationalism was a central site of women's public participation, and the causes of temperance, suffrage and Liberalism were significant for incorporating women into public debate and electoral politics.

A belief in the social and moral importance of the maternal and domestic was integral to middle-class women's culture, and the women's temperance movement illustrates the importance of gender and social class to the feminine public sphere. Female temperance reform responded to middle-class desires to maintain a cultural and social dominance, as evidenced by the British Women's interest in providing 'counter attractions' in order to draw working-class patrons away from public houses and into sober domestic entertainments. Female temperance reform was further influenced by middle-class women's participation in the public world of voluntary philanthropy, and the movement of women from charity to social reform cross-pollinated women's associations with similar reforming strategies. In turn, these methodologies were informed by themes of domesticity, and, for instance, female inebriate homes sought to rehabilitate female drinkers for life as domestic servants, wives and mothers. Indeed, while female temperance reformers used their public roles to promote values of female domesticity, they simultaneously created opportunities for meaningful careers outside the home, and their voluntary work might better be viewed as a professional pursuit rather than as an amateur hobby.

This study's fresh perspective on women's public lives further emphasises the breadth of the constitutional suffrage movement. Outside suffragists in the BWTASCU and the SWLF made important contributions to the women's suffrage campaign in Scotland. From 1893 and the BWTASCU's implementation of the American WCTU's 'do everything' policy, female temperance reformers in Scotland systematised their agitation for female political rights. This process was further encouraged by the ascendancy of prohibition as the international temperance community's preferred means of temperance reform. For female temperance reformers in Scotland, where local veto was the temperance community's prohibition goal, links between women's voting and prohibition gained greater meaning with the enfranchisement of female ratepayers in 1881. Local veto and women's municipal voting led many British Women to conclude that women's parliamentary enfranchisement would result in British-national legislation driven by Christian women's reforming impulses. The SWLF was a similarly important site of women's suffragism. As in the BWTASCU, the SWLF understood women's suffrage and temperance as complementary goals. Drawing on Liberal party networks in Scotland and Westminster, Liberal women vigorously pursued extra-parliamentary agitation for suffrage and temperance legislation. The SWLF was concerned to encourage women's formal political participation across electoral arenas, and Liberal women sought to broaden women's involvement in local and national democracy both as electors and representatives.

The BWTASCU and SWLF were actively pro-suffrage, organising dedicated suffrage departments and liaising with dedicated constitutional suffrage societies, yet suffrage did generate some controversy within these organisations. In the BWTASCU, the suffrage debate centred around the legitimacy of prohibition and the relationship between women's voting and legislation for prohibition. On one hand, anti-suffragists suggested that prohibition was an ineffective temperance reform strategy. On the other hand, by the late nineteenth and early twentieth centuries prohibition was increasingly understood as the only suitable course for temperance reform. Anti-suffragists and pro-suffragists alike looked abroad to support their arguments, and used the 1893 enfranchisement of women in New Zealand as evidence either that women's voting was key or irrelevant to legislation for social reform. In the SWLF, the anti-suffrage minority was treated with some ridicule in Liberal women's publications, and ultimately the SWLF stood by its founding principle to seek women's parliamentary enfranchisement. Similarly, the BWTASCU was in the vanguard of the British women's temperance by resisting internal pressure to abandon its pursuit of women's suffrage while maintaining the integrity of the organisation.

The role of the BWTASCU and SWLF in the women's suffrage campaign further reveals Scotland's divergence from English organised feminism. Walker has recently detailed the tensions over suffrage which marked the early years of the English WLF, and which ultimately led to a fracturing of the WLF in 1892.[1] The WLF had been established by Gladstonian Liberal women with networks to the Liberal inner circle. This moderate wing of the association dominated the executive from the founding of the WLF, and argued that suffrage was a non-party issue and therefore not appropriate for inclusion within the WLF's remit. The moderates came under increasing pressure from a group of progressive Liberal women associated with more radical Liberal MPs, and by 1891 the pro-suffrage progressive wing had gained enough advantage on the executive to force through a pro-suffrage amendment to the WLF constitution, which in turn led the moderates to stand down and to establish the Women's National Liberal Association.

While Walker's discussion demonstrates important parallels between Liberal women's organisations in Scotland and England, such as the affluent background of leading members, their close ties to MPs as well as the synergies between temperance and suffrage, it is similarly clear from my own research that the SWLF was a more significant site of outside suffragism than its sister organisation in England. Not only was women's right to vote incorporated as a founding objective of the SWLF, the suffrage issue was far less divisive than in England. While this issue eventually drove a wedge between moderates and progressives in England, there is no evidence of an equivalently strong opposition to the inclusion of suffrage in the SWLF's constitution, and indeed it has been shown that anti-suffragism within the SWLF was treated with derision in the Liberal women's press. The successful integration of women's suffrage into the SWLF's programme may be attributed, in part, to a more radical Liberal membership which more emphatically and uniformly understood Liberal principles of mass democratic participation as a mandate for women's enfranchisement. It has been shown that the SWLF considered Scotland and Scottish Liberals to be keepers of 'true' Liberalism, and to the extent that there was a more widespread acceptance of the expansion of the electorate among Scottish female Liberals this notion seems accurate. Walker's work highlights the importance of an adherence to Liberal democratic principles for the progressive faction in the WLF. In contrast, Bush's analysis of anti-suffrage women notes that anti-suffragists' challenges to the spread of democracy related to a 'feminine gentility' versus 'ignorant masses' mentality coupled with anti-Socialist feeling.[2] This characterisation of anti-suffrage rationale certainly reflects the arguments deployed by Lady Griselda Cheape of the St. Andrew's BWTASCU, the most vociferous anti-suffragist evident from the records of the organisations studied here. Yet it is clear from the records of the SWLF that in spite of abundant evidence for the prevalence of conservative, religiously-inspired notions of gender difference within this organisation, a more radical approach to mass democratic participation supported an overwhelming pro-suffrage majority within the SWLF.

The BWTASCU was, like the SWLF, strongly differentiated from the BWTA in England. Work on the BWTA in England shows a striking contrast with the BWTASCU. While the BWTASCU embraced an associ-ation with the American women's temperance 'Crusade' and sought to emulate Francis Willard's 'do everything' policy, the BWTA in England resisted what Barrow has identified as attempts by Lady Henry Somerset to 'Americanise' the organisation in the early 1890s.[3] Barrow argues that Somerset's efforts to introduce 'do everything' and particularly women's suffrage into the BWTA's programme was emblematic of Somerset's efforts to 'Americanise' the BWTA and drove those executive members committed to a 'single-issue' temperance organisation to split from the BWTA and to form the Women's Total Abstinence Union. While there is evidence of anti-suffragism within the BWTASCU, or at least resist-ance to including agitation for the vote in the reform programme, there is corresponding evidence that: Scoto-American connections eroded resistance to 'Americanisation' and 'do everything'; female temperance reformers in Scotland proudly celebrated their perceived connection with their American sisters; and a pro-suffrage majority successfully convinced the organisation that women's enfranchisement was vital to the temper-ance project. The comparative success of the pro-suffrage contingent in the BWTASCU versus the BWTA was further aided by the contempora-neous ascendency of prohibition and the municipal enfranchisement of women in Scotland in 1881. Barrow's analysis of resistance to 'do every-thing' in the BWTA suggests fears of 'Americanisation', antipathy towards Somerset's high-handed leadership as well as a greater commitment to moral versus legislative temperance reform played a role in the 1893 rift in the English organisation. In contrast, female temperance reformers in Scotland embraced 'do everything' and the policy's underlying approval of prohibition. The clear association between prohibition and the ability to choose representatives was further highlighted by women's newly gained access to the municipal vote and worked to politicise temperance women in Scotland as more in favour of suffrage agitation than their counterparts in England.

1870 to 1914 was a buoyant period for the formation and expansion of female associations: what then was the fate of the suffrage and temperance movements in the twentieth century?[4] With the outbreak of war, suffrage societies – militant and constitutionalist – adapted their operations to wartime concerns. The WSPU dissolved its organisation, while the NUWSS mobilised its branches in support of the war effort. In Scotland, the ENSWS sought to relieve the struggles of women in Leith whose husbands went to war, while the GWSAWS organised an exchange for voluntary workers and fund-raising schemes.[5] Women's voting rights were realised in the inter-war period; in 1918, a limited suffrage enfranchised women over thirty, and voting rights for men and women were equalised in 1928.

The BWTASCU continued its reforming work for most of the twentieth century. Immediately prior to the outbreak of war, Scottish temperance reformers celebrated the passage of the Temperance (Scotland) Act, 1913 which granted local veto powers, and prohibition remained key to the British Women's twentieth-century temperance reform ideology. Indeed, evidence from the twentieth-century minute books of the Glasgow Prayer Union suggests a certain continuity between the pre- and post-war temperance movements.[6] Between the 1930s and the 1980s the Glasgow Prayer Union's records continue to emphasise the central place of hymns and prayer for regular meetings, as well as the continued use of departments. The BWTASCU maintained its legacy of departments into the twentieth century with the most striking innovation being the development of a peace department. In the 1940s, 'fireside meetings' gained popularity in the BWTASCU. These gatherings were held in members' homes and were akin to the drawing-room meetings of the Victorian and Edwardian period. The *SWTN* was published throughout the twentieth century, but the magazine struggled to make sales. Ultimately, it seems that the British Women retained many of the cultural ideals that distinguished its pre-war ideology, and, for instance, a twentieth-century pamphlet presented the BWTASCU's aims as: to promote total abstinence; to lessen access to drink; to provide 'counter-attractions'; to reduce drink driving accidents; and to educate women to use their votes for the good of the community. In this way the British Women hoped to, 'preserve the sanctity of the home, to secure the happiness and safety of the people and especially of little children, to safeguard the weak, and to add to the spiritual and material prosperity of the nation'.[7] Thus, the

BWTASCU continued to seek the protection of the 'helpless' and to assert the centrality of domestic life.

The BWTASCU did adapt its reforming activities to changes in women's political status after 1928. Most importantly, citizenship departments were organised to deal with prohibition issues at the local and parliamentary levels. Citizenship departments inherited the work of various nineteenth-century departments – legal, legislative, municipal, parliamentary and women's suffrage – and were responsible for raising women's political awareness and harnessing the female electorate's support for prohibition. Citizenship departments were meant to turn claims of women's socially responsible voting into a reality, and these departments were ceaselessly vigilant against the political manoeuvrings of the liquor interests. For instance, in 1940 Mrs McDougall, Superintendent of the Citizenship Department reported, 'her success in having playing-cards (used at functions in City Chambers advertising liquor) changed over to those with photos of the King and Queen as the result of a protest which she made direct to the suitable quarter'.[8] So, in the mid-twentieth century the BWTASCU endeavoured to make good on promises of social reform through the women's vote. Indeed, the (limited) successes of local veto remain visible today in places such as Shawlands in south Glasgow where public houses remain a less prominent part of the urban landscape.

By the late twentieth century, the BWTASCU appears unsustainable, and from the 1980s minute books make repeated reference to the barriers of old age and illness to an effective organisation. In 1980, the Glasgow Prayer Union president reported that the celebration of the Kirkintilloch Branch's centenary was missed by many because, 'some of them [were] in different nursing homes'.[9] It seems that by the 1980s temperance reform no longer appealed to young middle-class women eager to influence their communities, and the ageing membership of the Glasgow Prayer Union disbanded in 1985, the Edinburgh Central Branch following suit in the early 1990s. The British Women did not fade silently from view, however, and when their records were deposited at The People's Story in Edinburgh visitors from around the globe came to witness the end of one of the world's longest running women's temperance organisations.

Notes

1 Walker, 'Gender, Suffrage and Party', 82–90.
2 Bush, *Women Against the Vote*, 15.
3 See Barrow, 'Teetotal Feminists' and 'British Women's Temperance Association (BWTA)', *Alcohol and Temperance in Modern History*, eds Blocker, Fahey and Tyrrell, 115.

4 For more on the wartime and inter-war suffrage campaign, see Pugh, *The March of the Women*, 284–88 and *Women and the Women's Movement*, chapter 2.
5 For more on the Scottish societies in wartime, see Leneman, *A Guid Cause*, especially chapter 12.
6 See GDU, *Minutes of Annual General Meetings* (1936–82). GCA TD 955/1/13.
7 BWTASCU, 'May We Introduce Ourselves?' (n.d.), 2. GCA TD 955/43/7.
8 GDU, *Minutes of Annual General Meetings* (1940). GCA TD 955/1/13.
9 GDU, *Minutes of Annual General Meetings* (1980). GCA TD 955/1/13.

Appendix 1

Legislation governing women's access to local government in Scotland, c.1870–1914

Legislation	Provisions	Public General Statutes Affecting Scotland
Education (Scotland) Act, 1872	Established a school board in every parish and burgh. Electors included all persons of lawful age whose names appeared on the valuation role of the burgh or parish and who were the owners or occupiers of lands or heritages with an annual value of £4.	35 & 36 Victoria, c.62
The Ballot Bill, 1872	All polls were to be taken using ballot papers and ballot boxes.	35 & 36 Victoria, c.33
Municipal Elections Amendment (Scotland) Act, 1881	Extended to Scotland the provisions of the English Act (1868) and stated that all terms importing the masculine gender included females for all purposes connected with the right to vote in the election of town councillors.	44 & 45 Victoria, c.30
Local Government (Scotland) Act, 1889	Established county councils for the administration and financial management of every county. Three year terms of office. Women not explicitly eligible to act as a county councillor or member of committee. A supplementary register was to be prepared every three years, simultaneous with the parliamentary register, including persons other than parliamentary electors entitled to vote in county council elections. Every woman, unmarried or married and not living in family with her husband and otherwise qualified as a parliamentary elector except through sex, was entitled to be placed in the supplementary register.	52 & 53 Victoria, c.50

Local Government (Scotland) Act, 1894	Allowed married women to be placed on the electoral register for county councils, municipal or parish councils if the husband and wife were not both registered with respect to the same property. Established parish councils in every parish. The parish electorate paid a special rate to be placed on the parish council register. Women, otherwise qualified for the county council were not disqualified by marriage if their property qualification was separate from their husbands'. No person was disqualified on account of sex or marriage to stand as a candidate or member of a parish council.	57 & 58 Victoria, c.58
Town Councils (Scotland) Act, 1900	Only qualified males eligible to act as councillors. All women (and peers) included as electors if they owned or occupied premises within the municipal boundary and possessed the qualifications entitling male commoners to vote for MPs and if they were not qualified with respect to the same property as their husbands.	63 & 64 Victoria, c.49
Town Councils (Scotland) Act, 1903	No new provisions for women's eligibility. Electorate extended to owners and occupiers within the municipal boundary of any burgh not returning or contributing to the return of MPs and who possessed the parliamentary franchise qualification but were on the parliamentary registration of the county only in respect of premises outwith the burgh.	3 Edward, c. 34
Qualification of Women (County and Town Councils) (Scotland) Act, 1907	Women no longer disqualified by sex or marital status from acting as a councillor in any town or burgh. Provisions and limits on women's scope for action. If a woman was elected councillor this post did not make her eligible to be elected or to act as burgh magistrate, judge in any police court, member of licensing court or court of appeal. If a woman was the chairman or provost: one, she might not act as a burgh magistrate or as a JP; and two, if she was provost then one more bailie than normal was elected to hold that post while the woman was provost.	7 Edward, c. 48
Education (Scotland) Act, 1908	Electorate was to include all those on the parish register as defined in the Local Government (Scotland) Act, 1894.	1 Edward, c. 63

County, Town and Parish Councils (Qualification) (Scotland) Act, 1914	Any person of either sex and of full age qualified to act as a county councillor if that person had resided in the county or burgh or parish for twelve months prior to the election. Women still subject to the limits set in the Qualification of Women (County and Town Councils) (Scotland) Act, 1907.	4 & 5 George, c. 39

Appendix 2

Database schema

Schema requirements

This system stores the details of female membership to several women's organisations active in late nineteenth-century Scotland. Each member may have a title, forename, initial and surname as well as a date of birth. This information is uneven, and many members may not have a complete set of these data. Members may have an address which includes street number, street, city and year(s) of known residence. While many members will not be linked to an address, members may be linked to different addresses in different years, and more than one member may share an address. Each member belongs to one or more organisations, and their membership to the same or different organisations may be spread over several – not necessarily contiguous – years. Each organisation has a name, location (e.g. Edinburgh or Glasgow), departments, committees and officers. Each organisation is likely to be active at multiple locations. The database should store the date different departments were started. Members may have roles on departments and as officers. A member may hold several positions in different organisations during the same or different years. Information on members and organisations comes from minutes books, annual reports and periodicals. These records may be stored at a museum, archive or library. Records have a title, authoring organisation, location and reference determined by the institution holding the record.

Entity-relationship diagram

The following entity-relationship diagram indicates the relationships linking the tables in the database schema.

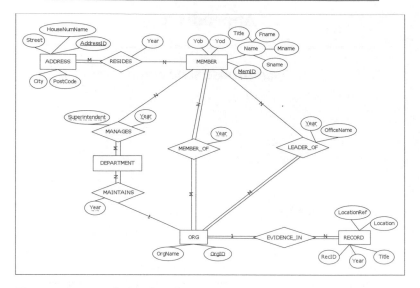

Figure 1: Entity-relationship diagram

Relational schema

Table: *A relational schema indicating the tables and their attributes as implemented in the database schema.*

ADDRESS	ADDRESSID	HOUSENUM-NAME	STREET	CITY	POSTCODE		
DEPT	DEPTID	DEPT NAME	ORGID#	START-YEAR	ENDYEAR		
DEPTLEADER	MEMID#	DEPTID#	START-YEAR	ENDYEAR			
MEMBER	MEMID	TITLE	FNAME	MNAME	SNAME	YOB	YOD
OFFICE	OFFICEID	OFFICENAME					
OFFICEHOLDER	MEMID#	OFFICEID#	ORGID#	START YEAR	END YEAR		
ORG	ORGID	ORGNAME					
ORGMEM	ORGID#	MEMID#	START YEAR	END YEAR			
ORGRECORD	RECID	ORGID#	TITLE	START YEAR	END YEAR	LOCA-TION	LOCA-TIONREF
RESIDENCE	MEMID#	STARTYEAR	ENDYEAR				

Appendix 3

Database assumptions regarding individuals' identities during data entry

Member	Organisations	Rationale
Brand, Miss	ENSWS 1907 SWLF 1899–1903	Determined records refer to same individual. Interest in suffrage: Brand listed as head of SWLF suffrage and poor law departments in 1901. Similar time frame for both sets of records.
Burton, Miss and Burton, Miss Ella	ENSWS 1870–92	Determined these are references to two different individuals.
	SWLF 1891–97	While reference to 'Miss Burton' seems a likely reference to Miss Mary Hill Burton discussed in *SLWM*, references to and 'Ella Burton' are confined to the ENSWS.
Falconer, Mrs A.	ENSWS 1907 SWLF 1908–14	Determined records refer to same individual. Name associated with Edinburgh (SWLF eastern VP). Similar time frame for both sets of records.
Fisher, Mrs and Garret Fisher, Mrs	ENSWS 1888 ENSWS 1892	Determined records refer to same individual. Name associated with Edinburgh. Inconsistent naming not uncommon in records. Similar time frame for both sets of records.
Forbes, Mrs	ENSWS 1888, 92 Edinburgh Central Branch 1889	Determined records refer to same individual. Name associated with Edinburgh. Similar time frame for both sets of records.
Hope, Miss Mary and Hope, Miss	ENSWS 1889 ENSWS 1877–78	Determined records refer to two different individuals. Suspect records differentiating between.

Member	Organisations	Rationale
Lang Todd, Mrs Ada	ENSWS 1892 SWLF 1891–1904	Determined records refer to same individual. Name associated with Edinburgh (SWLF eastern bills and literature departments). Similar time frame for both sets of records.
Lees, Miss Mary Carr	ENSWS 1907 Edinburgh Central Branch 1890–1902	Determined records refer to same individual. Name associated with Edinburgh. Similar time frame for both sets of records.
Maitland, Miss and Maitland, Miss Heriot	ENSWS 1880–81, 1885, 1887 ENSWS 1889	Determined records refer to two different individuals. Suspect records differentiating between sisters.
Matheson, Miss	ENSWS 1892, 1907	Determined records refer to same individual. Name associated with Edinburgh.
Miller Morison, Mrs Miller Morrison, Mrs	ENSWS 1889 ENSWS 1892	Determined records refer to same individual. Name associated with Edinburgh. Similar time frame for both sets of records. Spelling normalised to Morrison. Suspect 'Mrs Morrison' (ENSWS 1886) is also individual, but erred on side of caution.
Miller, Mrs John and Millar, Mrs	ENSWS 1887–89	Determined to be Mrs Grant A. Millar (d. of Duncan McLaren) m. to John Millar. Known involvement in suffrage.
Pringle, Mrs Robert and Pringle, Mrs	ENSWS 1889, 92 Edinburgh Central Branch 1888–93	Determined records refer to same individual. Name associated with Edinburgh. Similar time frame for both sets of records.
Wellstood, Mrs	ENSWS 1871–92 Edinburgh Central Branch 1897	Determined records refer to same individual. Name associated with Edinburgh. Similar time frame for both sets of records.
White Millar, Miss Grace and White Miller, Miss	ENSWS 1907 Edinburgh Central Branch 1893–1901	Determined records refer to same individual. Name associated with Edinburgh (White Miller and White Millar both listed as Edinburgh Central Branch YWCAs departments). Similar time frame for both sets of records. Spelling Deemed same person and name to 'White Miller'.

Member	Organisations	Rationale
and White Millar, Miss Grace	ENSWS 1907	Determined records refer to same individual. Name associated with Edinburgh (White Miller and White Millar both listed as Edinburgh Central Branch YWCAs departments). Similar time frame for both sets of records. Spelling Deemed same person and name to 'White Miller'.

Appendix 4

Duplicate entries of member names

Surname	Title	First name	Middle name	Organisation	Department	Start	End
Adam	Miss	Margaret		GWSAWS		1908	1911
Adam	Miss			SWLF		1909	1914
				SWLF	suffrage & local govt	1910	1911
				SWLF	suffrage & local govt	1913	1913
				SWLF	*SLW magazine*	1909	1911
				SWLF	temperance	1909	1911
				SWLF	temperance	1913	1913
Barton	Mrs			BWTASCU Glasgow		1898	1898
				BWTASCU Glasgow		1901	1901
Barton	Mrs	Helen		SWLF		1900	1913
				SWLF	education & industrialism	1905	1911
				SWLF	suffrage & local govt	1908	1909
				SWLF	general legislation	1900	1906
				SWLF	temperance	1908	1909
				SWLF	temperance	1913	1913
				SWLF	western organisation	1900	1905
Brown	Mrs			SWLF		1894	1894
Brown	Mrs			SWLF		1914	1914
Burn	Mrs			BWTASCU Edinburgh		1894	1894

Surname	Title	First name	Middle name	Organisation	Department	Start	End
Burn	Mrs	John		BWTASCU Edinburgh		1897	1903
				BWTASCU Edinburgh		1905	1905
Cook	Miss			BWTASCU Edinburgh		1897	1900
Cook	Miss	M.	E.	BWTASCU Edinburgh		1901	1901
Dalziel	Miss			SWLF		1905	1912
				SWLF	education & industrialism	1906	1911
				SWLF	suffrage & local govt	1907	1911
				SWLF	general legislation	1905	1906
				SWLF	general legislation	1910	1911
				SWLF	*SLWM*	1911	1911
Dalziel	Miss			GWSAWS		1908	1913
Ferguson	Mrs			BWTASCU Glasgow		1900	1900
Ferguson	Mrs			BWTASCU Edinburgh		1894	1901
Ferguson	Miss			BWTASCU Edinburgh		1903	1907
				BWTASCU Edinburgh	YWCAs	1903	1907
Ferguson	Miss			BWTASCU Glasgow		1909	1909
Frame	Mrs	Martha		GWSAWS		1902	1913
Frame	Mrs			SWLF		1911	1914
				SWLF	education & industrialism	1911	1911
				SWLF	education & industrialism	1913	1913
Greig	Mrs	I.	T.	GWSAWS		1902	1908
				GWSAWS	bills	1902	1902
Greig	Mrs	I.	T.	SWLF		1903	1911
				SWLF		1913	1914
				SWLF	general legislation	1903	1911
				SWLF	general legislation	1913	1913
				SWLF	temperance	1903	1911
				SWLF	temperance	1913	1913

Surname	Title	First name	Middle name	Organisation	Department	Start	End
				SWLF	eastern organisation	1906	1911
				SWLF	eastern organisation	1913	1913
Henderson	Mrs			BWTASCU Glasgow		1894	1897
				BWTASCU Glasgow		1912	1912
Henderson	Mrs	R.		BWTASCU Edinburgh		1894	1896
Latta	Mrs			GWSAWS		1908	1908
Latta	Mrs			SWLF		1910	1914
				SWLF	suffrage & local govt	1911	1911
				SWLF	suffrage & local govt	1913	1913
				SWLF	general legislation	1910	1911
				SWLF	general legislation	1913	1913
				SWLF	western organisation	1910	1911
				SWLF	western organisation	1913	1913
Laurie	Mrs			BWTASCU Glasgow		1895	1897
Laurie	Mrs			GWSAWS		1907	1914
Lewis	Mrs			BWTASCU Edinburgh		1888	1901
Lewis	Mrs	Walter		BWTASCU Edinburgh		1907	1909
				BWTASCU Edinburgh	musical	1907	1909
Lockhart	Miss	Elliot		BWTASCU Edinburgh		1890	1892
Lockhart	Miss			BWTASCU Edinburgh		1907	1914
Maitland	Miss			ENSWS		1880	1881
				ENSWS		1885	1885
				ENSWS		1887	1887
Maitland	Miss	Heriot		ENSWS		1889	1889
McLean	Miss			GWSAWS		1912	1914
McLean	Miss			BWTASCU Glasgow		1912	1913

Surname	Title	First name	Middle name	Organisation	Department	Start	End
Miller	Mrs	W.		BWTASCU Glasgow		1893	1897
				BWTASCU Glasgow	police office visiting	1893	1897
Miller	Mrs	William		BWTASCU Glasgow		1893	1902
				BWTASCU Glasgow	police office visiting	1893	1897
Mitchell	Mrs			SWLF		1903	1906
				SWLF	temperance	1903	1906
				SWLF	eastern organisation	1903	1906
Mitchell	Mrs			BWTASCU Glasgow		1912	1913
Paterson	Mrs	D.	W.	BWTASCU Edinburgh		1893	1894
Paterson	Mrs			ENSWS		1887	1887
				ENSWS		1892	1892
				ENSWS		1907	1907
Rose	Mrs	Hugh		SWLF		1894	1895
				SWLF	eastern organisation	1894	1895
Rose	Mrs			BWTASCU Edinburgh		1888	1896
Somerville	Mrs			ENSWS		1880	1880
Somerville	Mrs			BWTASCU Edinburgh		1897	1906
				BWTASCU Edinburgh	legal	1906	1906
				BWTASCU Edinburgh	municipal	1905	1906
				BWTASCU Edinburgh	prohibition on steamers	1897	1906
Steel	Mrs			SWLF		1891	1896
				SWLF		1899	1903
				SWLF	suffrage & poor law	1899	1902
				SWLF	suffrage & local govt	1903	1903
				SWLF	eastern organisation	1894	1896
				SWLF	eastern literature	1893	1896

Surname	Title	First name	Middle name	Organisation	Department	Start	End
Steel	Lady			ENSWS		1907	1907
				SWLF		1904	1906
				SWLF	education & industrialism	1906	1906
				SWLF	suffrage & local govt	1904	1906
				SWLF	eastern organisation	1905	1906
Stephen	Mrs	F.	J.	GWSAWS		1912	1913
Stephen	Mrs	Fred	J.	GWSAWS		1913	1913
Wilson	Mrs	John		BWTASCU Glasgow		1889	1902
				BWTASCU Glasgow		1913	1913
Wilson	Mrs	John		BWTASCU Edinburgh		1889	1889
				BWTASCU Edinburgh		1898	1902
				BWTASCU Edinburgh	social west	1898	1902

Appendix 5

Inter-organisational networks

Surname	Title	First name	Middle name	Organisation	Department	Start	End
Brand	Miss			ENSWS		1907	1907
				SWLF		1899	1904
				SWLF	education & industrialism	1899	1904
				SWLF	suffrage & poor law	1901	1901
Falconer	Mrs	A.		ENSWS		1907	1907
				SWLF		1892	1894
				SWLF		1906	1914
				SWLF	suffrage & local govt	1907	1911
				SWLF	suffrage & local govt	1913	1913
Forbes	Mrs			ENSWS		1888	1888
				ENSWS		1892	1892
				BWTASCU Edinburgh		1888	1889
Lang Todd	Mrs	Ada		ENSWS		1892	1892
				SWLF		1891	1894
				SWLF		1897	1904
				SWLF	education & industrialism	1899	1904
				SWLF	eastern bills	1892	1892
				SWLF	eastern organisation	1898	1899
				SWLF	eastern literature	1892	1892
				SWLF	eastern literature	1897	1899

Surname	Title	First name	Middle name	Organisation	Department	Start	End
Lees	Miss	Mary	Carr	ENSWS		1907	1907
				BWTASCU Edinburgh		1890	1902
				BWTASCU Edinburgh	decorative	1901	1902
				BWTASCU Edinburgh	municipal	1899	1899
				BWTASCU Edinburgh	rescue	1897	1897
McLaren	Dr	Agnes		ENSWS		1892	1892
				ENSWS		1880	1880
				ENSWS		1907	1907
				ENSWS		1870	1878
				GWSAWS		1902	1902
Pringle	Mrs	Robert		ENSWS		1889	1889
				ENSWS		1892	1892
				BWTASCU Edinburgh		1888	1893
Steel	Lady			ENSWS		1907	1907
				SWLF		1904	1906
				SWLF	education & industrialism	1906	1906
				SWLF	suffrage & local govt	1904	1906
				SWLF	eastern organisation	1905	1906
Wellstood	Mrs			ENSWS		1871	1871
				ENSWS		1873	1878
				ENSWS		1880	1880
				ENSWS		1882	1882
				ENSWS		1885	1885
				ENSWS		1889	1889
				ENSWS		1892	1892
				BWTASCU Edinburgh		1897	1897
White Miller	Miss	Grace		ENSWS		1907	1907
				BWTASCU Edinburgh		1893	1902
				BWTASCU Edinburgh	YWCAs	1897	1902

Surname	Title	First name	Middle name	Organisation	Department	Start	End
Wigham	Miss	Eliza		ENSWS		1870	1879
				ENSWS		1881	1882
				ENSWS		1884	1889
				ENSWS		1892	1892
				BWTASCU Edinburgh		1897	1898
				SWLF		1891	1894
				BWTASCU Edinburgh	legal	1897	1897
				SWLF	eastern bills	1892	1892
Millar	Mrs	Grant	A.	ENSWS		1887	1889
				BWTASCU Edinburgh		1897	1908
				BWTASCU Edinburgh	non-alcoholic wine	1897	1898
Lindsay	Mrs	Anna		BWTASCU Glasgow		1901	1901
				GWSAWS		1902	1902
				SWLF		1891	1894
				SWLF		1901	1902
				GNSWS		1885	1888
Aberdeen	Lady	Ishbel		BWTASCU Edinburgh		1897	1904
				GWSAWS		1902	1914
				SWLF		1891	1894
				SWLF		1903	1905
				SWLF	education & industrialism	1905	1905
Napier	Mrs	Isabel		BWTASCU Edinburgh		1898	1900
				BWTASCU Edinburgh		1906	1911
				SWLF		1893	1894
				BWTASCU Edinburgh	suffrage	1906	1911
Overton	Lady			BWTASCU Glasgow		1893	1902
				BWTASCU Glasgow		1908	1908
				BWTASCU Glasgow		1912	1913
				SWLF		1894	1894

Surname	Title	First name	Middle name	Organisation	Department	Start	End
Blackie	Miss	Marion	B.	GWSAWS		1902	1902
				SWLF		1898	1902
				SWLF		1912	1914
				SWLF	education & industrialism	1899	1902
				SWLF	general legislation	1902	1902
				SWLF	western bills	1898	1899
Wood	Mrs			GWSAWS		1903	1913
				SWLF		1903	1903
				SWLF		1905	1914
				SWLF	suffrage & local govt	1903	1903
				SWLF	suffrage & local govt	1905	1911
				SWLF	western organisation	1910	1911
				SWLF	western organisation	1913	1913
Forrester-Paton	Mrs			BWTASCU Edinburgh		1913	1914
				SWLF		1903	1914
				SWLF	*SLWM*	1903	1911
				SWLF	temperance	1903	1911
				SWLF	temperance	1913	1913
				SWLF	eastern organisation	1906	1907
Allan	Mrs			BWTASCU Edinburgh		1900	1901
				SWLF		1906	1907
				SWLF	suffrage & local govt	1906	1907
				SWLF	eastern organisation	1906	1907
Sutherland	Mrs			BWTASCU Edinburgh		1897	1907
				BWTASCU Glasgow		1892	1892
				BWTASCU Glasgow		1896	1896
				BWTASCU Glasgow		1900	1902

Surname	Title	First name	Middle name	Organisation	Department	Start	End
				BWTASCU Glasgow		1905	1906
				BWTASCU Edinburgh	rescue	1899	1903
				BWTASCU Edinburgh	rescue & habitual inebriates bill	1904	1906
				BWTASCU Edinburgh	rescue & prison	1907	1907
				BWTASCU Glasgow	legislative	1896	1896
				BWTASCU Glasgow	prison	1896	1896
Sutherland	Miss			BWTASCU Edinburgh		1898	1898
				BWTASCU Glasgow		1893	1897
				BWTASCU Glasgow	young ladies committee	1893	1897
Gemmill	Mrs			BWTASCU Edinburgh		1897	1910
				BWTASCU Edinburgh		1912	1914
				BWTASCU Glasgow		1893	1897
				BWTASCU Glasgow		1912	1913
				BWTASCU Edinburgh	counter attractions to public house	1907	1910
				BWTASCU Edinburgh	organisation & extension	1897	1905
				BWTASCU Edinburgh	social institutes	1903	1906
				BWTASCU Glasgow	work among lads	1893	1897
				BWTASCU Glasgow	young abstainer's union	1912	1913
Black	Mrs	Margaret		BWTASCU Edinburgh		1897	1902
				BWTASCU Glasgow		1894	1897
				BWTASCU Glasgow		1900	1901
				BWTASCU Edinburgh	education	1897	1902

Surname	Title	First name	Middle name	Organisation	Department	Start	End
				BWTASCU Glasgow	education	1894	1897
Harvie	Miss			BWTASCU Edinburgh		1898	1902
				BWTASCU Glasgow		1898	1898
				BWTASCU Glasgow		1900	1902
				BWTASCU Glasgow		1906	1907
				BWTASCU Glasgow		1909	1909
				BWTASCU Edinburgh	social west	1898	1902
Donaldson	Mrs			BWTASCU Edinburgh		1899	1914
				BWTASCU Glasgow		1895	1903
				BWTASCU Glasgow		1905	1908
				BWTASCU Glasgow		1911	1913
				BWTASCU Edinburgh	non-alcoholic wine	1899	1914
Lusk	Mrs			BWTASCU Edinburgh		1901	1901
				BWTASCU Glasgow		1899	1899
Gourlay	Mrs			BWTASCU Edinburgh		1904	1904
				BWTASCU Edinburgh		1906	1906
				BWTASCU Edinburgh		1908	1914
				BWTASCU Glasgow		1895	1902
				BWTASCU Glasgow		1908	1909
				BWTASCU Glasgow		1911	1913
				BWTASCU Edinburgh	infantile mortality	1908	1914
Linton	Mrs			BWTASCU Edinburgh		1911	1914
				BWTASCU Glasgow		1905	1909

Surname	Title	First name	Middle name	Organisation	Department	Start	End
				BWTASCU Glasgow		1912	1913
				BWTASCU Edinburgh	counter attractions to public house literature	1911	1914
				BWTASCU Glasgow	literature	1912	1913
Sinclair	Mrs			BWTASCU Edinburgh		1911	1914
				BWTASCU Glasgow		1882	1893
				BWTASCU Glasgow		1895	1899
				BWTASCU Glasgow		1912	1913
				BWTASCU Edinburgh	literature	1911	1914
Cameron-Corbett	Miss	Elsie		BWTASCU Edinburgh		1913	1914
				SFWSS Kilmarnock		1911	1911
				SFWSS Kilmarnock		1913	1914
Allan	Miss			BWTASCU Glasgow		1911	1912
				GWSAWS		1902	1914
Cockburn	Mrs	Janet		BWTASCU Glasgow		1881	1897
				BWTASCU Glasgow		1905	1913
				GWSAWS		1903	1914
McDairmid	Mrs			BWTASCU Glasgow		1912	1913
				GWSAWS		1902	1905
Cameron-Corbett MP	Mr			GWSAWS		1907	1914
				SFWSS Kilmarnock		1911	1912
Shakespeare	Miss			GWSAWS		1914	1914
				SFWSS Kilmarnock		1914	1914
Adam	Miss	Margaret		GWSAWS		1908	1911
				SWLF		1909	1914

Surname	Title	First name	Middle name	Organisation	Department	Start	End
				SWLF	suffrage & local govt	1910	1911
				SWLF	suffrage & local govt	1913	1913
				SWLF	*SLWM*	1909	1911
				SWLF	temperance	1909	1911
				SWLF	temperance	1913	1913
Barton	Mrs	Helen		BWTASCU Glasgow		1898	1898
				BWTASCU Glasgow		1901	1901
				SWLF		1900	1913
				SWLF	education & industrialism	1905	1911
				SWLF	suffrage & local govt	1908	1909
				SWLF	general legislation	1900	1906
				SWLF	temperance	1908	1909
				SWLF	temperance	1913	1913
				SWLF	western organisation	1900	1905
Dalziel	Miss			SWLF		1905	1912
				SWLF	education & industrialism	1906	1911
				SWLF	suffrage & local govt	1907	1911
				SWLF	general legislation	1905	1906
				SWLF	general legislation	1910	1911
				SWLF	*SLWM*	1911	1911
				GWSAWS		1908	1913
Ferguson	Mrs			BWTASCU Glasgow		1900	1900
				BWTASCU Edinburgh		1894	1901
Ferguson	Miss			BWTASCU Edinburgh		1903	1907
				BWTASCU Edinburgh	YWCAs	1903	1907
				BWTASCU Glasgow		1909	1909

Surname	Title	First name	Middle name	Organisation	Department	Start	End
Frame	Mrs	Martha		GWSAWS		1902	1913
				SWLF		1911	1914
				SWLF	education & industrialism	1911	1911
				SWLF	education & industrialism	1913	1913
Greig	Mrs	I.	T.	GWSAWS		1902	1908
				GWSAWS	bills	1902	1902
				SWLF		1903	1911
				SWLF		1913	1914
				SWLF	general legislation	1903	1911
				SWLF	general legislation	1913	1913
				SWLF	temperance	1903	1911
				SWLF	temperance	1913	1913
				SWLF	eastern organisation	1906	1911
				SWLF	eastern organisation	1913	1913
Henderson	Mrs	R.		BWTASCU Glasgow		1894	1897
				BWTASCU Glasgow		1912	1912
				BWTASCU Edinburgh		1894	1896
Latta	Mrs			GWSAWS		1908	1908
				SWLF		1910	1914
				SWLF	suffrage & local govt	1911	1911
				SWLF	suffrage & local govt	1913	1913
				SWLF	general legislation	1910	1911
				SWLF	general legislation	1913	1913
				SWLF	western organisation	1910	1911
				SWLF	western organisation	1913	1913
Laurie	Mrs			BWTASCU Glasgow		1895	1897
				GWSAWS		1907	1914

Surname	Title	First name	Middle name	Organisation	Department	Start	End
McLean	Miss			GWSAWS		1912	1914
				BWTASCU Glasgow		1912	1913
Mitchell	Mrs			SWLF		1903	1906
				SWLF	temperance	1903	1906
				SWLF	eastern organisation	1903	1906
				BWTASCU Glasgow		1912	1913
Paterson	Mrs	D.	W.	BWTASCU Edinburgh		1893	1894
				ENSWS		1887	1887
				ENSWS		1892	1892
				ENSWS		1907	1907
Rose	Mrs	Hugh		SWLF		1894	1895
				SWLF	eastern organisation	1894	1895
				BWTASCU Edinburgh		1888	1896
Somerville	Mrs			ENSWS		1880	1880
				BWTASCU Edinburgh		1897	1906
				BWTASCU Edinburgh	legal	1906	1906
				BWTASCU Edinburgh	municipal	1905	1906
				BWTASCU Edinburgh	prohibition on steamers	1897	1906
Steel	Lady			SWLF		1891	1896
				SWLF		1899	1903
				SWLF	suffrage & poor law	1899	1902
				SWLF	suffrage & local govt	1903	1903
				SWLF	eastern organisation	1894	1896
				SWLF	eastern literature	1893	1896
				ENSWS		1907	1907
				SWLF		1904	1906
				SWLF	education & industrialism	1906	1906

Surname	Title	First name	Middle name	Organisation	Department	Start	End
				SWLF	suffrage & local govt	1904	1906
				SWLF	eastern organisation	1905	1906
Wilson	Mrs	John		BWTASCU Glasgow		1889	1902
				BWTASCU Glasgow		1913	1913
				BWTASCU Edinburgh		1889	1889
				BWTASCU Edinburgh		1898	1902
				BWTASCU Edinburgh	social west	1898	1902

Appendix 6

Kinship networks

Surname	Title	First name	Middle name	Organisation	Start	End
Allan	Mrs	Alexander		BWTASCU Glasgow	1881	1897
Allan	Miss			BWTASCU Glasgow	1911	1912
				GWSAWS	1902	1914
Brown	Mrs			SFWSS Kilmarnock	1912	1914
Brown	Reverend	Henry		SFWSS Kilmarnock	1914	1914
Cameron-Corbett	Mrs			GWSAWS	1902	1914
Cameron-Corbett	Miss	Elsie		BWTASCU Edinburgh	1913	1914
				SFWSS Kilmarnock	1911	1911
				SFWSS Kilmarnock	1913	1914
Cockburn	Mrs	Janet		BWTASCU Glasgow	1881	1897
				BWTASCU Glasgow	1905	1913
				GWSAWS	1903	1914
Cockburn	Miss			BWTASCU Glasgow	1882	1897
Crawfurd	Mrs	Helen	Walker	SFWSS Kilmarnock	1911	1913
Crawfurd	Mr	Walter		SFWSS Kilmarnock	1911	1914
Denny	Colonel			GWSAWS	1902	1914
Denny	Miss			GWSAWS	1904	1905
Falconer	Miss	Agnes		SWLF	1892	1893
				SWLF	1892	1893
Falconer	Mrs	A.		ENSWS	1907	1907
				SWLF	1892	1894
				SWLF	1906	1914
				SWLF	1907	1911
				SWLF	1913	1913

Surname	Title	First name	Middle name	Organisation	Start	End
Forrester-Paton	Mrs			BWTASCU Edinburgh	1913	1914
				SWLF	1903	1914
				SWLF	1903	1911
				SWLF	1903	1911
				SWLF	1913	1913
				SWLF	1906	1907
Forrester-Paton	Miss	Catherine		BWTASCU Edinburgh	1906	1913
Latta	Mrs			GWSAWS	1908	1908
Latta	Professor			GWSAWS	1908	1914
McLaren	Mrs	Priscilla	Bright	ENSWS	1870	1889
				ENSWS	1892	1892
McLaren	Mrs	Charles		ENSWS	1888	1888
Millar (nee McLaren)	Mrs	Grant	A.	ENSWS	1887	1889
				BWTASCU Edinburgh	1897	1908
				BWTASCU Edinburgh	1897	1898
McLaren	Dr	Agnes		ENSWS	1892	1892
				ENSWS	1880	1880
				ENSWS	1907	1907
				ENSWS	1870	1878
				GWSAWS	1902	1902
Stevenson	Miss	Eliza		ENSWS	1872	1878
				ENSWS	1892	1892
Stevenson	Miss	Louisa		ENSWS	1877	1881
				ENSWS	1884	1884
				ENSWS	1886	1886
				ENSWS	1892	1892
				ENSWS	1907	1907
				ENSWS	1889	1889
Stevenson	Miss	Flora		ENSWS	1881	1881
				ENSWS	1887	1887
				ENSWS	1889	1889
Wigham	Mrs	Jane		ENSWS	1870	1878
Wigham	Miss	Eliza		ENSWS	1870	1879
				ENSWS	1881	1882

Surname	Title	First name	Middle name	Organisation	Start	End
				ENSWS	1884	1889
				ENSWS	1892	1892
				BWTASCU Edinburgh	1897	1898
				SWLF	1891	1894
				BWTASCU Edinburgh	1897	1897
				SWLF	1892	1892
Woyka	Mrs	Wilhel-mina		BWTASCU Glasgow	1881	1902
				BWTASCU Glasgow	1893	1897
				BWTASCU Glasgow	1893	1897
Woyka	Miss	Dora		BWTASCU Glasgow	1893	1897
				BWTASCU Glasgow	1908	1909
				BWTASCU Glasgow	1912	1913
				BWTASCU Glasgow	1893	1897

Bibliography

Abbreviations

BL	British Library
BWTASCU Collection	BWTASCU Collection, The People's Story, Edinburgh City Museums
GCA	Glasgow City Archives
GUA	Glasgow University Archives
GUL Sp. Coll.	Glasgow University Library Special Collections
LSF	Library of the Society of Friends
NAS	National Archives of Scotland
NLS	National Library of Scotland
WL	Women's Library

Annual reports, minute books, personal papers

BWTASCU. *Annual Reports*. 1888–1914. BWTASCU Collection.

——. *Book of the Bazaar*. 1905. BWTASCU Collection.

——. *May We Introduce Ourselves?*. N.d. GCA TD 955/43/7.

Book of Compiled Newsclippings, Glasgow. GCA TD 912.

ENSWS. *Annual Report and Annual Suffrage Meeting*. Edinburgh, 1868–78. WL 324. 6230604134 /18323; /18325; /18328; /18332; /18336; /18341; /18346; /18351; /18356; /18362.

——. *Annual Report and Annual Suffrage Meeting*. Edinburgh, 1892. City of Manchester Library M50/2/12.

——. *Annual Report*. Edinburgh: Darien Press, 1907. NLS HP 1.82.1728.

Foreign Mission Society. *Letter from William Stevenson to Margaret Blaikie*. 1898. NLS MSS 7922.

——. *Letter from William Stevenson to Margaret Blaikie*. 1902. NLS MSS 7926.

Glasgow Central Branch. *BWTASCU Minutes*. 1895–1905. GCA TD 955/15/1.

——. *BWTASCU Minutes*. 1905–12. GCA TD 955/15/2.

Glasgow District Union. *BWTA, Scottish Christian Branch, Third Annual Report and Handbook, Glasgow District Union*. Glasgow, 1905. GCA TD 955/1/1.

——. *BWTA, Scottish Christian Branch, Twelfth Annual Report and Handbook, Glasgow District Union*. Glasgow, 1914. GCA TD 955/1/1.

Glasgow Prayer Union. *Minute Books*. 1881–98, 1905, 1914. GCA TD 955/1/1.

Glasgow School Board. *Minutes of the Monthly Public Meetings of the Glasgow School Board*. 1884–1913. GCA D-ED 1.1.1.3–1.1.1.16.

GWSAWS. *Executive Committee Minute Books*. 1902–14. Mitchell Library 891036 /1/1; /1/2.

——. *Minute Books*. 1908–1914. BWTASCU Collection.

SFWSS Kilmarnock Branch. *Minute Books.* 1911–14. Ayrshire Collection, Ayrshire Archives.

SWLF *Executive Committee Minute Books* 1891–1913. Scottish Liberal Party and Scottish Liberal Democrats Collection, NLS Acc. 11765 /20; /21; /22; /23; /24; /25; /26; /27; /28.

SNSWS *Minute Books.* 1909–1914. Shetland Archives, D.1/32.

Papers of Archibald Cameron Corbett. *Album of Newsclippings.* GUA DC/26/19.

——. *Bundle of Letters.* GUA DC/26/41.

——. *Elsie's Papers.* GUA DC/26/12.

Public General Statutes Affecting Scotland. *Ballot Bill, 1872.* 35 & 36 Victoria, c. 33.

——. *County, Town and Parish Councils (Qualification) (Scotland) Act, 1914.* 4 & 5 George, c. 39.

——. *Education (Scotland) Act, 1872.* 35 & 36 Victoria, c. 62.

——. *Education (Scotland) Act, 1908.* 1 & 2 Edward, c. 63.

——. *Habitual Drunkards Act, 1879.* 42 & 43 Victoria, c. 19.

——. *Inebriates Act, 1888.* 51 & 52 Victoria, c. 19.

——. *Inebriates Act, 1898.* 61 & 62 Victoria, c. 60.

——. *Inebriates Act, 1900.* 63 & 64 Victoria, c. 28.

——. *Local Government (Scotland) Act, 1889.* 52 & 53 Victoria, c. 50.

——. *Local Government (Scotland) Act, 1894.* 57 & 58 Victoria, c. 58.

——. *Municipal Elections Amendment (Scotland) Act, 1881.* 44 & 45 Victoria, c. 30.

——. *Publican's Certificate (Scotland) Act, 1876.* 39 & 40 Victoria, c. 36.

——. *Qualification of Women (County and Town Councils) (Scotland) Act, 1907.* 7 & 8 Edward, c. 48.

——. *Temperance (Scotland) Act, 1913.* 3 & 4 George, c. 33.

——. *Town Councils (Scotland) Act, 1900.* 63 & 64 Victoria, c. 49.

——. *Town Councils (Scotland) Act, 1903.* 3 & 4 Edward, c. 34.

Robertson, Christina E. *BWTASCU: Its Origins and Progress.* BWTASCU, 1908. BWTASCU Collection.

Society of Friends. *Dictionary of Quaker Biography.* LSF.

——. *Digest of Births, Marriages and Burials in Scotland.* NAS CH 10/1/64.

Stevenson, Louisa. 'Women's Status in the Poor Law'. In *The International Congress of Women of 1899 Volume V: Women in Politics,* ed. Lady Ishbel Countess of Aberdeen, 64–70. London: T. Fisher Unwin, 1900. Mitchell Library.

Stewart, Eliza. *The Crusader in Great Britain, or, The History of the Origins and Organization of the British Women's Temperance Association.* Springfield, OH: The New Era Company, 1893. WL 178.10942 STE.

Newspapers and periodicals

Annual Monitor
The Ladies' Friend
League

Monthly Record
SLWM
Scottish Temperance Annual
Scottish Temperance Review
SWTN
WSJ

Books and articles

Abrams, Lynn. *The Orphan Country: Children of Scotland's Broken Homes from 1845 to the Present Day*. Edinburgh: John Donald Publishers Ltd., 1998.

Armstrong, Norma. *Edinburgh as it Was Volume II: The People of Edinburgh*. Hendon Hill, Lancashire: Hendon Publishing Company Limited, 1977. NLS 6.2551.

Aspinwall, Bernard. *Portable Utopia: Glasgow and the United States 1820–1920*. Aberdeen: Aberdeen University Press, 1984.

Bailey, Peter. *Leisure and Class in Victorian England: Rational Recreation and the Contest for Control, 1830–1885*. London: Methuen & Co. Ltd., 1978. Reprint, London: Methuen & Co. Ltd., 1987.

Banks, Olive. *Becoming a Feminist: The Social Origins of 'First Wave' Feminism*. Brighton: Wheatsheaf Books, 1986.

——. *Faces of Feminism: A Study of Feminism as a Social Movement*. Oxford: Martin Robertson, 1981.

Barrow, Margaret. 'Teetotal Feminists: Temperance Leadership and the Campaign for Women's Suffrage'. In *A Suffrage Reader: Charting Directions in British Suffrage History*, eds Claire Eustance, Joan Ryan and Laura Ugolini, 69–89. London: Leicester University Press, 2000.

Barrows, Susanna and Robin Room eds. *Drinking: Behaviour and Belief in Modern History*. Oxford: University of California Press, 1991.

Belchem, John and Nick Hardy. 'Second Metropolis: The Middle Class in Early Victorian Liverpool'. In *The Making of the British Middle Class?: Studies of Regional and Cultural Diversity since the Eighteenth Century*, eds Alan Kidd and David Nicholls, 58–71. Thrupp, Gloucestershire: Sutton Publishing Limited, 1998.

Blocker, Jack S. Jr. *American Temperance Movements: Cycles of Reform*. Boston: Twayne Publishers, 1989.

——. *'Give to the winds thy fears': The Women's Temperance Crusade, 1873–1874*. London: Greenwood Press, 1985.

——. *Retreat from Reform: The Prohibition Movement in the United States 1890–1913*. London: Greenwood Press, 1976.

Bordin, Ruth. *Woman and Temperance: The Quest for Power and Liberty, 1873–1900*. Philadelphia: Temple University Press, 1981.

Boussahba-Bravard, Myriam. 'Introduction'. In *Suffrage Outside Suffragism: Women's Vote in Britain 1880–1914*, ed. Myriam Boussahba-Bravard, 1–32. Basingstoke: Palgrave Macmillan, 2007.

Boydston, Jeanne. *Home and Work: Housework, Wages, and the Ideology of Labor in the Early Republic*. Oxford: Oxford University Press, 1990.

Bradley, Katherine. "'If the vote is good for Jack; why not for Jill?'": The Women's Suffrage Movement in Cornwall, 1870–1914'. Publication of the Institute of Cornish Studies, ed. Philip Payton, *Cornish Studies*, no. 8. Exeter: University of Exeter Press, 2000: 127–46.

Branca, Patricia. *Silent Sisterhood: Middle Class Women in the Victorian Home*. London: Croom Helm, 1975.

Brock, Jeanette M. *The Mobile Scot: A Study of Emigration and Migration 1861–1911*. Edinburgh: John Donald Publishers Ltd., 1999.

Brown, Callum. 'Popular Culture and the Continuing Struggle for Rational Recreation'. In *Scotland in the 20th Century*, eds T. M. Devine and R. J. Finlay, 210–29. Edinburgh: Edinburgh University Press, 1997.

——. *Religion and Society in Scotland since 1707*. Edinburgh: Edinburgh University Press, 1997.

Burton, Antoinette. 'Rules of Thumb: British History and "Imperial Culture" in Nineteenth- and Twentieth-Century Britain'. *Women's History Review* 3, no. 4 (1994): 483–501.

——. 'The White Woman's Burden: British Feminists and "the Indian Woman", 1865–1915'. In *Western Women and Imperialism: Complicity and Resistance*, eds Nupur Chaudhuri and Margaret Strobel, 137–57. Indianapolis: Indiana University Press, 1992.

Bush, Julia. *Edwardian Ladies and Imperial Power*. London: Leicester University Press, 2000.

——. *Women Against the Vote: Female Anti-Suffragism in Britain*. Oxford: Oxford University Press, 2007.

Caine, Barbara. *English Feminism 1780–1980*. Oxford: Oxford University Press, 1997.

Cannadine, David. *Class in Britain*. London: Yale University Press, 1998.

——. 'Victorian Cities: How Different?'. *Social History* 4 (1977): 457–82.

Checkland, Olive. *Philanthropy in Victorian Scotland: Social Welfare and the Voluntary Principle*. Edinburgh: John Donald Publishers, 1980.

Clark, Anna. *The Struggle for the Breeches: Gender and the Making of the British Working Class*. London: University of California Press, 1995.

Cowman, Krista and Louise A. Jackson eds. 'Middle-Class Women and Professional Identity'. *Women's History Review* 14, no. 2 (2005).

Daggers, Jenny. 'The Victorian Female Civilising Mission and Women's Aspirations towards Priesthood in the Church of England', *Women's History Review* 10, no. 4 (2001): 651–70.

Dalziel, Raewyn. 'Presenting the Enfranchisement of New Zealand Women Abroad'. In *Suffrage and Beyond: International Feminist Perspectives*, eds Melanie Nolan and Caroline Daley, 42–64. Auckland: Auckland University Press, 1994.

Daunton, Martin ed. *Charity, Self-Interest and Welfare in the English Past*. London: UCL Press, 1996.

Dingle, A. E. *The Campaign for Prohibition in Victorian England: The United Kingdom Alliance 1872–1895*. London: Croom Helm Ltd., 1980.

Doctor Agnes McLaren (1937–1913) Physician Convert Pioneer. 1953. NLS HP 1.86. 2696.

Dodd, Kathryn. 'Cultural Politics and Women's Historical Writing: The Case of Ray Strachey's *The Cause*'. *Women's Studies International Forum* 13, no. ½ (1990): 127–37.

Doern, Kirstin. '"Equal Questions": The "Woman Question" and the "Drink Question" in the Writings of Clara Lucas Balfour'. In *Women, Religion and Feminism in Britain 1750–1900*, ed. Sue Morgan, 159–75. Basingstoke: Palgrave Macmillan, 2000.

Duthie, John L. 'Philanthropy and Evangelism among Aberdeen Seamen, 1814–1924'. *The Scottish Historical Review* 63, no. 2 (1984): 155–73.

Dyer, Michael. *Men of Property and Intelligence: The Scottish Electoral System prior to 1884 Vol. 1*. Aberdeen: Scottish Cultural Press, 1996.

——. *Capable Citizens and Improvident Democrats: The Scottish Electoral System 1884–1929 Vol. 2*. Aberdeen: Scottish Cultural Press, 1996.

Epstein, Barbara Leslie. *The Politics of Domesticity: Women, Evangelism, and Temperance in Nineteenth Century America*. Middletown, CT: Weslyan University Press, 1981.

Eustance, Claire. 'Meanings of Militancy: The Ideas and Practice of Political Resistance in the Women's Freedom League, 1907–14'. In *The Women's Suffrage Movement: New Feminist Perspectives*, eds Maroula Joannou and June Purvis, 51–64. Manchester: Manchester University Press, 1998.

Eustance, Claire, Laura Ugolini and Joan Ryan eds. *A Suffrage Reader: Charting Directions in British Suffrage History*. London: Leicester University Press, 2000.

Evans, Neil. 'Urbanisation, Elite Attitudes and Philanthropy: Cardiff, 1850–1914'. *International Review of Social History* 27 (1982): 290–323.

Evans, Richard J. *The Feminists: Women's Emancipation Movements in Europe, America and Australasia 1840–1920*. London: Croom Helm, 1977.

Fraser, W. Hamish and Irene Maver eds. *Glasgow Volume II: 1830 to 1912*. Manchester: Manchester University Press, 1996.

——. *Scottish Popular Politics: From Radicalism to Labour*. Edinburgh: Polygon, 2000.

Fry, Michael. *The Scottish Empire*. East Lothian: Tuckwell Press, 2001.

Fulford, Roger. *Votes for Women: The Story of a Struggle*. London: Faber and Faber, 1957. Reprint, London: Readers Union, 1958.

Garner, Les. *Stepping Stones to Women's Liberty: Feminist Ideas in the Women's Suffrage Movement 1900–1918*. London: Heinemann Educational Books, 1984.

Giele, Janet Zollinger. *Two Paths to Women's Equality: Temperance, Suffrage, and the Origins of Modern Feminism*. London: Twayne Publishers, 1995.

Giles, Judy. *Women, Identity and Private Life in Britain, 1900–50*. Basingstoke: Macmillan, 1995.

Gleadle, Kathryn. *The Early Feminists: Radical Unitarians and the Emergence of the Women's Rights Movement, 1831–51.* Basingstoke: Macmillan, 1995.

Gordon, Eleanor and Gwyneth Nair. 'The Economic Role of Middle-Class Women in Victorian Glasgow'. *Women's History Review* 9, no. 4 (2000): 791–814.

——. *Public Lives: Women, Family, and Society in Victorian Britain.* London: Yale University Press, 2003.

Gorsky, Martin. *Patterns of Philanthropy: Charity and Society in Nineteenth-Century Bristol.* Woodbridge, Suffolk: Royal Historical Society and The Boydell Press, 1999.

Gray, Robert. 'The Platform and the Pulpit: Cultural Networks and Civic Identities in Industrial Towns, c.1850–70'. In *The Making of the British Middle Class?: Studies of Regional and Cultural Diversity since the Eighteenth Century*, eds Alan Kidd and David Nicholls, 130–47. Thrupp, Gloucestershire: Sutton Publishing Limited, 1998.

Grimshaw, Patricia. *Women's Suffrage in New Zealand.* Auckland: Auckland University Press, 1987.

Gunn, Simon. 'The Ministry, the Middle Class and the "Civilising Mission" in Manchester, 1850–80'. *Social History* 21, no. 1 (1996): 22–36.

——. *The Public Culture of the Victorian Middle Class: Ritual and Authority and the English Industrial City 1840–1914.* Manchester: Manchester University Press, 2000.

Gusfield, Joseph. 'Benevolent Repression: Popular Culture, Social Structure, and the Control of Drinking'. In *Drinking: Behavior and Belief in Modern History*, eds Susanna Barrows and Robin Room, 399–424. Oxford: University of California Press, 1991.

——. *Symbolic Crusade: Status Politics and the American Temperance Movement.* London: University of Illinois Press, 1970.

Haggis, Jane. '"A heart that has felt the love of God and longs for others to know it": Conventions of Gender, Tensions of Self and Constructions of Difference in Offering to be a Lady Missionary'. *Women's History Review* 7, no. 2 (1998): 171–92.

Hall, Catherine and Leonore Davidoff. *Family Fortunes: Men and Women of the English Middle Class, 1780–1850.* London: Unwin Hyman Ltd., 1987.

Hannam, June. '"I had not been to London": Women's Suffrage – A View from the Regions'. In *Votes for Women*, eds June Purvis and Sandra Stanley Holton, 226–45. London: Routledge, 2000.

Harper, Marjory. *Emigration from North-East Scotland Volume One: Willing Exiles.* Aberdeen: Aberdeen University Press, 1988.

Harrison, Brian. *Drink and the Victorians: The Temperance Question in England 1815–1872.* London: Faber and Faber Limited, 1971.

——. *Separate Spheres: The Opposition to Women's Suffrage in Britain.* London: Croom Helm, 1978.

Harrison, Patricia Greenwood. *Connecting Links: The British and American Woman Suffrage Movements, 1900–1914.* London: Greenwood Press, 2000.

Heilmann, Ann ed. 'Words as Deeds: Literary and Historical Perspectives on

Women's Suffrage'. *Women's History Review* 11, no. 4 (2002); and 12, no. 1 (2003).

Hirshfield, Claire. 'Fractured Faith: Liberal Party Women and the Suffrage Issue in Britain, 1892–1914'. *Gender & History* 2, no. 2 (1990): 174–97.

Hollis, Patricia. *Ladies Elect: Women in English Local Government 1865–1914.* Oxford: Clarendon Press, 1987.

——. 'Women in Council: Separate Spheres, Public Space'. In *Equal or Different: Women's Politics 1800–1914*, ed. Jane Rendall, 192–213. Oxford: Basil Blackwell Ltd., 1987.

Holton, Sandra Stanley. 'British Freewomen: National Identity, Constitutionalism and Languages of Race in Early Suffrage Histories'. In *Radical Femininity: Women's Self-Representation in the Public Sphere*, ed. Eileen Janes Yeo, 149–71. Manchester: Manchester University Press, 1998.

——. *Feminism and Democracy: Women's Suffrage and Reform Politics in Britain 1900–1918.* Cambridge: Cambridge University Press, 1986.

——. 'Kinship and Friendship: Quaker Women's Networks and the Women's Movement'. *Women's History Review* 14, no. 3&4 (2005): 365–84.

——. 'The Making of Suffrage History'. In *Votes for Women*, eds June Purvis and Sandra Stanley Holton, 13–33. London: Routledge, 2000.

——. 'The Suffragist and the "Average Woman"'. *Women's History Review* 1, no. 1 (1992): 9–24.

Holton, Sandra Stanley and June Purvis eds. *Votes for Women.* London: Routledge, 2000.

Innes, Sue and Jane Rendall. 'Women, Gender and Politics'. In *Gender in Scottish History Since 1700*, eds Lynn Abrams, Eleanor Gordon, Deborah Simonton and Eileen Janes Yeo, 43–83. Edinburgh: Edinburgh University Press, 2006.

Isettes, Charles A. 'A Social Profile of the Women's Temperance Crusade: Hillsboro, Ohio'. In *Alcohol, Reform and Society: The Liquor Issue in Social Context*, ed. Jack S. Blocker Jr., 101–10. London: Greenwood Press, 1979.

Isichei, Elizabeth. *Victorian Quakers.* London: Oxford University Press, 1970.

James, Mark. 'Temperance'. In *The Oxford Companion to Scottish History*, ed. Michael Lynch, 595–96. Oxford: Oxford University Press, 2001.

Joannou, Maroula and June Purvis eds. *The Women's Suffrage Movement: New Feminist Perspectives.* Manchester: Manchester University Press, 1998.

John, Angela V. and Claire Eustance eds. *The Men's Share?: Masculinities, Male Support and Women's Suffrage in Britain, 1890–1920.* London: Routledge, 1997.

Jones, Colin. 'Some Recent Trends in the History of Charity'. In *Charity, Self-Interest and Welfare in the English Past*, ed. Martin Daunton, 51–64. London: UCL Press, 1996.

Jones, Gareth Stedman. *Outcast London: A Study in the Relationship between Classes in Victorian Society.* Oxford: Oxford University Press, 1971; Penguin Books, 1984.

Jordan, Ellen. *The Women's Movement and Women's Employment in Nineteenth Century Britain.* London: Routledge, 1999.

Kennedy, Thomas C. *British Quakerism 1860–1920: The Transformation of a Religious Community*. Oxford: Oxford University Press, 2001.

Kent, Susan Kingsley. *Sex and Suffrage in Britain 1860–1914*. Princeton: Princeton University Press, 1987. Reprint, London: Routledge, 1990.

Kidd, Alan. 'Philanthropy and the "Social History Paradigm"'. *Social History* 21, no. 4 (1996): 180–92.

——. *State, Society and the Poor in Nineteenth-Century England*. London: Macmillan Press Ltd., 1999.

Kidd, Alan and David Nicholls eds. *Gender, Culture and Consumerism: Middle-Class Identity in Britain 1800–1940*. Manchester: Manchester University Press, 1999.

——. *The Making of the British Middle Class? Studies of Regional and Cultural Diversity since the Eighteenth Century*. Thrupp, Gloucestershire: Sutton Publishing Limited, 1998.

Kinchin, Juliet. 'The Drawing Room'. In *The Scottish Home*, ed. Annette Carruthers, 155–80. Edinburgh: National Museums of Scotland Publishing, 1996.

King, Elspeth. *Scotland Sober and Free: The Temperance Movement 1829–1979*. Glasgow: Glasgow Museums and Art Galleries, 1979.

——. 'The Scottish Women's Suffrage Movement'. In *Out of Bounds: Women in Scottish Society, 1800–1945*, eds Esther Breitenbach and Eleanor Gordon, 121–50. Edinburgh: Edinburgh University Press, 1992.

Klein, Lawrence E. 'Gender and the Public / Private Distinction in the Eighteenth Century: Some Questions about Evidence and Analytic Procedure'. *Eighteenth Century Studies* 29, no. 1 (1995): 97–109.

Kneale, James. 'The Place of Drink: Temperance and the Public, 1856–1914'. *Social & Cultural Geography* 2, no. 1 (2001): 43–59.

Koven, Seth. 'Borderlands: Women, Voluntary Action and Child Welfare in Britain 1840 to 1914'. In *Mothers of a New World: Maternalist Politics and the Creation of Welfare States*, eds Seth Koven and Sonya Michel, 94–135. London: Routledge, 1993.

Kraditor, Aileen S. *The Ideas of the Women's Suffrage Movement, 1890–1920*. London: Columbia Press, 1967.

Landes, Joan B. 'The Public and the Private Sphere: A Feminist Reconsideration'. In *Feminists Read Habermas: Gendering the Subject of Discourse*, ed. Johanna Meehan, 91–116. London: Routledge, 1995.

Lambert, W. R. *Drink and Sobriety in Victorian Wales c.1820–c.1895*. Cardiff: University of Wales Press, 1983.

Leneman, Leah. 'Dundee and the Women's Suffrage Movement: 1907–1914'. In *The Remaking of Juteopolis: Dundee circa 1891–1991*, ed. Christopher Whatley, 80–95. Dundee: Abertay Historical Society, 1992.

——. *A Guid Cause: The Women's Suffrage Movement in Scotland Revised Edition*. Edinburgh: Mercat Press, 1995.

——. 'A Truly National Movement: The View from Outside London'. In *The Women's Suffrage Movement: New Feminist Perspectives*, eds Maroula Joannou and June Purvis, 37–50. Manchester: Manchester University Press, 1998.

——. 'The Scottish Churches and "Votes for Women"'. *Records of the Scottish Church History Society* 24, no. 2 (1991): 237–62.

Levine, Philippa. *Victorian Feminists 1850–1900*. London: Hutchison Education, 1987.

Lewis, Jane. *Women in England 1870–1950: Sexual Division and Social Change*. Sussex: Wheatsheaf Books, 1984.

Liddington, Jill and Jill Norris. *One Hand Tied Behind Us: The Rise of the Women's Suffrage Movement*. London: Virago Press, 1978.

Lister, Ruth. *Citizenship: Feminist Perspectives*. Basingstoke: Macmillan, 1997.

Lloyd-Morgan, Ceridwen. 'From Temperance to Suffrage?'. In *Our Mothers' Land: Chapters in Welsh Women's History, 1830–1939*, ed. Angela V. John, 135–58. Cardiff: University of Wales Press, 1991.

MacDonald, Lesley A. Orr. *A Unique and Glorious Mission: Women and Presbyterianism in Scotland 1830–1930*. Edinburgh: John Donald Publishers Ltd., 2000.

Mahood, Linda. *The Magdalenes: Prostitution in the Nineteenth Century*. London: Routledge, 1990.

——. *Policing Gender, Class and Family Britain, 1850–1940*. London: UCL Press, 1995.

Malcolm, Elizabeth. 'Ireland'. In *Alcohol and Temperance in Modern History: An International Encyclopedia*, eds Jack S. Blocker, Jr., David M. Fahey and Ian R. Tyrrell, 321–24. Oxford: ABC-CLIO, 2003.

——. 'Ireland Sober, Ireland Free': Drink and Temperance in Nineteenth-Century Ireland*. Syracuse: Syracuse University Press, 1986.

Marshall, Susan E. 'In Defense of Separate Spheres: Class and Status Politics in the Anti-Suffrage Movement'. *Social Forces* 65, no. 2 (1986): 327–51.

Martin, Jane. *Women and the Politics of Schooling in Victorian and Edwardian England*. London: Leicester University Press, 1999.

Martin, Moira. 'Single Women and Philanthropy: A Case Study of Women's Associational Life in Bristol, 1880–1914'. *Women's History Review* 17, no. 3 (2008): 419–34.

Masson, Ursula. '"Political conditions in Wales are quite different …": Party Politics and Votes for Women in Wales, 1912–15'. *Women's History Review* 9, no. 2 (2000): 369–88.

Mayhall, Laura E. Nym. 'Creating the "Suffragette Spirit": British Feminism and the Historical Imagination'. *Women's History Review* 4, no. 3 (1995): 319–44.

——. *The Militant Suffrage Movement: Citizenship and Resistance in Britain, 1860–1930*. Oxford: Oxford University Press, 2003.

Mayhall, Laura E. Nym, Philippa Levine and Ian Christopher Fletcher eds. *Women's Suffrage in the British Empire: Citizenship, Nation and Race*. London: Routledge, 2000.

McAlpine, Joan C. *The Lady of Claremont House: Isabella Elder Pioneer and Philanthropist*. Glendaruel: Argyll Publishing, 1997.

McCarthy, Kathleen D. 'Parallel Power Structures: Women and the Voluntary Sphere'. In *Lady Bountiful Revisited: Women, Philanthropy and Power*, ed.

Kathleen D. McCarthy, 1–34. London: Rutgers University Press, 1990.

McClintock, Anne. *Imperial Leather: Race, Gender and Sexuality in the Colonial Contest*. London: Routledge, 1995.

McLaren, Miss E. T. *Recollections of the Public Work and Home Life of Louisa and Flora Stevenson*. Edinburgh: Andrew Elliot, 1914. NLS NF.1181.e.36.

McLaughlin, Patrick M. 'Inebriate Reformatories in Scotland: An Institutional History'. In *Drinking: Behavior and Belief in Modern History*, eds Susanna Barrows and Robin Room, 287–314. Oxford: Oxford University Press, 1991.

McLeod, Hugh. *Class and Religion in the Late Victorian City*. London: Croom Helm, 1974.

McPhee, Carol and Ann FitzGerald eds. *The Non-Violent Militant: Selected Writings of Teresa Billington-Greig*. London: Routledge & Kegan Paul, 1987.

Midgley, Clare. 'Anti-Slavery and the Roots of "Imperial Feminism"'. In *Gender and Imperialism*, ed. Clare Midgley, 161–79. Manchester: Manchester University Press, 1998.

——. 'Female Emancipation in an Imperial Frame: English Women and the Campaign against Sati (Widow-Burning) in India, 1813–30'. *Women's History Review* 9, no. 1 (2000): 95–121.

——. *Feminism and Empire: Women Activists in Imperial Britain, 1790–1865*. Abingdon, Oxon: Routledge, 2007.

——. *Women against Slavery: The British Campaigns, 1780–1870*. London: Routledge, 1992.

Moore, Lindy. 'Feminists and Femininity: A Case Study of WSPU Propaganda and Local Response at a Scottish By-Election'. *Women's Studies International Forum* 5, no. 6 (1982): 675–84.

Morgan, David. *Suffragists and Liberals: The Politics of Woman Suffrage in England*. Oxford: Basil Blackwell, 1975.

Morgan, Simon. '"A sort of land debatable": Female Influence, Civic Virtue and Middle-Class Identity, c.1830–c.1860'. *Women's History Review* 13, no. 2 (2004): 195–6.

——. *A Victorian Woman's Place: Public Culture in the Nineteenth Century*. London: Tauris Academic Studies, 2007.

Morgan, Sue. 'Faith, Sex and Purity: The Religio-Feminist Theory of Ellice Hopkins'. *Women's History Review* 9, no. 1 (2000): 13–34.

——. *A Passion for Purity: Ellice Hopkins and the Politics of Gender in the Late Victorian Church*. Bristol: Centre for Comparative Studies in Religion and Gender, 1999.

Morton, Graeme. *Unionist Nationalism: Governing Urban Scotland 1830–60*. East Linton: Tuckwell, c1999.

Murdock, Catherine Gilbert. *Domesticating Drink: Women, Men, and Alcohol in America 1870–1940*. London: Johns Hopkins University Press, 1998.

Murphy, Cliona. 'The Religious Context of the Women's Suffrage Campaign in Ireland'. *Women's History Review* 6, no. 4 (1997): 549–65.

——. *The Women's Suffrage Movement and Irish Society in the Early Twentieth Century*. London: Harvester Wheatsheaf, 1989.

Nenadic, Stana. 'The Victorian Middle Classes'. In *Glasgow Volume II: 1830 to 1912*, eds W. Hamish Fraser and Irene Maver, 265–99. Manchester: Manchester University Press, 1996.

Nolan, Melanie and Caroline Daley eds. *Suffrage and Beyond: International Feminist Perspectives*. Auckland: Auckland University Press, 1994.

Oldfield, Audrey. *Woman Suffrage in Australia: A Gift or a Struggle?* Cambridge: Cambridge University Press, 1992.

O'Neill, William. *Everyone Was Brave: The Rise and Fall of Feminism in America*. Chicago: Quadrangle Press, 1969.

——. *The Woman Movement: Feminism in the United States and England*. London: George Allan and Unwin Ltd., 1969.

Pankhurst, Christabel. *Unshackled: The Story of How We Won the Vote*. London: Hutchinson & Co. Ltd., 1959.

Pankhurst, E. Sylvia. *The Suffragette Movement: An Intimate Account of Persons and Ideals*. London: Longman Group, 1931. Reprint, London: Virago Press, 1988.

Parker, Alison M. '"Hearts uplifted and minds refreshed": The Woman's Christian Temperance Union and the Production of Pure Culture in the United States, 1880–1930'. *Journal of Women's History* 2, no. 2 (1999): 135–58.

Pateman, Carole. *The Disorder of Women: Democracy, Feminism and Political Theory*. Cambridge: Polity Press, 1989.

Pederson, Sarah. 'The Appearance of Women's Politics in the Correspondence Pages of Aberdeen Newspapers, 1900–14'. *Women's History Review* 11, no. 4 (2002): 657–74.

Perkin, Harold. *The Rise of Professional Society: England Since 1880*. London; New York: Routledge, 1989.

Prochaska, F. K. *Women and Philanthropy in Nineteenth Century England*. Oxford: Oxford University Press, 1980.

Pugh, Martin. *The March of the Women: A Revisionist Analysis of the Campaign for Women's Suffrage, 1866–1914*. Oxford: Oxford University Press, 2000.

——. *Women and the Women's Movement in Britain 1914–1999 Second Edition*. London: MacMillan Press Ltd, 2000.

Raeburn, Antonia. *The Militant Suffragettes*. Newton Abbot: Victorian (& Modern History) Book Club, 1974.

——. *The Suffragette View*. Newton Abbot: David & Charles Ltd., 1976.

Rendall, Jane. 'Citizenship, Culture and Civilisation: The Languages of British Suffragists, 1866–1874'. In *Suffrage and Beyond: International Feminist Perspectives*, eds Melanie Nolan and Caroline Daley, 127–50. Auckland: Auckland University Press, 1994.

——. 'The Citizenship of Women and the Reform Act of 1867'. In *Defining the Victorian Nation: Class, Race, Gender and the British Reform Act of 1867*, eds Catherine Hall, Keith McClelland and Jane Rendall, 119–78. Cambridge: Cambridge University Press, 2000.

——. *The Origins of Modern Feminism: Women in Britain, France and the United States, 1780–1860*. London: Macmillan Press Ltd., 1985.

——. 'Women and the Public Sphere'. *Gender & History* 11, no. 3 (1999): 475–88.

Rose, Michael E. 'Culture, Philanthropy and the Manchester Middle Classes'. In *City, Class and Culture: Studies of Social Policy and Cultural Production in Victorian Manchester*, eds Alan Kidd and K. W. Roberts, 103–17. Manchester: Manchester University Press, 1985.

Rosen, Andrew. *Rise Up, Women!: The Militant Campaign of the Women's Social and Political Union 1903–1914*. London: Routledge & Kegan Paul, 1974.

Ross, Ellen. 'Good and Bad Mothers: Lady Philanthropists and London Housewives before the First World War'. In *Lady Bountiful Revisited: Women, Philanthropy, and Power*, ed. Kathleen D. McCarthy, 174–98. London: Rutgers University Press, 1990.

——. *Love and Toil: Motherhood in Outcast London, 1870–1918*. Oxford: Oxford University Press, 1993.

Rowbotham, Judith. '"Soldiers of Christ"? Images of Female Missionaries in Late Nineteenth-Century Britain: Issues of Heroism and Martyrdom'. *Gender & History* 12, no. 1 (2000): 82–106.

Rowbotham, Sheila. *Hidden from History: 300 Years of Women's Oppression and the Fight Against It*. London: Pluto Press Ltd., 1973.

Rubinstein, David. *Before the Suffragettes: Women's Emancipation in the 1890s*. Brighton: The Harvester Press, 1986.

Ryan, Mary P. *Women in Public: Between Banners and Ballots, 1825–1880*. London: Johns Hopkins University Press, 1992.

Shiman, Lilian Lewis. '"Changes Are Dangerous": Women and Temperance in Victorian England'. In *Religion in the Lives of English Women, 1760–1930*, ed. Gail Malmgreen, 193–215. London; Sydney: Croom Helm, 1986.

——. *Crusade Against Drink in Victorian England*. Basingstoke: Macmillan, 1988.

Simonton, Deborah. *European Women's Work: 1700 to the Present*. London: Routledge, 1998.

Sinclair, Andrew. *Prohibition: The Era of Excess*. London: Faber and Faber, 1962.

Smith, Bonnie G. *Ladies of the Leisure Class: The Bourgeoises of Northern France in the Nineteenth Century*. Princeton: Princeton University Press, 1981.

Smith, Charles J. *Historic South Edinburgh Volume 1*. Haddington: Charles Skilton Ltd., 1978. NLS H3.201.1889.

——. *Historic South Edinburgh Volume 3*. Haddington: Charles Skilton Ltd., 1986. NLS H3.201.1889.

Smith-Rosenburg, Carroll. 'The Female World of Love and Ritual: Relations between Women in Nineteenth Century America'. *Signs* 1 (1975): 1–29.

Smitley, Megan. 'Feminist Anglo-Saxonism?: The Representation of "Scotch" Women in the English Women's Press in the Late Nineteenth Century'. *Cultural and Social History* 4, no. 3 (Sept 2007): 341–59.

——. '"Inebriates", "Heathens", Templars and Suffragists: Scotland and Imperial Feminism, 1870–1914'. *Women's History Review* 11, no. 3 (2002): 455–80.

——. 'Mary White'. In *Alcohol and Temperance in Modern History: An International Encyclopedia Vol. 2*, eds Jack S. Blocker, David Fahey and Ian R. Tyrrell, 657–58. Santa Barbara, CA: ABC-CLIO, 2003.

Stacy, Margaret and Marion Price. *Women, Power and Politics*. London: Tavistock Publications, 1981.

Summers, Anne. *Damned Whores and God's Police Revised Edition*. Harmondsworth, England: Penguin Books Ltd., 1994.

Taylor, Barbara. *Eve and the New Jerusalem: Socialism and Feminism in the Nineteenth Century*. London: Virago Press Ltd., 1983. Reprint, London Virago Press Ltd., 1991.

Thorne, Susan. *Congregational Missions and the Making of an Imperial Culture in Nineteenth-Century England*. Stanford: Stanford University Press, 1999.

Tilly, Louise A. 'Gender, Women's History, and Social History'. *Social Science History* 13, no. 4 (1989): 439–62.

Trainor, Richard H. 'The Elite'. In *Glasgow Volume II: 1830 to 1912*, eds W. Hamish Fraser and Irene Maver, 227–64. Manchester: Manchester University Press, 1996.

——. 'The Middle Class'. In *The Cambridge Urban History of Britain Volume III 1840–1950*, ed. Martin Daunton, 673–713. Cambridge: Cambridge University Press, 2000.

Tyrrell, Ian. *Sobering Up: From Temperance to Prohibition in Antebellum America, 1800–1860*. London: Greenwood Press, 1979.

——. *Woman's World Woman's Empire: The Women's Christian Temperance Union in International Perspective, 1880–1930*. London: University of North Carolina Press, 1991.

Valverde, Mariana. '"Racial poison": Drink, Male Vice, and Degeneration in First-Wave Feminism'. In *Women Suffrage in the British Empire: Citizenship, Nation and Race*, eds Laura E. Nym Mayhall, Philippa Levine and Ian Christopher Flectcher, 33–50. London: Routledge, 2000.

Varty, Carmen Nielson. '"A career in Christian charity": Women's Benevolence in a Mid- Nineteenth-Century Canadian City'. *Women's History Review* 14, no. 2 (2005): 243–64.

Vicinus, Martha. *Independent Women: Work and Community for Single Women, 1850–1920*. London: Virago Press, 1985.

Vickery, Amanda. 'Golden Age to Separate Spheres?'. *Historical Journal* 36, no. 1 (1993): 383–414.

Wach, Howard M. 'Unitarian Philanthropy and Cultural Hegemony in Comparative Perspective: Manchester and Boston, 1827–1848'. *Journal of Social History* 26, no. 3 (1993): 539–57.

Wahrman, Dror. *Imagining the Middle Class: The Political Representation of Class in Britain, c. 1780–1840*. Cambridge: Cambridge University Press, 1995.

Walker, Linda. 'Gender, Suffrage and Party: Liberal Women's Organisations, 1880–1914'. In *Suffrage Outside Suffragism: Women's Vote in Britain 1880–1914*, ed. Myriam Boussahba-Bravard, 77–102. Houndsmills, Basingstoke: Palgrave Macmillan, 2007.

——. 'Party Political Women: A Comparative Study of Liberal Women and the Primrose League, 1890–1914'. In *Equal or Different: Women's Politics 1800–1914*, ed. Jane Rendall, 165–91. Oxford: Basil Blackwell, 1987.

Walker, William M. 'The Scottish Prohibition Party and the Millennium'. *International Review of Social History* 18 (1973): 353–79.

Ward, David. 'Environs and Neighbours in the "Two Nations": Residential Differentiation in Mid-Nineteenth-Century Leeds'. *Journal of Historical Geography* 6, no. 2 (1980): 133–62.

Wood, Claire. 'Campaigning Women and Bad, Bad Men: Otago's Campaign for Female Suffrage'. In *Mrs Hocken Requests … Women's Contributions to the Hocken Collection*, ed. Rosemary Entwistle, 11–18. Otago: Otago University Press, 1993.

Yeo, Eileen Janes. 'Protestant Feminists and Catholic Saints in Victorian Britain'. In *Radical Femininity: Women's Self-Representation in the Public Sphere*, ed. Eileen Janes Yeo, 127–48. Manchester: Manchester University Press, 1998.

Unpublished work

Brewster, Lynn. 'The Women's Suffrage Campaign from a Local Perspective: Stirling and its Environs 1871–1914'. Unpublished M.A. Dissertation, Faculty of Arts, University of Glasgow, 2000.

Brown, Callum. 'Religion and the Development of an Urban Society: Glasgow 1780–1914'. Unpublished Ph.D. Thesis, Faculty of Social Sciences, University of Glasgow, 1981.

Logan, Norma Davies. 'Drink and Society: Scotland 1870–1914'. Unpublished Ph.D. Thesis, Faculty of Arts, University of Glasgow, 1983.

Ryan, Jane. 'Sex and the Saltmarket – Public Discussion of Glasgow Fair 1820–1870'. Unpublished M.A. Dissertation, Faculty of Arts, University of Glasgow, 2002.

Smitley, Megan. '"Woman's Mission": The Temperance and Women's Suffrage Movements in Scotland, c1870–1914'. Unpublished Ph.D. Thesis, Faculty of Arts, University of Glasgow, 2002.

——. 'Women in Victorian and Edwardian Politics: The Case of the Municipal Vote in Scotland, 1881–1914'. Unpublished paper presented to Institute of Historical Research, Women's History Seminar, 7 May 2004.

Index